A Study Guide

to Educating
Young Children

SECOND EDITION

Mary Hohmann

EXERCISES for ADULT LEARNERS

HIGH/SCOPE® PRESS

Ypsilanti, Michigan

Published by

HIGH/SCOPE® PRESS
A division of the High/Scope Educational Research Foundation
600 North River Street
Ypsilanti, Michigan 48198-2898
(734) 485-2000, FAX (734) 485-0704
press@highscope.org

Holly Barton and Lynn Taylor, *High/Scope Press Editors*
Pattie McDonald, *Editorial Assistant*
Linda Eckel, *Cover design, text design, and production*

Library of Congress Cataloging-in-Publication Data
Hohmann, Mary.
    A study guide to Educating young children : exercises for adult
        learners / Mary Hohmann.—2nd ed.
        p. cm.
    Includes bibliographical references (p.) and index.
    ISBN 1-57379-163-6 (soft cover: alk. paper)
    1. Active Learning—handbooks, manuals, etc. 2. Early childhood education—
Handbooks, manuals, etc. 3. Perry Preschool Project (Ypsilanti, Mich.)—Handbooks, manuals, etc. 4. Children and adults—Handbooks, manuals, etc. 5. Education, Preschool—
Handbooks, manuals, etc. 6. Day care centers—Handbooks, manuals, etc. I. Title:
Educating young children. II. Hohmann, Mary. Educating young children. III. High/Scope
Educational Research Foundation. IV. Title.
LB1027.23.H65 2002
371.39—dc21   2002002350

Printed in the United States of America
10 9 8 7 6 5 4 3 2 1

To trainers, teachers, child care providers, and students using and studying the High/Scope educational approach

Contents

PART 2:
THE ACTIVE LEARNING ENVIRONMENT 47

5 Arranging and Equipping Spaces for Active Learners 49

6 The High/Scope Daily Routine—A Framework for Active Learning 65

7 The High/Scope Plan-Do-Review Process 71

Planning Time 71

Work Time 78

Acknowledgments

earning about teaching and learning is an ongoing and shared experience among High/ Scope consultants. The collective wisdom and support of the following people have made the writing of this book possible: Julie Austin, Michelle Graves, Philip Hawkins, Charles Hohmann, Diana Jo Johnston, Carol Markley, Beth Marshall, Susan Terdan, David Weikart, and Linda Weikel at the High/Scope Foundation; Barbara Carmody in California; Betsy Evans in Massachusetts; Joan Sharp and Rachel Underwood in England; and Serena Johnson, Pam Lafferty, and Malek Pirani at High/Scope UK in London.

Many people have also tried out various versions of these exercises—Joan Brink and her students at Sienna Heights College, Adrian, Michigan; the participants in the Moultrie, Georgia, Lead Teacher Training Project; the participants in the 1991, 1992, and 1994 Ypsilanti Training of Trainers Projects; and the participants in the Binghamton, New York, Lead Teacher Training Project. A heartfelt thanks to you all!

A Study Guide
to *Educating*
Young Children
SECOND EDITION

nservice training can result in improved practice if teachers are engaged in participatory,
active learning experiences.

—*Training for Quality, p. 163*

Introduction

Active Learning for Adults

Over the years, High/Scope staff, teachers, and trainers have discovered that active learning is not just for children. From our own research and experiences as learners and teachers, we are convinced that human beings of all ages need to construct knowledge in a way that allows them both to relate new ideas to what they already know and to reconsider their own assumptions and beliefs in light of new information they have gathered.[1] Using this book, *A Study Guide to Educating Young Children: Exercises for Adult Learners,* is one way that adults, alone or in groups, can explore the ideas and strategies presented in the text *Educating Young Children: Active Learning Practices for Preschool and Child Care Programs.*

Who Needs a Study Guide?

There are many ways to learn about the High/Scope approach to preschool education—through reading, taking a class, participating in inservice training, observing High/Scope programs in action on site and on videotapes, observing children, joining a High/Scope teaching team, and trying out active learning support strategies in your own setting. *A Study Guide to Educating Young Children* is designed to support adults engaged in any of these learning endeavors.

For **students** in a college course using *Educating Young Children* as a text, study guide exercises can serve as a way to become familiar with active learning practices, to guide child

observations, to try out support strategies with young children at home or in a preschool setting, and to make important connections between all the elements of the High/Scope approach.

For **preschool staff and child care providers** who are implementing the High/Scope approach on their own, the study guide can provide an active, step-by-step way to explore and experience the concepts and ideas presented in *Educating Young Children.* The study guide exercises can lead teaching teams through a collective examination of their personal beliefs and assumptions about teaching and learning and aid them in developing their implementation plans.

Trainers and college teachers might incorporate some of the study guide exercises into their workshops and courses as small-group activities or discussions, or they might ask their students or trainees to select and do the study guide exercises they find most relevant or challenging. The exercises that students or trainees choose to do as assignments might become the basis for group discussion at their next class or training meeting. Some study guide exercises can be modified to suit the training needs of a particular group of teachers or students; other exercises can serve as a springboard for creating additional, original text-related training activities.

Whether students, practitioners, trainers, or college teachers, study guide users will want to select those exercises that are suited to their particular needs and interests. Some may work their way through all the chapters in order, while others may begin with a topic of particular interest and proceed in their own fashion, selecting chapters and exercises in a sequence that makes sense to them. Some study guide users may feel compelled to do every exercise in a particular chapter, whereas others may find it more useful to pick and choose exercises based on the time available

---

[1] *Epstein, Ann S., **Training for Quality: Improving Early Childhood Programs Through Systematic Inservice Training** (Ypsilanti, MI: High/Scope Press, 1993).*

or previous experience. If you are a trainer, for example, and all your teachers are already materials experts, you would very likely acknowledge their collective expertise, skip exercise 10 ("Materials Expert") in Chapter 5, and go on to another, less familiar exercise or topic.

How Is This Guide Organized?

Because this study guide is designed to be used as a supplement to the text *Educating Young Children (EYC)*, the chapters of the two books are coordinated. For example, Chapter 1 in both *EYC* and the study guide is entitled "Active Learning: The Way Children Construct Knowledge," Chapter 2 in both books is entitled "Establishing a Supportive Climate: The Basics of Positive Adult-Child Interactions," and so on.

Each study guide chapter consists of a variety of interactive exercises designed to help study guide users make sense of ideas presented in the text by connecting those ideas with their own experiences and observations of young children. Types of exercises in each chapter include hands-on explorations and experiences with materials; child studies; analysis of photographs and case studies in terms of curriculum elements; recollections and reflections about curriculum topics; construction of definitions; relating child observations to curriculum topics; trying out support strategies; and making implementation plans.

Materials needed to carry out most of the exercises in this study guide include the *Educating Young Children* text, since many exercises require the use of photographs, discussions, explanations, and checklists on specific pages of *EYC;* easy-to-find toys and household and natural

materials; and a notebook for recording the answers to study guide exercises. As answers are recorded in the notebook, it will become the study guide user's personal journal of thoughts and observations about preschool teaching and learning. In addition to these materials, study guide users will need one or more young children to interact with and observe and, ideally, occasional access to an early childhood setting to observe, analyze, and plan around. Some exercises specifically call for having a partner or some teammates to work with. You may find that other exercises also lend themselves to being done with a partner or teammates, since talking things over with someone often makes it easier to formulate questions and answers and make discoveries.

A small number of exercises suggest making an audiotape or videotape or using a computer and preschool software; there are notes forewarning the reader of this. Occasionally, a study guide exercise refers to, but does not require you to have, one of these High/Scope publications: the *High/Scope Program Quality Assessment (PQA): Preschool Version* (2001 Field-Test Edition); the *High/Scope Child Observation Record (COR) for Ages 2$\frac{1}{2}$–6;* and *Supporting Young Learners 2: Ideas for Child Care Providers and Teachers.* Information on these and other useful supplementary materials—publications, videotapes, and recordings—appears at the end of each chapter.

Where Are the Answers?

Most of the exercises in this study guide do not have specific answers. Instead they include questions that are open-ended, and call for actions, recollections, reflections, and creation of plans

and definitions in one's own words. As a study guide user, you will often be led back to the text *Educating Young Children* for working definitions, strategies, and examples and then asked to apply these concepts or to use them as a basis for analysis. Coming up with answers means constructing knowledge based on what you already know, on your close reading and interpretation of the text, on your interactions with and observations of children, and on the insights and experiences of others in your class, inservice training, or early childhood setting. Seriously thinking about what you are doing—being willing to analyze, question, contextualize, and try out ideas—will lead you to answers that are interesting, unique, and useful.

When a study guide exercise does call for a specific answer, the answer is given at the end of the chapter in which the exercise appears.

Learning about the High/Scope approach to early childhood teaching and learning is an active, ongoing process. We hope the exercises in *A Study Guide to Educating Young Children* will lead you to new insights about young children and will strengthen your understanding of the important role adults play in supporting and guiding each child through this active learning journey.

Part 1

The Active Learning Approach

Given that children learn through their own experiences and discoveries, what is the role of adults in the active learning environment? In the broadest sense, adults are supporters of development, and as such their primary goal is to encourage active learning on the part of the child. Adults both attend to what children learn and how they learn it—and they empower children to take control of their own learning. . . . While children interact with materials, people, ideas, and events to construct their own understanding of reality, adults observe and interact with children to discover how each child thinks and reasons. Adults strive to recognize each child's particular interests and abilities, and to offer the child appropriate support and challenges.

—**Educating Young Children**, *p. 20*

1

Active Learning: The Way Children Construct Knowledge

Experiencing Active Learning

▶ A. For this exercise in *exploring materials,* you will need a partner and some objects(s) or material(s) that both of you find interesting (for example, a paper bag, sand and/or water, some rocks or shells, a tree, a bicycle, a chair, a ball, marbles, clay, a musical instrument, a Venetian blind, popcorn, a watermelon, a bar of soap, bubble-blowing materials).

❶ With your partner, take time to explore your object(s) or material(s) with all your senses, doing as many things as you think of with it. When you have completed your exploration, talk together about what you have done, and record your discoveries and reflections.

❷ Turn to the checklist entitled "Essential Ingredients of Active Learning: A Summary" on p. 40 of *EYC.* Read through the checklist's sections on *choice, materials, manipulation,* and *language from the child,* mentally changing "child" or "children" to "I" or "we" as you read. List the statements from the checklist that describe your experiences with the object(s) or material(s) you just explored.

▶ B. For this exercise in *discovery,* you and your partner will need pieces of positive and negative Velcro, and if possible, a magnifying glass.[2]

❶ Together examine both positive and negative Velcro pieces, looking at them through the magnifying glass. What similarities and differences do positive and negative Velcro exhibit?

❷ Based on what you see, draw a picture showing how Velcro works, how it "sticks together."

❸ Discuss how what you just did with the Velcro relates to active learning, and record your answer.

▶ C. In your own life, what are some active learning experiences you can recall?

Photographs of Active Learners

Review the discussion of the five ingredients of active learning on *EYC* pp. 37–40. Then examine the front and back cover photographs of *EYC* and the photographs on pp. 2–40 of *EYC.*

▶ A. Which photograph(s) particularly strike you? Why?

▶ B. Explain what these photographs convey to you about each of the following five ingredients of active learning.

❶ Materials: What materials are children using?

❷ Manipulation: What are children doing with materials?

❸ Choice: What choices are children making?

❹ Language from the child: What people are children talking with?

[2]*This exercise is adapted from "Fabric Fasteners" in Blackwell, Frank F., and Charles Hohmann,* **High/Scope K–3 Curriculum Series: Science** *(Ypsilanti, MI: High/Scope Press, 1991), pp. 130–131.*

⑤ Adult support: What are adults doing to support children's learning?

▶ C. Find a photograph of yourself as a child at play. (If this is not possible, find a photograph of another young family member, or find a magazine photograph of a child at play.) Which ingredients of active learning are evident in the photograph you have selected?

Exercise 3

Active Learners You Have Observed

In *EYC* (pp. 17–18), active learning is defined as direct action on objects; reflection on actions; intrinsic motivation, invention, and generativity; and problem solving.

▶ A. Think of a child or children you have seen engaged in each of the four aspects of active learning:

① Give an example of a child engaged in *direct action on objects*.

② Give an example of a child *reflecting on his or her actions*.

③ Give an example of a child exhibiting *intrinsic motivation, invention*, and *generativity*.

④ Give an example of a child *problem solving*.

▶ B. Are children naturally active learners? Why or why not?

▶ C. Are adults naturally supportive of active learning? Why or why not?

Exercise 4

Young Children and Adults Think Differently, or Do They?

On p. 18 of *EYC* the insert entitled "Young Children and Adults Think Differently" describes some of the ways preschool children's thinking diverges from adult thinking. Occasionally, however, adults themselves abandon logic to return to their own early ways of thinking, thus giving themselves some appreciation for children's intuitive explanations of "why things are."

▶ A. For each type of thinking described below, give one example of **a preschooler's use** of such thinking, and give one example of **your own use** of such thinking.

① *It's alive!* Thinking that an inanimate object is alive, or attributing lifelike qualities to an inanimate object

② *Concrete definitions.* Knowing only one meaning of a word, or focusing on only one meaning of a word

③ *Blending intuitive and scientific thought.* Using magical thinking

④ *One thing at a time.* Focusing on one idea or one feature of an object at a time

⑤ *Judging by appearances.* Drawing a conclusion based on appearances

▶ B. Page 33 of *EYC* includes a discussion of why it is important for adults to accept children's answers and explanations, even though they may be "wrong" according to adult logic. In your opinion, what is important for learning—being able to think and reason, knowing the correct answers, both, or neither? Why?

Exercise 5

Key Experiences as Action Statements

Read through the list of preschool key experiences on *EYC* p. 22. What relationship do you see between active learning and this list of action statements?

Exercise 6

Child Study: Watching and Listening to an Active Learner

For 10–20 minutes, observe a preschool-aged child at play alone or with others. As you watch and listen, record your observations by checking the appropriate items in the adaptation of the checklist from *EYC* p. 40 that is provided on p. 9 of this study guide. If you check an item, note the verifying evidence (for example, if you check "Child chooses materials," you might write, "Jack selected blocks and pillows to build a house"). If you do not check the item, note why you did not (for example, "Adult *told* Jack to build with blocks and pillows").

Exercise 7

Adult Feelings About Child Initiative

Some adults are uncomfortable with what they see as the potential for messiness, noise, and motion in settings that support child initiative.

Child's Name_____ Date_____

Location_____ Time of Day_____

Time Observed_____

Choice: The child chooses what to do.
___Child initiates activities that grow from personal interests and intentions:

___Child chooses materials:

___Child decides what to do with materials:

Materials: There are abundant materials that the child can use in many ways.
___Child uses a variety of materials:

___Child has space to use materials:

___Child has time to use materials:

Manipulation: Adults encourage the child to manipulate objects freely.
___Child actively explores with all senses:

___Child discovers relationships through direct experiences:

___Child transforms and combines materials:

___Child uses age-appropriate tools and equipment:

___Child uses large muscles:

Language from the child: The child describes what he or she is doing.
___Child talks about his or her experiences:

___Child talks using his or her own words:

Other adults enjoy seeing the creativity and persistence children show as they follow their own interests in such settings. The behaviors listed in the following exercises A–I are typical of children in active learning settings (discussed on *EYC* pp. 24–29). For each behavior, list the **cons** (reasons some adults might discourage children's engagement in that particular self-motivated action), and list the **pros** (reasons some adults might encourage that particular type of initiative in preschoolers).

▶ A. Children initiate activities that grow from personal interests and intentions.

▶ B. Children choose materials and decide what to do with them.

▶ C. Children explore materials actively with all their senses.

▶ D. Children discover relationships through direct experience with objects.

▶ E. Children transform and combine materials.

▶ F. Children use age-appropriate tools and equipment.

▶ G. Children use their large muscles.

▶ H. Children talk about their experiences.

▶ I. Children talk about what they are doing in their own words.

Materials for Active Learning

Active learners of preschool age enjoy exploring and playing with appealing materials, including practical everyday objects; natural and found materials; tools; messy materials; heavy, large materials; and easy-to-handle materials (discussed in *EYC*, pp. 29–31). By doing the following exercises you may remind yourself why children find these materials so attractive.

▶ A. Think back to your own childhood and what objects and materials you most enjoyed playing with then. Make a list of your favorite playthings. How does your list correspond to the types of materials described in the opening paragraph of this exercise?

▶ B. Gather together a collection of natural, found, and everyday objects (including, for example, sticks, stones, shells, buttons, spoons, sponges, leaves, flowers, bells) and a collection of small plastic objects (including, for example, toy animals, beads, blocks, toy people, toy vehicles). Explore each of the two collections with all your senses. Which collection is the more interesting? Why?

▶ C. Go to your toolbox, workbench, or shop or to the tool section of a store. Pick up and try out the tools that interest you. Next, find a child's set of plastic tools. Pick them up and try them out. Which tools are more appealing, the real tools or the plastic tools? Why?

▶ D. Find or buy a tube or squeeze bottle of one or more of the following: white glue, mustard,

ketchup, shampoo, hand cream, toothpaste. Find a work space on a table or floor, cover it generously with newspaper, roll up your sleeves, and if you wish, put on an old shirt, smock, or apron. Now, setting aside the rules of propriety generally associated with these substances, squeeze, explore, mix, dribble, make designs, cover your hands, and experiment until your containers are empty. When you have completed your play, reflect on and record your experiences—what did you discover about the materials? About yourself? About why preschoolers might enjoy exploring messy materials?

Remembering Supportive Adults

Look at the *adult support* strategies in the checklist on p. 40 of *EYC* (discussed on pp. 29–35).

▶ A. Think about the adults who supported you in some way at some time from birth through childhood. What strategies (from this list or otherwise) did they use, and what effect did their use of these strategies have on you?

▶ B. What support strategies from this list do you wish they had used more frequently?

Identifying Adult Support

Read "An Active Learning Experience: Observing and Supporting Callie" on *EYC* pp. 39–40.

▶ A. What *adult support* strategies from the checklist on *EYC* p. 40 did Callie's teacher, Ann, use? How did she use them?

▶ B. What in particular strikes you about the way Ann supported Callie's active learning?

Self-Study: Supporting Children's Active Learning

▶ A. Review the *adult support* strategies in the checklist on p. 40 of *EYC* (discussed on pp. 29–35). Then, with a preschool child (or group of children), try out some of these strategies for supporting children's active learning. Record the **strategies you tried,** and for each strategy, explain **what you found out** about the child (or children), about the strategy, and/or about yourself. Organize your answers in a chart with these headings:

Support Strategy Tried	*Findings/Lessons Learned*

▶ B. Would you like to increase the support you provide to active learners? If so, how would you do this? What support strategies might you try? If not, why not?

Recognizing the Ingredients of Active Learning in Everyday Situations

▶ A. Read scenarios (1)–(3), analyzing each one for the ingredients of active learning. Use the checklist from *EYC* p. 40, which is reproduced on p. 9 of this study guide, and write 1, 2, or 3 beside each item to indicate if it applies to scenario (1), (2), or (3) respectively.

❶ As Sam, Mike's teacher, sits next to him at the art table, Mike tries to tape three papers together to form the pages of a "book," but the middle paper keeps falling out. "Uh-oh!" Mike says. "Uh-oh," Sam observes, "some of the paper fell out."

Mike then looks around and picks up a stapler. He pushes down on the stapler to fasten the papers together but then cannot see any staple in his papers. He pushes down again on the stapler, harder this time, but still does not see a staple in his papers. He bends over, pushes the stapler slowly, watches the staple come out, and then realizes that his papers are underneath the stapler instead of between its "jaws." Finally he positions the papers between the jaws, pushes down on the stapler, removes the papers, and sees the resulting staple holding his "book" together. "Look! It worked!" he says to Sam.

"You got the staple to go through all the papers," Sam replies. Mike then continues to staple until he has 15 staples in place.

❷ Mrs. Lu (a teacher) and a small group of children are working with bowl-shaped grape-fruit rinds, straw, toothpicks, yarn, pipe cleaners, and construction paper.

"I'm making a nest," says Elise as she fills a grapefruit rind with straw. "Yes, I see you are," says Mrs. Lu.

"Mine's gonna be a basket with this for a handle," says Lynette, twisting together some pipe cleaners. "Ah, You're twisting pipe cleaners together," says Mrs. Lu.

Marketta selects a grapefruit rind, turns it over so it looks like a dome, and pokes toothpicks into it. Mrs. Lu pokes toothpicks into her grapefruit rind. Mike watches them both, and then he tries the same thing but also winds yarn around his toothpicks. Meanwhile, Troy fills his grapefruit rind with straw, toothpicks, pipe cleaners, and crumpled pieces of paper. When it is full, he dumps it out and fills it up again.

❸ Alex, Kevin, and Brendan are playing on the climber. Alex and Kevin capture Beth, their teacher, and lead her through an opening into a space under the climber. "You're locked in jail," Alex tells her. "You can't get out." "On, no!" says Beth.

A little later Beth says, "I'm getting hungry in this jail. Is there anything to eat?" "You get icky food," Alex says, as he and Kevin hand her some pretend food. Beth tastes her pretend food: "Ick! I don't like icky food!" Tearing it out of her mouth, she throws it to the ground, saying "I don't want icky food!" "That's all you get in jail," Alex tells her.

When Alex and Kevin leave the "jail" to get more icky food, Brendan motions to Beth to escape. She climbs through another opening and starts to run away, but Kevin and Alex recapture her and bring her back to the climber jail. "This time we have to hold you," says Alex, grabbing one of Beth's hands while Kevin grabs the other. "You are locked up." Beth stays in "jail" while Brendan tries to distract Alex and Kevin.

▶ B. Would you expect to see all five ingredients of active learning in every active learning experience? Why or why not? Would you expect to see all 40 items from the active learning checklist (*EYC*, p. 40) in every active learning experience? Why or why not?

Defining Key Concepts

When you are familiar with the contents of *EYC* Chapter 1 and have completed several or all of exercises 1–12 in this chapter of the study guide, define these terms in your own words:

▶ A. Active learning

▶ B. Developmentally appropriate learning opportunities

▶ C. Construction of knowledge

Active Learning Issues to Ponder and Write About

▶ A. When, where, and how did you learn to ride a bicycle (or to acquire some equally challenging childhood skill)? How does that experience relate to your understanding of active learning?

Essential Ingredients of Active Learning: A Summary

Choice: The child chooses what to do.

_____ Children initiate activities that grow from personal interests and intentions.

_____ Children choose materials.

_____ Children decide what to do with materials.

Materials: There are abundant materials that children can use in many ways.

_____ Children use a variety of materials.

_____ Practical everyday objects

_____ Natural and found materials

_____ Tools

_____ Messy, sticky, gooey, drippy, squishy materials

_____ Heavy, large materials

_____ Easy-to-handle materials

_____ Children have space to use materials.

_____ Children have time to use materials.

Manipulation: Adults encourage children to manipulate objects freely.

_____ Children explore actively with all their senses.

_____ Children discover relationships through direct experience.

_____ Children transform and combine materials.

_____ Children use age-appropriate tools and equipment.

_____ Children use their large muscles.

Language from the child: The child describes what he or she is doing.

_____ Children talk about their experiences.

_____ Children talk about what they are doing in their own words.

Adult support: Adults recognize and encourage children's intentions, reflections, problem solving, and creativity.

_____ Adults form partnerships with children.

_____ Put themselves on children's physical level.

_____ Follow children's ideas and interests.

_____ Converse in a give-and-take style.

_____ Adults seek out children's intentions.

_____ Acknowledge children's choices and actions.

_____ Use materials in the same way children are using them.

_____ Watch what children do with materials.

_____ Ask children about their intentions.

_____ Adults listen for and encourage children's thinking.

_____ Listen to children as they work and play.

_____ Converse with children about what they are doing and thinking.

_____ Focus on children's actions.

_____ Make comments that repeat, amplify, and build on what the child says.

_____ Pause frequently to give children time to think and gather their thoughts into words.

_____ Accept children's answers and explanations even when they are "wrong."

_____ Adults encourage children to do things for themselves.

_____ Stand by patiently and wait while children take care of things independently.

_____ Show understanding of children's mishaps.

_____ Refer children to one another for ideas, assistance, and conversation.

_____ Encourage children to ask and answer their own questions.

▶ B. What choices did you make as a child? What were your parents' or guardians' attitudes toward giving children choices? Why is or isn't it important for young children to make choices and decisions?

▶ C. Do children construct knowledge when they are in settings that are not geared to active learning? If so, what kinds of knowledge do they construct? If not, what do they do in such settings?

▶ D. Educational theorist John Dewey[3] said, "Enforced quiet and acquiescence prevent pupils from disclosing their real natures." What does this statement mean to you? Why are children's real natures valued in active learning settings?

▶ E. Brain research supports active learning. How?

▶ F. What excites you about teaching and learning in an active learning setting? What worries you about teaching and learning in an active learning setting?

---

[3]*Dewey, John, **Experience and Education** (New York: Macmillan, 1938, Reprint 1963), p. 62.*

Related Publications

Blackwell, Frank F., and Charles Hohmann. 1991. *High/Scope K–3 Curriculum Series: Science.* Ypsilanti, MI: High/Scope Press.

Frede, Ellen. 1984. *Getting Involved: Workshops for Parents,* 43–75. Ypsilanti, MI: High/Scope Press.

Hohmann, Charles. 1996. *Foundations in Elementary Education: Overview.* Ypsilanti, MI: High/Scope Press.

Hohmann, Charles. 1996. "In the Elementary School—Play Sparks Learning." In *Supporting Young Learners 2: Ideas for Child Care Providers and Teachers,* Nancy A. Brickman, ed., 173–74. Ypsilanti, MI: High/Scope Press.

Post, Jacalyn. 1996. "Science: Here, There, and Everywhere." In *Supporting Young Learners 2: Ideas for Child Care Providers and Teachers,* Nancy A. Brickman, ed., 193–200. Ypsilanti, MI: High/Scope Press.

Post, Jacalyn, and Mary Hohmann. 2000. "Active Learning and Key Experiences for Infants and Toddlers." In *Tender Care and Early Learning: Supporting Infants and Toddlers in Child Care Settings,* 21–54. Ypsilanti, MI: High/Scope Press.

Weikart, David P. 1996. "'Driving Master Brian': Supporting Children's Thinking." In *Supporting Young Learners 2: Ideas for Child Care Providers and Teachers,* Nancy A. Brickman, ed., 23–26. Ypsilanti, MI: High/Scope Press.

Weikel, Linda. 1996. "Talking With Parents About Play and Learning." In *Supporting Young Learners 2: Ideas for Child Care Providers and Teachers,* Nancy A. Brickman, ed., 163–72. Ypsilanti, MI: High/Scope Press.

Related Videos

The High/Scope Approach for Under Threes, U.S. Edition. 1999. Color videotape, part 3, "Choosing & Doing," 15 min. London, England: High/Scope Institute U.K. (Available from High/Scope Press, Ypsilanti, MI)

High/Scope K–3 Curriculum Series: Active Learning. 1991. Color videotape, 17 min. Ypsilanti, MI: High/Scope Press.

Supporting Children's Active Learning: Teaching Strategies for Diverse Settings. 1989. Color videotape, 13 min. Ypsilanti, MI: High/Scope Press.

One of the High/Scope Curriculum's major goals is to assist adults in establishing and maintaining settings where they can interact positively with children, so children can work and play with people and materials free of fear, anxiety, boredom, and neglect.

—***Educating Young Children***, *p. 43*

Establishing a Supportive Climate: The Basics of Positive Adult-Child Interactions

Understanding the Concept of "Sense of Self"

A child's sense of self provides the foundation for social interactions. Exercises A and B are designed to examine the definition of this important but abstract concept.

▶ A. Based on the brief description of sense of self in *EYC* on pp. 43–44 and on your own experience, write your own working definition of "sense of self."

▶ B. To expand your understanding of sense of self, go to the library and examine one or more of the books listed below to find out what psychologists mean by this concept. If these books are not available, try an alternative approach to your research. For example, search the Internet or library for books or articles that are available on this subject; talk with a psychologist in your community about sense of self; talk with a family member or an experienced early childhood practitioner about this topic. Record your findings, and add to your own definition of "sense of self," if appropriate.

- *Childhood and Society* by Erik Erikson (1950)

- *Attachment. Attachment and Loss,* Volume 1, by John Bowlby (1969)

- *The Psychological Birth of the Human Infant* by Margaret Mahler, Fred Pine, and Anni Bergman (1975)

- *Patterns of Attachment: A Psychological Study of the Strange Situation* by Mary Ainsworth, D. Salter, Mary Blehar, Everett Waters, and Sally Wall (1978)

- *First Feelings* by Stanley and Nancy Greenspan (1985)

- *The New Peoplemaking* by Virginia Satir (1988)

- *Beyond Self-Esteem: Developing a Genuine Sense of Human Value* by Nancy E. Curry and Carl N. Johnson (1990)

- *Emotional Intelligence: Why It Can Matter More Than IQ* by Daniel Goleman (1995)

- *Becoming Attached* by Robert Karen (1998)

Building Blocks of Human Relationships: Trust, Autonomy, Initiative, Empathy, Self-Confidence

As people interact positively with one another, they generally exhibit some degree of trust, autonomy, initiative, empathy, and self-confidence in a variety of ways, depending on their developmental level and life experiences. With a partner or several others, discuss and record your answers to the following:

▶ A. Consider people you have encountered and how they interact with others. Record anecdotes of how **trust, autonomy, initiative, empathy,** and **self-confidence** are expressed at the various ages listed in (1)–(8) on p. 16. Use a chart like the one shown to organize your answers.

Age	Trust	Autonomy	Initiative	Empathy	Self-Confidence

❶ Infant

❷ Toddler

❸ Preschooler

❹ Early elementary school

❺ Late elementary school

❻ Early teen

❼ Late teen

❽ Adult

▶ B. What strikes you about your group of anecdotes as a whole?

▶ C. How are trust, autonomy, initiative, empathy, and self-confidence important to human beings throughout their lives? Think about and briefly record examples of how you exhibit each one of these capacities.

▶ D. How is *active learning* related to the development of a child's sense of self, including the capacities for trust, autonomy, initiative, empathy, and self-confidence?

A Closer Look at Empathy and Self-Esteem

Read "The Beginnings of Empathy" by Daniel Goleman on p. 46 of *EYC* and "An Unsentimental View of Self-Esteem" by Mike Schmoker on p. 47 of *EYC*.

▶ A. What strikes you about these two statements? How do the findings reported relate to your own observations and experiences?

▶ B. How might the development of empathy affect, or influence, the development of self-esteem?

Contrasting Social Climates and Interaction Styles

Laissez-faire, *directive*, and *supportive* climates (described on *EYC* pp. 47–52) are characterized by distinctive adult-child interaction styles.

▶ A. What types of social climates and adult-child interaction styles characterized your own early school years?

▶ B. How does the chart "Contrasting Climates for Children" (*EYC* p. 49) relate to the delinquency findings of the High/Scope Preschool Curriculum Study (discussed on *EYC* p. 8–9)?

▶ C. Read "In the Eye of the Beholder: Dressing in Two Different Social Climates" on *EYC* p. 50.

  ❶ What strikes you about this scenario?

  ❷ What types of social climates and adult-child interactions are represented in the homes of Lyle and Gus?

  ❸ What social climate and interaction style prevails in your household early in the morning when people are leaving for work and school?

▶ D. What type of social climate and adult-child interaction style are you striving to create (or will you strive to create) in the early childhood setting you prepare for children? Why?

Experiencing the Elements of Support and Their Opposites

For the following exercises, you will need a partner and a ball made out of wadded-up newspaper wrapped round and round with tape. With your partner and ball, do exercises A–F:

▶ A. *Keep Away* and *Toss and Catch:*

  • For five minutes, play a game of Keep Away in which one person tries to grab or snatch the ball from the other person, who tries to maintain possession of the ball.

  • Next play a game of Toss and Catch in which you throw the ball directly to your partner, who throws it back to you, and so forth.

After you have played both games, discuss and record how each game affected you. In which game did you *share control* of the ball?

▶ B. *Target Practice:*

  • Find a challenging target to hit or toss your ball into, and each take several turns trying to hit the target. When you are not throwing the ball, point out what your partner is doing wrong and how he or she might improve.

  • Then continue with more turn taking, but this time, when it is not your turn with the ball, support and encourage your partner's efforts to hit the target.

After you have played both versions of Target Practice, discuss and record how each version of the game affected you. In which version were you *focusing on each other's strengths and interests?*

▶ C. *Sharing Information About Balls:*

  • Take turns giving each other a brief lecture about balls.

  • Next talk together for a few minutes about ball games you have played in your past.

Discuss and record how these two ways of exchanging information affected you. Which exchange was more *authentic?* Why?

▶ D. *Rolling Balls:*

  • Make an inclined plane by holding a book or some other flat object in a slanted position. Take turns, with one person holding the inclined plane in a steady position and the other person rolling the ball down the plane.

  • Next sit opposite each other on the floor or at a table, and roll the ball back and forth between you.

Discuss and record how these two ball-rolling experiences affected you. Which experience was more *playful?* Why?

▶ E. *Fixing the Ball:*

  • One of you sits or stomps on the ball. The other person scolds and shames the ball flattener and says that since the ball is ruined, you can't play ball together any more.

  • Next, one of you sits or stomps on the ball, but together you figure out a way to repair it. After repairing the ball, make up and play a new ball game together.

Discuss and record how these two approaches to ball flattening affected you. Which one focused on *problem solving?*

▶ F. Based on these experiences, discuss and record the conclusions you can draw about how sharing control, focusing on interests, being authentic, being playful, and taking a problem-solving approach to conflict contribute to supportive adult-child interactions.

Exercise 6

Adults and Children Sharing Control

One strategy that creates supportive adult-child interactions is the *sharing of control between adults and children:* Adults take cues from children, participate with children on children's terms, learn from children, and relinquish control by consciously giving control to children. (These strategies are discussed in *EYC* on pp. 52–55.)

▶ A. Look at the photographs on *EYC* pp. 36 and 189. How are adults sharing control with children in these two situations?

▶ B. Find at least six other photographs in *EYC* that show situations in which adults and children share control. List the page number of each photograph, and describe how adults are sharing control with children in each situation.

▶ C. From your own childhood, recall a situation in which an adult shared control with you. Briefly describe the situation and how it affected you.

▶ D. Recall a situation in which you as an adult shared control with a child. Briefly describe the interaction.

▶ E. The idea of sharing control with children makes some adults uneasy. Why might this be so?

▶ F. What are some of the benefits of sharing control with children?

Exercise 7

Sharing Conversational Control

To consider the issue of sharing control with children during conversations, read "Sharing Conversational Control" on p. 218 of *EYC*.

▶ A. With a partner take turns trying out the following five conversational moves:

- *Move 1, enforced repetition.* Direct your partner to repeat something you tell him or her to say. For example, you might give this directive to your partner: "Say 'I'm sorry' to Roger." or "Tell Aisha to give you the blanket." After directing your partner to make several enforced repetitions, switch roles so your partner now directs you to repeat several statements.

- *Move 2, closed questions.* Ask your partner several closed questions, that is, questions that leave no choice because they have only one right answer. For example, you might ask "What is your name?" Wait for your partner to respond, then ask another closed question. Then switch roles so your partner asks you closed questions.

- *Move 3, open questions.* Ask your partner several open questions, that is, questions that have many possible answers. For example, you might ask your partner "What do you plan to do this weekend?" Give your partner an opportunity to respond, then ask another open question. Switch roles with your partner so your partner asks you open questions.

- *Moves 4 and 5, contributions and acknowledgments.* Begin a conversation with your partner by making a contribution, that is, an observation or statement. For example, you might begin with an observation ("There are several new restaurants in town . . .") or a statement about yourself ("I had the best meal last night . . ."). After you have completed your contribution, pause for your partner's contribution or acknowledgment. An acknowledgment is a word, phrase, or gesture that lets the speaker know you are listening. It might be a nod of the head or a "placeholder" comment, such as "I see!" Continue your conversation together, using *only* contributions and acknowledgments. Listen carefully to each other as you take turns speaking.

With your partner, discuss and record the experiences you just had with the five conversational moves—enforced repetition, closed questions, open questions, contributions, and acknowledgments.

▶ B. In an active learning setting, which conversational moves would be most effective in promoting the active learning ingredient *language from the child?* Why?

Focusing on Children's Strengths

In supportive adult-child interactions, adults *focus on children's strengths*. They do this by looking for children's interests, viewing situations from the child's perspective, sharing children's interests with parents and staff, and planning around children's strengths and interests. (For a discussion of these strategies, see *EYC* pp. 55–57).

▶ A. List your strengths and interests.

▶ B. Read the insert on *EYC* pp. 306–307 entitled "Key Experience Notes." Based on the anecdotes in these notes, list Jonah's strengths and interests.

▶ C. There are many children who appear repeatedly in photographs throughout *EYC*, for example, Julia (p. 10) and Mikey (p. 36). Choose Julia, Mikey, or some other child frequently pictured in *EYC*, and find and examine all the *EYC* photographs of that child. Beside each photo's page number, list everything the photo reveals about the child's strengths and interests.

▶ D. How are the strengths and interests you recorded for Jonah (in exercise B) and your photo child (in exercise C) related to the key experiences (listed on *EYC* p. 22)?

▶ E. Why do you think adults in active learning settings focus on children's strengths rather than on their deficits?

Child Study: Observing a Child's Strengths and Interests

Find a preschool child at play, and observe the child for 10–20 minutes. As you watch and listen, write down what you see the child doing and hear the child saying. Afterward, use a child study format like this one to record what your observations lead you to conclude about the child's strengths and interests.

| *Child's Name*_____ *Date*_____ |
| *Location*_____ |
| *Time of Day*_____ |
| *Time Observed* _____ |

What Child Does and Says	*Child's Strengths and Interests*

Forming Authentic Relationships With Children

Authenticity is an important element of supportive adult-child interactions. Adults in active learning settings share themselves with children, respond attentively to children's interests, give children specific feedback, and both ask honest questions and respond to questions honestly. (For a discussion of these strategies, see *EYC* pp. 57–59.)

▶ A. When you think about authenticity, what person in your life comes to mind. Why?

▶ B. Read psychologist Carl Rogers's description of an authentic teacher on p. 57 of *EYC*. In your own words, what does he mean by "transparent realness"?

▶ C. What does it mean to share yourself with young children? How does sharing yourself with young children relate to your own strengths and interests (listed for exercise 8A on this page)?

▶ D. Of the five conversational moves you explored in exercises 7A and 7B on p. 18, which ones encourage authentic conversation? How?

▶ E. Look at the photo sequence on *EYC* pp. 14–15. What specific feedback might Beth, the teacher, give to Erica, the child?

▶ F. What specific feedback might you give to the children in the following *EYC* photos?

   ❶ Matthew on *EYC* p. 47
   ❷ Jalèssa (bottom photo) on *EYC* p. 51
   ❸ Frances on *EYC* p. 101
   ❹ Stacey on *EYC* p. 165
   ❺ Chris on *EYC* p. 177
   ❻ Saraya on *EYC* p. 249
   ❼ Jeff on *EYC* p. 384
   ❽ James on *EYC* p. 389

▶ G. What honest question might you ask of Carlos (*EYC* p. 179) as he looks through his "spy glasses"?

▶ H. Why is authenticity an important element in positive adult-child interactions?

Making a Commitment to Supporting Children's Play

In supportive adult-child interactions, adults *make a commitment to supporting children's play,* because it is through play that children engage with their world. In active learning settings, adults observe and understand the complexity of children's play, and they themselves are playful with children. (See *EYC* pp. 59–61, 201–202, and 210–213 for a discussion of these strategies.)

▶ A. The *EYC* photos on pp. 201–202 illustrate four major types of play—exploratory play, constructive play, pretend play, and games. Find at least four other photos in *EYC* that illustrate each type of play. Categorize them by recording the page numbers of the photos in a chart like this.

Exploratory	Constructive	Pretend	Games

▶ B. Describe one or more specific examples of young children engaging in each type of play—exploratory play, constructive play, pretend play, and simple games.

▶ C. Find a photograph of yourself as a child at play (or make a mental picture of yourself as a child at play). What type of play were you engaged in? What memories of play does your photograph (or mental picture) evoke?

▶ D. Throughout your life, what have you learned through play?

▶ E. What playful adults do you remember from your childhood? How did each one of them play with you?

▶ F. Find at least six photographs of playful adults in *EYC*, and beside the page number of each photo, describe how the adult is playing with children.

▶ G. Some adults feel uncomfortable playing with children. (See "What? **Me** Play? You've **Got** to Be Kidding!" on *EYC* p. 213.) List your concerns about playing with children. List the benefits you see in adult-child play partnerships.

▶ H. Sometimes children's play is disturbing. (See "The Other Side of Play" on *EYC* p. 61.) Describe a play episode that made you uncomfortable. How might an adult share control, focus on children's strengths, be authentic, be playful, and/or adopt a problem-solving approach during the episode you described?

Child Study: Observing Types of Play

Find a preschool child at play, and observe the child for 10–20 minutes. As you watch and listen, write down what you see the child doing and hear the child saying. Afterward, use a child-study format like the following to record the type(s) of play the child was involved in.

Child's Name_____ Date_____
Location_____
Time of Day_____
Time Observed _____

What Child Does and Says	Types(s) of Play

Playing With Children's Toys and Materials

Many of the children's toys and materials in an active learning setting (such as blocks, scissors, paper, dress-up clothes, sand and water) are so open-ended that they appeal to people of all ages. By yourself or with a friend, go into an early childhood setting after the children have left, and spend at least 30 minutes playing with as many things as you want to. After you have finished playing (and have put away your playthings), reflect on your experience, and record what you found out about yourself as a player.

Exercise 14

Adopting a Problem-Solving Approach to Social Conflict[4]

Supportive adult-child interactions call for adults to adopt a *problem-solving approach to social conflict*. This means approaching social conflicts calmly; acknowledging children's feelings; gathering information; restating the problem; asking for and choosing a solution; and giving follow-up support. (For a discussion of these strategies, see *EYC* pp. 61–64 and 403–407, *Supporting Young Learners 2* pp. 27–56, and *You Can't Come to My Birthday Party! Conflict Resolution With Young Children*.)

▶ A. With a partner, recall and describe how conflicts were resolved when you were a child.

▶ B. In general, would you say that in your own childhood experience with social conflicts, adults used a *laissez-faire* approach (that is, they took the role of *turtles*, figuratively pulling their heads in under their shells and leaving you to resolve disputes on your own); adults used a *directive* approach (that is, they took the role of *sharks*, figuratively using their sharp teeth to correct or punish you); adults used a *supportive* approach (that is, they took the role of *owls*, patiently taking time to engage you in the problem-solving process); or adults used a combination of these approaches?[5]

▶ C. As described below, act out each of the following two scenarios three times with a partner.

Tracey, a preschooler, has overwatered the ivy plant. A lot of water is flowing from the bottom of the pot onto the floor.

Kim, a preschooler, is playing with some little plastic animals instead of getting dressed for outside time.

- First have one person assume the role of the child and the other person take the role of the adult. In these roles, act out the first scenario three times: The first time, the adult acts as a *turtle*; the second time, the adult acts as a *shark*; and the third time, the adult acts as an *owl*.

- Then switch roles for the second scenario, and repeat the scenario three times, so the "new" adult can try out the roles of *turtle*, *shark*, and *owl*, and the "new" child can experience how each type of interaction feels.

With your partner, discuss and record how these role plays affected you. Which type of adult role (turtle, shark, or owl) resulted in the most mutually satisfying interaction? Why?

▶ D. Read "Uh-oh, Rachel. I'm Tellin' On You!" on *EYC* p. 63, and read over the steps for resolving conflicts discussed on *EYC* p. 405. Then, on a chart like the following, list steps (1)–(6) below, and check whether each step was **present** or **absent** in Mrs. William's interaction with the children. For any step that was absent, briefly describe **how she might have included it.**

Step	Present	Absent	How to Include Step

❶ Approach the situation calmly.

❷ Acknowledge children's feelings.

❸ Gather information.

❹ Restate the problem.

❺ Ask for ideas for solutions, and choose one together.

❻ Be prepared to give follow-up support.

▶ E. In a problem-solving approach to conflict, how do adults share control with children? Why is shared control an important element of the problem-solving process?

▶ F. How do adults focus on children's interests and strengths during the problem-solving process? Why are children's interests and strengths important to the problem-solving process?

---

[4]*For further exercises on this topic, see this study guide's Chapter 12, "Initiative and Social Relations," pp. 156–168.*

[5]*The originator of the "turtle, shark, owl" exercise is High/Scope certified trainer Betsy Evans, director and head teacher of Giving Tree School in Gill, Massachusetts.*

G. What role does adult authenticity play in the steps of conflict resolution? Why is authenticity important to solving problems?

H. In an active learning setting, how does a problem-solving approach to conflict relate to the development of children's capacities for trust, autonomy, initiative, empathy, and self-confidence?

Exercise 15

Using the Elements of Support in Everyday Situations

Before doing exercises A and B, read "Using the Elements of Support: Moving a Group of Children from Place to Place" on *EYC* pp. 64–65 for a description of how one teaching team applies the elements of support in a specific classroom situation.

A. In the scenario of Jason and the sand (*EYC* pp. 382–383), how did Jason's teacher use the elements of support—sharing control, focusing on strengths, authenticity, playfulness, a problem-solving approach to conflict—to help him solve his problem?

B. Describe how you might use the elements of support in scenarios (1) and (2).

❶ *It is cleanup time. Some children are putting toys away. Some children are playing with puzzles under the table. Some children are holding hands, looking out the window and singing.*

❷ *At the beginning of the day, Sammy and his mom arrive with four grocery bags full of empty boxes, cartons, and containers they have been saving for children to use at the center.*

Exercise 16

Self-Study: Trying Out Supportive Adult-Child Interaction Strategies

A. Review the "Strategies for Creating Supportive Climates: A Summary" in the checklist on *EYC* p. 66 (discussed on pp. 52–65). Then, with a preschool child (or children), try out some of these strategies for creating supportive climates and positive adult-child interactions. Record the strategies you tried, and for each strategy, explain what you learned from the adult-child interaction it produced. Organize your answers in a chart with these headings:

Strategy Tried	*Reflections on Findings*

B. Think about the elements of support—sharing of control between adults and children, focusing on children's strengths, forming authentic relationships with children, making a commitment to supporting children's play, and adopting a problem-solving approach to social conflict.

❶ Which of these elements of support are you already using with children? For each element you use, give an example of how you do so.

❷ Which elements of support would you like to strengthen in your interactions with children? For each element, how might you do this?

Exercise 17

"Sense of Self" Revisited

After completing some or all of the exercises in this chapter, re-read the definition of "sense of self" you wrote in exercise 1. Then, respond to the following questions about an adult sense of self.

A. For an adult, what is the relationship between being authentic and one's sense of self?

B. How is an adult's sense of self different from a young child's sense of self?

C. What role does an adult's sense of self play in adult-child interactions?

Exercise 18

Self-Assessment: Supportive Adult-Child Interactions

Assess your own interactions with children by setting up a video camera and recording yourself (or have someone videotape you) while you support children's play. Afterward, as you watch the videotape, make notes about your interaction, and decide how you would rate yourself on a scale of 1–5 on the items from the High/Scope Program Quality Assessment (PQA): Preschool Version, which appear on the next two pages. In item III-G mentally change the phrase "throughout the day" to "during this play session/interaction."

PQA Item III-D. Adults use a variety of strategies to encourage and support child language and communication.

Supporting evidence/anecdotes:

☐ Adults control or disrupt conversations with children (e.g., lecture or quiz children, interrupt, talk over, dominate, redirect topic).

☐ Adults sometimes share control of conversations with children.

☐ Adults share control of conversations with children (e.g., let children initiate conversations, take turns, wait patiently for children to form thoughts without interrupting).

☐ Adults do not observe and listen to children; children are told to be quiet so they can listen to adults or follow directions.

☐ Adults sometimes observe and listen to children.

☐ Adults observe and listen to children throughout the day (e.g., wait for child to speak first, remain quiet until child indicates he or she is done talking).

☐ Adults ignore children when they talk; adults give directives.

☐ Adults sometimes converse with children in a give and take manner.

☐ Adults converse with children in a give and take manner. They make comments, observations, acknowledgments, and seek children's ideas.

☐ Adults ask children many questions, especially closed-ended or leading questions with predetermined correct answers (e.g., "What color is this circle?").

☐ Adults ask a moderate number of questions; questions are both closed-ended and open-ended.

☐ Adults ask children questions sparingly; questions are open-ended (i.e., to discover child's ideas and thought processes); questions relate directly to what the child is doing.

1	2	3	4	5

PQA Item III-F. Adults participate as partners in children's play.

Supporting evidence/anecdotes:

☐ Adults do not participate in children's play.

☐ Adults sometimes participate as partners in children's play.

☐ Adults participate as partners in children's play.

☐ Adults attempt to dominate children's play (e.g., by redirecting play around adult ideas, telling children what to play with, how to play, or who to play with).

☐ Adults use some strategies as partners in children's play.

☐ Adults use a variety of strategies as partners in children's play:
• Observe and listen before and after entering children's play
• Assume roles as suggested by children
• Follow the children's cues about the content and direction of play
• Imitate children
• Match the complexity of children's play
• Offer suggestions for extending play
• Stay within the children's play theme

1	2	3	4	5

PQA Item III-G. Adults encourage children's initiatives throughout the day.

Supporting evidence/anecdotes:

☐ Adults do not encourage children's initiatives.

☐ Adults sometimes encourage children's initiatives.

☐ Adults encourage children's ideas, suggestions, and efforts by
  • Listening to children
  • Encouraging children to talk about what they are doing
  • Trying out and imitating children's ideas
  • Using children's words
  • Commenting specifically on children's work

☐ Adults impose their own ideas of what children should be learning and doing.

☐ Adults sometimes encourage and support children's strengths and interests.

☐ Throughout the day, adults encourage and support children's strengths and interests.

1	2	3	4	5

PQA Item III-L. Children participate in resolving conflicts.

Supporting evidence/anecdotes:

☐ Adults shame, scold, and/or punish children in conflict.

☐ Adults provide children in conflict with statements about manners or morals.

☐ Adults treat conflict situations with children matter-of-factly:
  • Approach children calmly and stop any hurtful actions.
  • Acknowledge children's feelings.

☐ Adults decide what the problem is without input from the children or don't state the problem at all.

☐ Adults state the problem with some confirmation from the children (e.g., "Did you take that from her?")

☐ Adults involve children in identifying the problem:
  • Gather information from the children (what happened, what upset the child).
  • Restate the problem.

☐ Adults solve problems for children without explanation.

☐ Adults sometimes impose their own ideas about how conflicts should be resolved and choose a solution.

☐ Adults involve children in the process of finding and choosing a solution for a problem:
  • Ask the children for solutions and encourage them to choose one together.
  • Be prepared to give follow-up support when children act on their decisions.

1	2	3	4	5

Supportive Interaction Issues to Ponder and Write About

▶ A. To what extent are sharing control between children and adults and sharing control between adults valued by our society?

▶ B. Are young children entitled to a supportive climate with supportive adult-child interactions? Why or why not?

▶ C. Violence, abuse, neglect, are part of many children's lives today. How important is it for these children to participate in supportive adult-child interactions? Why?

▶ D. *Know yourself. To thine own self be true.* In active learning settings, how do these two adages apply to early childhood educators and their interactions with young children?

▶ E. Is there a role for criticism in early childhood teaching and learning? If there is, what is it, and how can it occur within the context of supportive adult-child interactions? If there is not, why isn't there? Can people learn from their mistakes without being criticized? If yes, how? If no, why not?

▶ F. What is the role of playfulness in creativity, teamwork, science, the arts, and teaching and learning? To what extent does our current society value playful adults? Playful children?

▶ G. Think of a family, social, study, or work group that you belong to. What do you imagine would happen if all the members of the group focused on one another's strengths?

▶ H. If, from a very young age, children consistently experience a problem-solving approach to conflict, what impact might they have on society when they are adults?

▶ I. Look at the sets of teaching strategies in the checklists on pp. 40 and 66 of *EYC*. What relationship do you see between the descriptions of what adults do in the two lists?

Related Publications

"Adult-Child Interaction." 1996. Ch. 1 in *Supporting Young Learners 2: Ideas for Child Care Providers and Teachers,* Nancy A. Brickman, ed., 3–56. Ypsilanti, MI: High/Scope Press.

Evans, Betsy. 2002. *You Can't Come to My Birthday Party! Conflict Resolution With Young Children.* Ypsilanti, MI: High/Scope Press.

Graves, Michelle. 1999. "A Child Development Approach to Rules and Limits." *High/Scope Extensions* (November/December): 1–3.

High/Scope Program Quality Assessment (PQA): Preschool Version (Field-Test Edition). 2001. Ypsilanti, MI: High/Scope Press.

Hohmann, Charles, and Warren Buckleitner. 1992. "Interactions That Promote Learning." In *High/Scope K–3 Curriculum Series: Learning Environment,* 53–78. Ypsilanti, MI: High/Scope Press.

Hohmann, Mary. 1991. "Social Development in the High/Scope Approach." In *Supporting Young Learners: Ideas for Preschool and Day Care Providers,* Nancy A. Brickman and Lynn S. Taylor, eds., 14–25. Ypsilanti, MI: High/Scope Press.

Hohmann, Mary. 1996. "Let Them Speak! Conversing With Children." In *Supporting Young Learners 2:*
Ideas for Child Care Providers and Teachers, Nancy A. Brickman, ed., 7–14. Ypsilanti, MI: High/Scope Press.

Post, Jacalyn, and Mary Hohmann. 2000. "Supportive Adult-Child Interactions." In *Tender Care and Early Learning: Supporting Infants and Toddlers in Child Care Settings,* 57–95. Ypsilanti, MI: High/Scope Press.

Powell, Amy. 1991. "Be Responsive!" In *Supporting Young Learners: Ideas for Preschool and Day Care Providers,* Nancy A. Brickman and Lynn S. Taylor, eds., 26–34. Ypsilanti, MI: High/Scope Press.

Tompkins, Mark. 1991. "'Special' Children: Building on Their Strengths." In *Supporting Young Learners: Ideas for Preschool and Day Care Providers,* Nancy A. Brickman and Lynn S. Taylor, eds., 53–60. Ypsilanti, MI: High/Scope Press

Related Videos

Adult-Child Interactions: Forming Partnerships With Children. 1996. Color videotape, 60 min. Ypsilanti, MI: High/Scope Press.

The High/Scope Approach for Under Threes, U.S. Edition. 1999. Color videotape, parts 4–6, "Supportive Styles of Interaction," "Effective Communication," and "Social Conflict," 20 min. London, England: High/Scope Institute U.K. (Available from High/Scope Press, Ypsilanti, MI)

Supporting Children in Resolving Conflicts. 1998. Color videotape, 24 min. Ypsilanti, MI: High/Scope Press.

The High/Scope approach recognizes the important role families play in young children's development. We want children to know who they are—to be well rooted in their home cultures. If we do our jobs well as parents, educators, and caring adults, we will enable children to understand their own families and learn from others.

—*Educating Young Children*, p. 69

Involving Families in Active Learning Settings

Creating an Active Learning Environment Based on Family Life

Our own families influence the way we understand the families of children in our care. From our experiences with the families we grew up in, we construct our own understanding of what families are and how they interact. With a partner or group of friends, discuss and record your answers to the following:

► A. Recall your own childhood family. What did you learn about the concept of family from your own family experiences?

► B. For exercises (1)–(5), imagine that you are creating an active learning early childhood center that you yourself would enjoy attending as a preschooler.

❶ What *materials* from your family's home or community would you include in your center (for example, materials you as a child played with or would particularly have liked to play with)?

❷ What *choices* reflecting your family life might you as a child make as you play and converse in your center?

❸ What *language* or dialect from home would you speak and expect to hear? What forms of nonverbal communication from home would you expect adults at the center to understand?

❹ What positive *adult support* strategies from home would you want adults to practice?

❺ How would you want the staff of your early childhood center to support the members of your family?

► C. To what extent do the choices you have made in your life reflect or not reflect your childhood family experiences (for example, choices you have made about education, work, relationships, religion, dress, food, and recreation)?

Extending the Elements of Support to Families

Since the family is essential to the child's life and well-being, our interactions with family members call for the same principles of support that guide our interactions with children. Therefore, supporting family involvement in a High/Scope early childhood center involves shared control between children and adults, a focus on children's and families' strengths, authenticity on the part of adults, and a commitment to children's family-inspired play. The following exercises examine some of the issues involved in providing this kind of support to children and families whose experiences may be different in some way from our own.

► A. Read the dialogue in the middle of p. 72 of *EYC*, and answer these questions:

❶ What ideas about birth do Jana, Teri, and Beth express?

❷ How might these children have formed their ideas about the birth process?

❸ From what you know about adult support and shared control, why didn't their teacher, Mr. Levy, "correct" Jana and Beth?

▶ B. As she talks about the M. family (*EYC* pp. 72–73), home visitor Sally W. says, "[Initially] I was terrified. Their lives were so different from mine." Think of a family you know that is very different from your own family. List any things about this family that might frighten or concern you. List the strengths this family possesses.

▶ C. Authenticity on the part of adults involves responding to children's comments and ideas nonjudgmentally. When Lerone (*EYC* p. 73) talks about not liking Marla because she does not have any hair, Ms. Holmes accepts his concern about Marla's appearance and supplies the facts behind Marla's hair loss. Based on Ms. Holmes's conversation and what you know about active learning and adult support, how might you respond to the following comments by preschool children?

❶ "If God made everything, who made God?"

❷ "Uh-oh! She didn't eat her greens! She's gonna get sick, isn't she teacher?"

❸ "Don't suck your finger. 'Cause that means you're a baby and your teeth'll fall out!"

❹ "Boys don't play with dolls! Only girls do that!"

❺ "My mom says not to paint 'cause I might get my clothes dirty."

▶ D. Some family-inspired play, like Bonnie Lou's visits to the "metal hospital" (*EYC* p. 73), may be somewhat unsettling to adults. From the child's perspective, however, having a family member in a hospital, residential treatment program, or jail may simply be accepted as a fact of life, just as some children accept as a fact of life that a family member is away at school, at a job, or in the armed services.

❶ Recall your own childhood. What are some times when family members were absent from your family? When you attended a family event, such as a wedding, funeral, reunion, picnic, or holiday celebration? When you witnessed an event you didn't understand?

❷ To what extent did you incorporate these experiences into your play or imagination?

❸ What kinds of interactions did you have or do you wish you could have had with a supportive adult at these times?

❹ How can you use your own early childhood experiences and knowledge of active learning to support children who are involved in family-inspired play?

Exercise 3

Valuing Families

Read "Bringing Family Art to Early Childhood Settings" (*EYC* p. 75) and "Parents Join the Team" (*EYC* p. 93), and look at the photographs of parents on *EYC* pp. 26, 68, 79, and 83.

▶ A. How do early childhood staff value families in these situations?

▶ B. What strengths and interests might members of your childhood family contribute to the early childhood center you created for exercise 1B?

▶ C. One way to value absent family members is through communication. How can we communicate with and encourage children to communicate with family members who are institutionalized, traveling, or living away from the child's home?

▶ D. "Parents are as important as teachers in educating their child—education must be a partnership."[7] Why do you agree or disagree with this preschool teacher's statement?

Exercise 4

Examining Who We Are and Where We Came From[8]

Though we are all unique individuals, our immediate and extended families influence who we are, what we believe, and how we act. Therefore, both to understand ourselves and to understand how the children in our care are also shaped by their families, it is important to examine our roots.

▶ A. Use a chart like the one at the top of the next page to list the family birthplaces you know or can discover.

[7]Smith, Teresa, *Parents and Preschool* (Ypsilanti, MI: High/Scope Press, 1980), p. 105.

[8]This exercise, which High/Scope originally used in the May/June 1988 **High/Scope Extensions** curriculum newsletter, was adapted, with permission, from Williams, Leslie R., and Yvonne De Gaetano, **ALERTA: A Multicultural, Bilingual Approach to Teaching Young Children** (Menlo Park, CA: Addison-Wesley, 1985), pp. 54–58.

Yourself							
Mother				Father			
Grandmother		Grandfather		Grandmother		Grandfather	
GGMom	GGDad	GGMom	GGDad	GGMom	GGDad	GGMom	GGDad

▶ D. Share your personal culture chart with someone else who has also done this exercise. Talk together about your perceptions of each other's personal culture, and record your reflections.

▶ E. If you are team-teaching, ask each member of your team to do parts A–C of this exercise, and then do exercise D by all talking together about your findings. (You could also do this exercise with parents on a home visit or during a parent meeting.) What did you discover about team members (or parents)?

▶ F. Based on your findings about yourself, what filters or blinders might you have unconsciously acquired as part of your belief system? That is, what in your own experience, personal culture, and set of beliefs might influence what you see, expect to see, and understand about people who may be operating from a different set of practices, attitudes, and beliefs?

Exercise 5

Home Visiting

One important way to learn about and value children and their families is through home visits. Exercises A–F examine this form of supportive interaction.

▶ A. Think for a moment about some family you know well (besides your own). How did you get to know this family?

▶ B. Read about Sally W.'s visit to the M. family (*EYC* pp. 72–73 and 76–77).

▶ B. Based on the family birthplace data you have collected, what strikes you about your family origins?

▶ C. To examine your culture, answer questions (1)–(3) about yourself and briefly record your answers in a "personal culture chart" with these headings.

What? (Things)	*How?* (Practices)	*Why?* (Beliefs About the World)

❶ *What things* are important to me, make me feel "at home," secure? For example, you might consider foods, music, clothing, art, dance, stories/writing, household items.

❷ *How do I behave* in various roles, on various occasions? How do I express myself? For example, you might reflect on holidays and celebrations, customs and traditions, recreation, child-rearing practices, health practices, language, self-expression.

❸ *What beliefs/attitudes make me behave the way I do?* For example, you might think about your beliefs and attitudes concerning religion, education, work, community, family, friends.

❶ What strikes you about this family?

❷ What strikes you about Sally's approach to the M. family?

▶ C. Look at the home visit photographs on EYC pp. 77–78. What do they say about the home visitor's role?

▶ D. What kinds of information do Mrs. Ernal and Mr. Milton record (EYC pp. 78–79) about children and families during their home visits? What relationship can you see between their notes and the emphasis an active learning approach places on people's strengths and interests?

▶ E. Read "Establishing a Supportive Climate With Parents" (EYC p. 79).

❶ How do these strategies relate to the elements of support discussed in EYC Chapter 2?

❷ Why is there an overlap between the strategies we use to support children and the strategies we use to support their families?

❸ How have you or could you use these strategies with parents?

▶ F. With some adults who make home visits, talk about the pros and cons of visiting families in their homes.

❶ What have been their concerns about home visits?

❷ What do they find to be benefits of home visits?

▶ G. If possible, arrange to make a home visit to the home of a preschooler you know, perhaps one of the children you observed for a child study exercise in Chapter 1 or Chapter 2. Listen, take cues from family members, and find out all you can about family interests and pursuits. Record your findings and reflections.

Exercise 6

Taking Part in Community Life

Participating in the life of the community provides opportunities to meet children and their families in "real life" outside the early childhood center.

▶ A. Think back to your own school days. When did you see your teachers outside the classroom? What impact did these out-of-school sightings and interactions have?

▶ B. What characterizes the community in which you currently live? Where and when do you or might you encounter young children and their families?

▶ C. What are the benefits and what are the drawbacks of living in the community where you teach?

Exercise 7

Learning About Children Through Observation

As you observe children, you gather information about their personal cultures—*what things* they like to play with, *how they play* and interact, and *what they believe* about the world.

▶ A. Read through one teaching team's observations of Billy (EYC p. 85), and record their observations in a personal culture chart like the one you made for yourself (exercise 4C on p. 29).

▶ B. Read through the "Key Experience Notes" on Jonah (EYC pp. 306–307), and record in a personal culture chart what you learn about Jonah's personal and family culture.

▶ C. What have you found out about the personal and family culture of your study child (from Chapter 1 or Chapter 2) or of your home visit child (from exercise 5G on this page)? Record your findings in a personal culture chart.

Exercise 8

Reaching Out to Families

There are many ways to welcome families into the early childhood setting. (See discussion on reaching out to families, EYC pp. 80–81 and 93.) For each strategy in exercises A–I, describe ways you have already used the strategy to include families in your program and/or describe ways you could use the strategy to reach out to families in the future.

▶ A. Sharing anecdotes verbally

▶ B. Planning family gatherings

▶ C. Publicly acknowledging families

▶ D. Conversing at drop-off/pickup

▶ E. Encouraging family lunch hours

F. Sending home brief anecdotes

G. Sending home a newsletter

H. Including families on field trips

I. Including families in the center

Exercise 9

Creating Positive Relationships With Families

One way to create positive relations with families is to encourage adult family members to work with children in the early childhood setting. (See "Parents Join the Team," *EYC* p. 93.)

A. Read the following scenario,[9] and describe how each of the elements of support in exercises (1)–(5) came into play in this series of adult-child, adult-adult interactions.

At a social gathering for parents of children in one preschool classroom, a non-English-speaking mother asked a friend to let the teacher know she would like to work in the classroom on Fridays. The teacher welcomed the mother's involvement.

Once in the classroom, the mother shadowed her son, scolding him when he did something she considered inappropriate, such as not sharing a toy. One day, when the son became involved in a physical conflict with another boy, the mother scolded her son in her native language, brought both children to the teacher, and in-

dicated that a fight had occurred. The teacher then knelt at the boys' physical level, held one hand of each boy, and began a problem-solving conversation. The mother stayed close, observing the interaction.

Several weeks later, the mother was again present when a physical conflict occurred. The teacher observed her as she took the hand of each child and sat down on the floor with them. Then the mother said, "Talk." Although the mother was unable to verbally facilitate the conversation, she had clearly indicated what needed to occur.

During the period in which she was a classroom volunteer, the mother began to learn the English language as well as the language of the children. She spent increasing amounts of time playing with her son and his friends.

❶ Shared control

❷ Focus on strengths

❸ Authenticity

❹ Commitment to supporting play

❺ Problem-solving approach to conflict

B. One teaching team made a point of including mothers in the classroom on a daily basis. They summed up their open, give-and-take approach this way: "If she's a good mother, it helps the group. If she's a poor mother, it helps her."[10] How does or doesn't this philosophy of parent involvement support an active learning approach to teaching and learning?

C. One teaching team collected daily anecdotes on their children (*EYC* pp. 95–102); used

the *High/Scope Child Observation Record (COR) for Ages 2½–6* (described on *EYC* p. 98); and at parent conferences, shared with parents the Parent Report Form that is included in the COR. Read their Parent Report Form describing Dan H. (on the next page). How might sharing this kind of information about Dan help his teachers, Julie and Carol, build a positive relationship with his parents?

Exercise 10

Seeking Our Better Selves

It is our job as teachers to look for the best in children and their families. One of the surest ways to encounter competence and creativity, for example, is to seek and expect to find it.

A. The way we describe people influences how we see and treat them. (See discussion on *EYC* pp. 83–84.) Record all the ways you can describe the people listed in exercises (1)–(4). First list the **positive,** descriptive words, and then list the **negative,** judgmental words you might use.

❶ Yourself

❷ Your family

❸ A child you know

❹ The child's family

B. Which set of descriptors would you rather have people keep in mind as they interact with you, your family, the child you know, and the child's family? Why?

---

[9]*This scenario was written by High/Scope consultant and teacher Barbara Carmody. It first appeared in the High/Scope Extensions curriculum newsletter, May/June 1995, p. 6.*

[10]*Smith, Teresa,* **Parents and Preschool** *(Ypsilanti, MI: High/Scope Press, 1980), p. 64.*

Parent Report Form

The High/Scope Child Observation Record (COR) is designed for use with children aged 2 years 6 months to 6 years 0 months in early childhood settings. After keeping anecdotal records of the child's behaviors in regular program activities over several weeks or months, the teachers complete this form by noting behaviors that best characterize the child's experiences in each of six general curriculum areas. The teachers focus on child-initiated behaviors, that is, actions that the child undertakes independently rather than in response to adult directions. Some of the observations teachers have made about your child in each of the six areas are summarized below.

Child's name: Dan H.
Date of Birth: 8/18/91 Age: 4
Date observations began: 9-11-95
Date this form completed: 3-5-96
Class: High/Scope Preschool
Completed by: Julie A. and Carol B.

I. Initiative

Dan indicates a desired activity, place of activity, material, or playmates with a short sentence. On his own, he uses materials or organizes active play involving two or more steps.

11/2: At work time in the block area, Dan built a "hideout" with large hollow blocks. Then he wrote with markers on several pieces of paper, taped the papers to his hideout, and said to Carol, "Look at all those signs on my hideout. They say mean stuff!" (The signs consisted of lines of scribbles.)

3/5: At planning time Dan said, "I'm going to hide Scott." Then he went to the block area and hid Scott under the beanbags and a sheet.

II. Social Relations

Dan sustains interactions with familiar adults and with other children. Classmates identify him as a friend. He sometimes attempts to solve problems with other children by negotiation or other socially acceptable means.

12/9: At work time in the block area, Dan and Scott built a "spaceship" with all the hollow blocks. They placed "lookouts" (dinosaurs and farm animals) all around on the blocks. Then they went to the art area to make "signs" for their spaceship. Dan filled a piece of paper with rows of I's and L's.

1/5: At work time Dan and Kyle put on hats and gloves. They told Michelle she could be the "audience" and sit on the "lawn." Dan was wearing "protection" because he was setting up fireworks. When some of the fireworks got close to Michelle, he explained, "Don't worry. They pop in the sky!"

2/9: At small-group time, when Kyle wanted an alligator that Dan had and suggested that they take turns with it, Dan said, "I know! We could both use it together. We could make one big house for all the animals." And they did.

III. Creative Representation

Dan uses materials to make or build things that include at least three details. He engages in cooperative pretend play with other children.

9/22: At work time in the block area, Dan and Petey used the hollow blocks to make a "helicopter." It included a propeller (two long planks crossed on top) that Dan described as "that thing that makes it go up," "a seat in the back for the drivers," "a big computer," and "seats for other people."

11/10: At work time in the block area, Dan and Rochelle built a "bridge" with the wooden planks that went from the art area to the "refrigerator"— a block structure with cylinder blocks for "beer" and "orange juice."

IV. Music and Movement

Dan exhibits body coordination. He manipulates small objects with precision.

9/11: At outside time, Dan pulled Scott in the wagon around the blacktop.

3/4: At small-group time, Dan made a "birthday cake" using scrap materials, glitter, and glue. He squeezed glue on foam pieces and then placed cardboard tubes and straws vertically in small groups in the pool of glue on top of the foam. Finally, he squeezed more glue on the foam and sprinkled glitter on top of it.

V. Language and Literacy

Dan participates in classroom conversations. He uses sentences that include two or more ideas. He picture-reads, telling about the story from the pictures on the cover or in the book. Dan copies or writes identifiable letters and his own name.

9/27: At greeting-circle time, Dan "read" the book *Will You Play with Me?* to Julie. He pointed to the pictures, told the story, and turned the pages.

10/17: At work time in the block area, Dan said to Carol, "Do you know why I have my gloves on? So I won't get electrocuted in case I have to touch some wires!"

12/18: At work time in the block area, Dan made a "hideout" with Heidi and Axel, using all the hollow blocks and unit blocks. Then he made a sign by writing his name and two lines of I's and L's. Reading the sign, he said, "It says, 'Don't come in unless we're home!'"

VI. Logic and Mathematics

Dan uses comparison words and counts over 10 objects. He also uses words that describe the direction of movement of things.

9/13: At small-group time, as he played with three plastic horses, Dan said, "Here's the biggest (pointing to the biggest horse), and then no more biggest (pointing to the other two smaller horses)."

11/9: At work time in the block area, as Dan walked on a hollow block structure, he said, "That's the beginning. Here you walk up and have to balance. (He was on a ramp.) And then you don't have to balance. (He was standing on a flat block.)"

3/1: At work time Dan brought Julie a "birthday cake" he made from pegs and a pegboard. He counted 25 "candles" as he pointed to each peg.

C. In your life, who are the people who have seen and anticipated the best in you? What effect has their belief in you had?

D. What roles do you see for children's family members in the early childhood center you created in exercise 1B on p. 27?

Exercise 11

"Hot Button" Issues

Within many families there are "hot button" issues that can cause conflict between family members, between generations, and between families and nonfamily members. For example, disagreements often arise over differing perspectives on bedtimes, mealtimes, limit setting (see *EYC* p. 84), pacifiers and other comfort items, dress, tidiness, and relationships to authority.

A. Think of a "hot button" issue you have experienced, and explore it from the perspectives listed in exercises (1)–(3).

❶ Generational perspectives: On this issue, what is your view? Your parents' view? Your grandparents' view?

❷ Communal perspectives: On this issue, what is your family's approach? Your neighbor's approach? Your community's (school's, church's) approach?

❸ Philosophical perspectives: Concerning this issue, what would be a supportive approach? A directive approach? A laissez-faire approach?

B. What does this exercise suggest to you about the perspectives you might find among the staff and families at an early childhood center on these or similar issues?

C. How might the five elements of support listed in exercises 9A(1)–(5) on p. 31 help you deal with a broad range of beliefs and expectations around a particular issue?

Exercise 12

Self-Assessment: Parent Involvement

One way to assess the extent to which parents are involved in an active learning early childhood setting is to use Section V items from the High/Scope Program Quality Assessment (PQA): Preschool Version. If you are currently teaching, use these items (given on the next two pages) to make notes and to rank on a scale of 1–5 your own parent involvement undertakings.

Exercise 13

Family Involvement Issues to Ponder and Write about

A. What is a family?

B. In our society, many people hope that a child's family will be an ongoing partner in the child's education and experience. At the same time, they believe that the child's task is to become increasingly independent. How might these seemingly contradictory points of view work together? How might they influence the way early childhood staff interact with families?

C. Traditional Navajo weavers weave a spirit path—an almost invisible thread of contrasting color—from one edge of their cloth to the other. The spirit path represents change, creativity, life itself; it thus permits the power of the universe to flow in and out of the weaving and allows traditions to shift to make way for new ideas and customs. To what extent are families static, unchanging? To what extent are they dynamic, growing, open to new possibilities? To what extent is your image of families (your own, others') static? To what extent is it dynamic?

D. What draws together early childhood staff members and the families of the children they serve? What pulls them apart?

E. If home is parents' territory and the early childhood setting is teachers' territory, where can parents and teachers meet on equal ground? What is the impact on children when teachers, parents, or both relinquish some of their power and control over "their territories"?

F. What kinds of experiences enable people to enjoy and interact positively with families whose practices and beliefs are different from their own?

G. When you were a young child, how did you view your family? Has your view of your family changed over the years? If it has changed, how and why?

H. Why is or isn't family involvement in early education worth the effort it takes on the part of families and teaching teams?

I. Read about "talking story" (*EYC* p. 185). How might you use this way of communicating with families who find questions intimidating or who believe that questions are rude and disrespectful?

PQA Item V-A. The program provides a variety of opportunities for parents to become involved in the program.

Supporting evidence/anecdotes:

☐ There are no activities or materials to help parents become involved in the program.

☐ The program provides some parent-oriented activities or materials to help parents become involved in the program.

☐ There are many parent involvement options consistent with a variety of parent interests and time constraints, e.g., parents may
- Volunteer in the classroom
- Bring in materials
- Attend parent meetings and workshops
- Serve on parent advisory councils
- Meet with teachers to discuss children's progress
- Support children's learning at home
- Read or contribute to a parent newsletter

☐ The program does not encourage parent participation.

☐ The program sometimes encourages parent participation.

☐ The program encourages parent participation (e.g., providing child care, arranging transportation, scheduling events at times convenient for parents, making reminder phone calls the day before, networking parents with one another).

| 1 | 2 | 3 | 4 | 5 |

PQA Item V-D. Staff and parents exchange information about the curriculum and children's development.

Supporting evidence/anecdotes:

☐ Staff and parents do not exchange information about the curriculum and children's development.

☐ Staff provide parents with information about the curriculum and children's development (e.g., an information packet is given or mailed to parents, staff tell parents how the program works).

☐ Staff and parents exchange information about the curriculum and children's development (e.g., staff send regular mailings or newsletters about the program and invite parent reactions, staff and parents interact during program workshops, staff and parents exchange frequent informal comments about activities, staff invite observations and answer questions from parents about the program).

☐ Staff do not seek input from parents about the program and children's development.

☐ Staff sometimes seek input from parents about the program and children's development.

☐ Staff seek input from parents about the program and children's development.

| 1 | 2 | 3 | 4 | 5 |

PQA Item V-E. Staff and parents interact informally to share information about the day's activities and children's experiences.

Supporting evidence/anecdotes:

☐ Staff and parents do not interact informally.

☐ Staff and parents sometimes interact informally.

☐ Staff and parents frequently interact informally to update each other about the child's recent experiences (e.g., conversing during drop-off and pickup times, bringing in or sending home things the child has made, sending notes, making calls).

☐ Staff communicate with parents in a blunt, distracted, or disinterested manner.

☐ Staff communicate respectfully with parents.

☐ Staff use an interested and unhurried manner to communicate clearly, honestly, and respectfully with parents about the program, their children, and issues of interest or concern.

1	2	3	4	5

PQA Item V-F. Staff and parents share information about how to promote and extend children's learning and social development at home.

Supporting evidence/anecdotes:

☐ Staff and parents do not exchange ideas or materials to support children's learning and social development at home.

☐ Staff and parents exchange some ideas or materials to support children's learning and social development at home.

☐ Staff and parents exchange many ideas and materials to support children's learning and social development at home (e.g., ideas and materials might pertain to the educational potential of ordinary household objects, how everyday family activities can be social learning experiences, how to promote language development).

☐ Staff do not seek input from parents about how they are supporting children's development at home.

☐ Staff sometimes seek input from parents about how they are supporting children's development at home.

☐ Staff seek input from parents about supporting children's development and additional resources.

1	2	3	4	5

Related Publications

Adams, Marilyn, and Bonnie Freeman. 1991. "Multicultural Education." In *Supporting Young Learners: Ideas for Preschool and Day Care Providers,* Nancy A. Brickman and Lynn S. Taylor, eds., 47–52. Ypsilanti, MI: High/Scope Press.

Banks, Nita. 1999. "Involving Parents in Curriculum Planning: A Head Start Story." *High/Scope Extensions* (March/April), 1–3.

Carmody, Barbara. 1996. "Elementary School—When the Parent Is No Longer Apparent." "Modeling to the Role Model." In *Supporting Young Learners 2: Ideas for Child Care Providers and Teachers,* Nancy A. Brickman, ed., 159–62. Ypsilanti, MI: High/Scope Press.

"The Family Connection." 1996. Ch. 4 in *Supporting Young Learners 2: Ideas for Child Care Providers and Teachers,* Nancy A. Brickman, ed., 145–174. Ypsilanti, MI: High/Scope Press.

Frede, Ellen. 1984. *Getting Involved: Workshops for Parents.* Ypsilanti, MI: High/Scope Press.

Freeman, Bonnie Lash, and Marilyn Adams Jacobson. 1991. "Multicultural Education: What It Is, How to Do It." In *Supporting Young Learners: Ideas for Preschool and Day Care Providers,* Nancy A. Brickman and Lynn S. Taylor, eds., 47–52. Ypsilanti, MI: High/Scope Press.

Graves, Michelle. 2000. *The Teacher's Idea Book 4: The Essential Parent Workshop Resource.* Ypsilanti, MI: High/Scope Press.

Greene, Ed. 1991. "Continuity: Building Bridges Between Settings." In *Supporting Young Learners: Ideas for Preschool and Day Care Providers,* Nancy A. Brickman and Lynn S. Taylor, eds., 229–36. Ypsilanti, MI: High/Scope Press.

High/Scope Educational Research Foundation. 2001. *You & Your Child* (parent newsletter series). Ypsilanti, MI: High/Scope Press.

High/Scope Program Quality Assessment (PQA): Preschool Version (Field-Test Edition). 2001. Ypsilanti, MI: High/Scope Press.

Lafferty, Pam. 1998. "Building Bridges With Parents." *High/Scope Extensions* (January/February), 1–3.

Markley, Carol. 1997. "Preparing for Successful Parent Conferences." *High/Scope Extensions* (March/April): 1–3.

Marshall, Beth. 1996. "Classrooms That Reflect Family Experiences." In *Supporting Young Learners 2: Ideas for Child Care Providers and Teachers,* Nancy A. Brickman, ed., 137–142. Ypsilanti, MI: High/Scope Press.

Olmsted, Patricia P., and David P. Weikart. 1994. *Families Speak: Early Childhood Care and Education in 11 Countries.* Ypsilanti, MI: High/Scope Press.

Olmsted, Patricia P., and Marilyn Adams Jacobson. 1991. "Parent Involvement: It's Worth the Effort." "Involving Busy Parents." In *Supporting Young Learners: Ideas for Preschool and Day Care Providers,* Nancy A. Brickman and Lynn S. Taylor, eds., 237–48. Ypsilanti, MI: High/Scope Press.

Post, Jacalyn, and Mary Hohmann. 2000. "The Caregiver Team and Their Partnership With Parents." In *Tender Care and Early Learning: Supporting Infants and Toddlers in Child Care Settings,* 295–355. Ypsilanti, MI: High/Scope Press.

Smith, Teresa. 1980. *Parents and Preschool.* Ypsilanti, MI: High/Scope Press.

Terdan, Susan M. 1996. "The 'Parent-First' Approach to Home Visits." In *Supporting Young Learners 2: Ideas for Child Care Providers and Teachers,* Nancy A. Brickman, ed., 151–58. Ypsilanti, MI: High/Scope Press.

Tizard, Barbara, Jo Mortimore, and Bebb Burchell. 1983. *Involving Parents in Nursery and Infant Schools.* Ypsilanti, MI: High/Scope Press.

Weikart, David P. 1996. "Parent-Child Relationships: A Foundation for Learning." In *Supporting Young Learners 2: Ideas for Child Care Providers and Teachers,* Nancy A. Brickman, ed., 145–50. Ypsilanti, MI: High/Scope Press.

Weikel, Linda. 1991. "Talking With Parents About Play and Learning." In *Supporting Young Learners 2: Ideas for Child Care Providers and Teachers,* Nancy A. Brickman, ed., 163–72. Ypsilanti, MI: High/Scope Press.

Teamwork is an interactive process. Working as a team, adults use many of the same strategies that they use as they work with children. At its best, teamwork is a process of active learning that calls for a supportive climate and mutual respect.

—***Educating Young Children***, *p. 89*

4

Working in Teams: Adult Collaboration to Promote Active Learning

Working as a Team

With a partner, do each of the following two activities.

- *Blind walk:* As a team, choose a place or an object to walk to that is 10 feet or more away from you. Then, both of you cover your eyes, join hands, and walk to your destination without benefit of sight.

- *Letter count:* Find a newspaper and select one page. Then choose a letter of the alphabet, and as a team, count the number of times the letter you have chosen appears in print on the newspaper page you have selected.

Together, discuss and record the advantages of doing each of these two activities as a team.

Recalling Team Experiences

Our own experiences with people and how we view authority may influence the way we perceive our role as members of early childhood teaching teams. With a partner or several friends, discuss the following:

▶ A. Recall some teams or groups you have worked within. For each team or group you recall, answer exercises (1)–(4).

❶ What was the team's or group's purpose?

❷ What was the team's or group's interaction style (directive/hierarchical, supportive/participatory, or laissez-faire/low key)?

❸ How did the team or group solve problems?

❹ What effect did team or group membership have on you?

▶ B. In an active learning early childhood program, adults adopt a supportive/participatory adult-child interaction style and a problem-solving approach to conflict. Why does or doesn't it make sense for the adults to use this same interaction style and problem-solving approach among themselves?

Observing Teaching Teams

▶ A. Observe an early childhood teaching team during a team meeting (this could be the team you are a member of). Who is on the team? When does the team meet? Who else joins the team from time to time?

▶ B. Why is or isn't it important for support staff to meet with the teaching team to coordinate their interactions with a particular child?

▶ C. To what extent might it be possible to treat parents who work in the classroom as part of the teaching team and to include them in team meetings on the days they volunteer? Give a rationale for your point of view.

Choosing to Collaborate

The way we regard and interact with people is generally the result of conscious or unconscious choices we make. For example, encountering a young woman wearing a lip ring, one could think, "Her lip ring is so unsettling to me, I don't even want to look at her, much less speak to her." Or one could think, "Well, if I watch and speak with her, maybe I will be able to find out why she enjoys wearing a lip ring." For examples of similar choices, read "Breaking Down Barriers to Collaboration" (*EYC* p. 96).

▶ A. List some individual characteristics you have encountered in other people, and based on each characteristic you list, describe the positive and negative choices you could make regarding that person. Organize your answers in a chart with these headings:

Characteristic	Choice to Erect Barriers	Choice to Collaborate

▶ B. How might the choices you make about personal characteristics of teaching team members affect the way you interact with them? To what extent can you change your attitude towards people?

Learning to Level: Open Communication[11]

To do this exercise, you will need two other people for role-play partners. Together read "Communicate openly" (*EYC* pp. 94–95). Then, as described in the insert on the next page, assign roles, and role-play the "Team-Planning Scenario" in three different ways. Identify the communication pattern you selected for each of the three role plays. For each pattern, describe the effect it had on your interactions with team members.

Gathering Accurate Information About Children

The reason that teaching teams form, choose to collaborate, and strive to communicate as *levelers* is to be able to focus their energies and abilities on understanding and supporting the children in their care. Read the discussion about gathering accurate information on children on *EYC* pp. 95–98. Then do the following exercises with a partner.

▶ A. Choose one of the key experience chapters (Chapters 10–19) in *EYC*. Read the anecdotes/ observations at the beginning of each key experience in the chapter you choose. What characterizes all of these anecdotal observations about children?

[11]*The terms and inspiration for this exercise come from Satir, Virginia, **The New Peoplemaking** (Mountain View, CA: Science and Behavior Books, 1988), pp. 80–115.*

▶ B. Look at the *EYC* photograph on p. 294, and read the following three anecdotes (observations) about what Misha (the child in the photo) is doing.

- *Observation 1:* Misha painted by herself in the art area at work time. She was very focused on her task and made deliberate brush strokes in a variety of colors.

- *Observation 2:* Misha made a colorful large painting at the easel at work time in the art area. She seemed to have a clear idea of what she wanted to accomplish. She made a distinct geometric rainbow-like design instead of covering the entire paper with layers of paint.

- *Observation 3:* At work time in the art area on a large sheet of paper at the easel, Misha painted a series of three-sided figures (like square, backwards C's) that varied in color and size. She surrounded the smallest figure in the middle by successively larger figures.

Which of the three anecdotes provides the most accurate information about what Misha is doing? Why?

▶ C. Look at the *EYC* photos on pp. 33, 249, and 292. For each child (Markie on p. 33, Tasha on p. 249, and Trevor on p. 292) write an anecdote (brief factual note) to describe what he or she is doing. (After you have written your anecdotes, for reference, you may wish to look at the sample anecdotes for these photographs given at the end of this chapter, on p. 45.)

▶ D. Choose three other photographs in *EYC*. Make up a name for each child you observe, and write an observation/anecdote for each photograph. Use a chart like the following (on p. 42) to record your answers. Have a partner look at your photographs, read, and respond to the accuracy of your anecdotes.

Team-Planning Scenario

Two of you play co-teachers in a preschool classroom. The third person on your team plays the education specialist who has been working with them in the classroom that day. One teacher is afraid that the program's emphasis on children's play, planning, and problem solving will not prepare children for "real school." The other teacher has worked with this approach, has seen its effect on children, and feels very comfortable with it. The education specialist wants the program to be developmentally appropriate. One teacher has raised her concerns at the team's daily team-planning meeting.

- Decide who will play **the teacher concerned about "real school"**; who will play **the teacher who supports children's initiatives and active learning;** and who will play **the education specialist** who advocates developmental appropriateness. Then have each character select one of the following ineffective communication patterns to use in his or her role:

  Placater—*Verbal behavior:* No matter what you really think or feel, agree with everyone else, so they will not get angry with you. Apologize for what you say. Assume that you are responsible for everything that goes wrong. *Nonverbal behavior:* Get down on your knees. Wring your hands and hold them out as though begging. Assume the posture of a victim. Look happy, but feel worthless.

  Blamer—*Verbal behavior:* Find fault with everything anyone says, so they will know they can't push you around. Cut everyone down. Talk in a loud, tyrannical voice. Make "you" statements, such as "You never . . ." Ask questions like "Why do you always . . . ?" but do not wait for answers. *Nonverbal behavior:* Point your finger accusingly. Put your other hand on your hip. Look mean, but feel like a rotten person.

  Computer—*Verbal behavior:* Use a lot of big words, even if you don't know what they mean, so everyone will think you really know a lot and will be afraid to question you. Talk calmly and reasonably but without feeling. The important thing is to keep talking and to sound intelligent. *Nonverbal behavior:* Sit stiffly upright and remain as motionless as possible. Keep your hands and face still. Look superior, but feel stupid.

  Distracter—*Verbal behavior:* Change the topic and bring up irrelevant topics, so you do not have to deal with anything real or uncomfortable. Do not respond to the point. Use a singsong voice. *Nonverbal behavior:* Keep busy moving your arms, legs, body, and face. Stand up, sit down, walk around, sort out the things in your purse or briefcase, pick lint off someone else's garment, and so forth. Look clownish, but feel scared.

- **Role Play 1:** Role-play the "Team-Planning Scenario" for about 5 minutes. Assume the roles, and use the communication patterns you have selected.

- **Role Play 2:** Role-play the "Team-Planning Scenario" again. Keep the same roles, but this time each character should select a different one of the four communication patterns to use.

- **Role Play 3:** Repeat the "Team-Planning Scenario" again. Keep the same roles, but this time sit in a circle while each person communicates as a **leveler,** as described below.

  Leveler—*Verbal behavior:* Say what you mean, sharing your thoughts and feelings in an honest, straightforward manner. Give your full attention to others as they speak. *Nonverbal behavior:* Keep your facial expressions and the way you move in harmony with what you are saying. For example, when you feel concerned, you look concerned.

EYC Photograph	Anecdote/Observation

▶ E. How does making factual, nonjudgmental observations of children relate to the *leveler* style of communication described on p. 41?

▶ F. Turn to *EYC* p. 306. In the "Key Experience Notes" on that page, read the Jonah anecdote for 1/21 under "Initiative and Social Relations" (see also the related anecdote for 3/28 under "Language and Literacy"). Is it possible to write factual, nonjudgmental anecdotes about children's struggles with social conflict? Why or why not?

Exercise 7

Child Study: Observing a Child's Actions and Language

Find a preschool child at play and observe the child for 10–20 minutes. As you watch and listen, make brief notes and/or sketches about what the child is **doing and saying.** After you have completed your observation, based on your brief notes, compose a series of readable, factual **anecdotes** about the child. Another way you might approach this observation is to watch and listen for 1 minute, then write for 1 minute about what you have seen and heard. Repeat this process until your 10 or 20 minutes are up, then take time to turn your notes into readable, factual anecdotes that someone else could read and understand. Use a format like the following.

Child's Name_____ Date_____
Location_____
Time of Day_____
Time Observed _____

Notes, Jottings, Sketches	Factual, Readable Anecdotes

Exercise 8

Interpreting Observations

After observing children to gather accurate information about what they are saying and doing, the next step is to ask "So what? What does this mean? What do I do with this information?" With a partner do the following exercises based on Vanessa's play episodes and the discussion on *EYC* pp. 99–102.

▶ A. Pick out at least three things that the teaching team observed about Vanessa, and connect their **observations,** their **interpretations** of her actions, and the **support strategies** they planned to try. Organize your answer in a chart like the following (which includes one example):

Observation	Interpretation	Support Strategies
V. calls, "Look it!" (5 times)	—Uses language to call attention to her accomplishments. —Seeks out Karl's acknowledgment	Be attuned to V. as she plays, so when she looks for adult acknowledgment, an adult is there to converse with her.

▶ B. Select three of the photograph children you have already written anecdotes about for exercise 6C or 6D. In a chart like the one below, for each child, write your **observation/anecdote,** make an **interpretation** of the anecdote using the key experiences (*EYC* p. 22) as your guide, and design or select (from *EYC*) a **support strategy** to try with the observed child.

Child	Observation/ Anecdote	Interpretation/ Key Experience	Support Strategy

▶ C. This time, look over the observations you wrote about your study child (exercise 7 on this page). Select three anecdotes/observations, and record them again in a chart like the following. Then, for each **anecdote/observation,** decide what it means in terms of **key experiences,** and design or select a **support strategy** to try. (For lists of support strategies related to each of the key experiences, see *EYC* pp. 339, 373, 407, 430, 445, 462, 472, 486, 507, and 523.)

Study Child:		
Observation/ Anecdote	Interpretation/ Key Experience	Support Strategy

▶ D. Read through the "Key Experience Notes" about Jonah (*EYC* pp. 306–307). From what you know about him through these anecdotes, what are some things Jonah might enjoy doing at small-group time? For each thing you name, cite the supporting anecdote(s).

Sharing Team Responsibilities

Do the following exercises with a partner.

▶ A. If you are or have been part of an early childhood teaching team or have watched a teaching team in action, use a chart like the following to show how the team's sharing of duties and responsibilities helps make the day run smoothly for adults and children. (Look at the lists in the insert on *EYC* p. 102.)

Responsibility/ Duty	Who Is Responsible	Rotation Schedule

▶ B. What common agreements and procedures has your team (or a team you have observed) reached regarding each of the in-class situations described in exercises (1)–(5)?

❶ Maintaining contact with each other.

❷ One adult needs to leave the room.

❸ One adult is too upset to mediate a conflict.

❹ A child prefers one of the adults over the others on the team.

❺ Supporting classroom volunteers.

▶ C. A teaching team works together most effectively when members are able to build an egalitarian working relationship. What factors may work against equality? What factors may work for equality?

Including Volunteers on the Team

Read *EYC* pp. 103–105, which recount the story of Mrs. Jones's experiences as a volunteer member of an early childhood teaching team. Then discuss the following questions with a partner, and record your answers.

▶ A. Why does the team include Mrs. Jones in their daily team-planning meeting on the days she volunteers in the classroom?

▶ B. In what specific ways do team members support Mrs. Jones?

▶ C. What are Mrs. Jones's strengths and contributions to the team?

Self-Assessment: Teamwork

Items IV-B and IV-D of the High/Scope Program Quality Assessment (PQA): Preschool Version provide one way to assess your current teaching team (or to think about team-teaching situations you might encounter). On these items (given on the next page), rate your team on a scale of 1–5 and make notes that support your ratings.

Teamwork Issues to Ponder and Write About

▶ A. "To trust means not just to tolerate a variety of viewpoints, acting as an impartial referee, assuring equal air time to all. It means to try to *connect,* to enter into each student's perspective."[12] How does this definition of trust by Belenky and her colleagues relate to the work of teaching teams?

▶ B. What do the following quotations by Rensis Likert and Gordon Lippitt, cited on *EYC* p. 95, say about individual differences among team members?

Likert: A major human asset in productive teams is the "capacity to use differences for purposes of innovation and improvement, rather than allowing differences to develop into bitter, irreconcilable, interpersonal conflict."

Lippitt: "In an effective group, persons are willing to express their differences openly. Such expressions create authentic communication and more alternatives for a quality decision."

▶ C. What are the pros and cons of teamwork?

▶ D. Why is teamwork important for adults in an early childhood setting? What effect does adult teamwork have on children?

▶ E. What are the advantages of *daily* team planning in this child-observation-based educational approach?

▶ F. How would you work as a team if you spoke only English and your team member spoke only Spanish?

---

[12]Belenky, Mary Field, Blythe McVicker Clinchy, Nancy Rule Goldberger, and Jill Mattuck Tarule, **Women's Ways of Knowing: The Development of Self, Voice, and Mind** *(New York: Basic Books, 1986), p. 227.*

PQA Item IV-B. Staff use a team-teaching model and share responsibilities for planning and implementing program activities.

Supporting evidence/anecdotes:

☐ Staff do not have regularly scheduled planning sessions.

☐ The head/lead teacher plans all activities.

☐ Assistants and aides play only nonteaching roles (e.g., wipe tables, prepare materials).

☐ Staff meet once or twice a week to plan.

☐ The head/lead teacher sometimes plans activities with other members of the teaching team.

☐ Assistants and aides sometimes conduct and/or participate in children's activities.

☐ Staff meet daily to discuss and make plans for the next day.

☐ Teaching team members participate equally in planning activities.

☐ Teaching team members conduct and participate in children's activities.

1	2	3	4	5

PQA Item IV-D. Staff record and discuss anecdotal notes as the basis for planning for individual children.

Supporting evidence/anecdotes:

☐ Staff do not record anecdotal notes about children.

☐ Notes are subjective and reflect personal judgments rather than recording what children are doing and saying.

☐ Notes focus on children's negative behaviors and deficits (what children do incorrectly, or cannot do).

☐ Staff do not use anecdotal notes to plan for individual children.

☐ Staff do not share anecdotal information with parents.

☐ Staff sometimes record anecdotal notes about children.

☐ Notes are sometimes objective.

☐ Notes sometimes focus on children's strengths.

☐ Staff sometimes use anecdotal notes to plan for individual children.

☐ Staff sometimes share anecdotal information with parents.

☐ Staff record and discuss anecdotal notes about children daily.

☐ Notes are objective and reflect what children are doing and saying throughout the day.

☐ Notes focus on children's strengths (what children are doing).

☐ Staff use anecdotal notes to plan for individual children.

☐ Staff share anecdotal information with parents.

1	2	3	4	5

Related Publications

Buckleitner, Warren, Bonnie Freeman, and Ed Greene. 1991. "Effective Team Teaching: Working Together Works Better." "Sharing Your Workload: Creating a Sensible Division of Labor." In *Supporting Young Learners: Ideas for Preschool and Day Care Providers,* Nancy A. Brickman and Lynn S. Taylor, eds., 189–97. Ypsilanti, MI: High/Scope Press.

Buckleitner, Warren, and Susan M. Terdan. 1991. "Getting Started: The First Day of the Rest of the Year." In *Supporting Young Learners: Ideas for Preschool and Day Care Providers,* Nancy A. Brickman and Lynn S. Taylor, eds., 220–25. Ypsilanti, MI: High/Scope Press.

"Child Observation, Team Planning, Assessment." 1996. Ch. 7 in *Supporting Young Learners 2: Ideas for Child Care Providers and Teachers,* Nancy A. Brickman, ed., 267–302. Ypsilanti, MI: High/Scope Press.

Gerecke, Katie. 1997. "High/Scope's Approach to Children With Special Needs." *High/Scope Extensions* (January/February): 1–3.

Graves, Michelle. 1996. "Planning Around Children's Interests." *High/Scope Extensions* (May/June): 1–3.

Graves, Michelle. 1996. *The Teacher's Idea Book 2: Planning Around Children's Interests.* Ypsilanti, MI: High/Scope Press.

Graves, Michelle. 1998. "Toys From Home: One Teaching Team's Dilemma." *High/Scope Extensions* (May/June): 1–3.

Hannibal, Sam, Michelle Graves, Carol Beardmore, Barbara Carmody, and Mary Hohmann. 1996. "Building a Teaching Team." In *Supporting Young Learners 2: Ideas for Child Care Providers and Teachers,* Nancy A. Brickman, ed., 269–74. Ypsilanti, MI: High/Scope Press.

High/Scope Child Observation Record (COR) for Ages 2½–6. 1992. Ypsilanti, MI: High/Scope Press. (Also available in COR for Windows 95/98 and COR-Mac formats.)

High/Scope Program Quality Assessment (PQA): Preschool Version (Field-Test Edition). 2001. Ypsilanti, MI: High/Scope Press.

Hohmann, Charles. 1996. "Saving Time With the COR–PC or the COR–Mac." In *Supporting Young Learners 2: Ideas for Child Care Providers and Teachers,* Nancy A. Brickman, ed., 283–84. Ypsilanti, MI: High/Scope Press.

Hohmann, Mary. 1991. "Observation and Feedback: Why They're So Important for You, for Children." In *Supporting Young Learners: Ideas for Preschool and Day Care Providers,* Nancy A. Brickman and Lynn S. Taylor, eds., 198–204. Ypsilanti, MI: High/Scope Press.

Marshall, Beth. 1996. "Anecdotes: Focusing in on Children." "Anecdote-Writing Hints." In *Supporting Young Learners 2: Ideas for Child Care Providers and Teachers,* Nancy A. Brickman, ed., 285–92. Ypsilanti, MI: High/Scope Press.

Neill, Polly. 1999. "The High/Scope PQA: Assessing Program Quality Through Classroom Observations." *High/Scope Extensions* (September): 1–3.

Post, Jacalyn, and Mary Hohmann. 2000. "The Caregiver Team and Their Partnership With Parents." In *Tender Care and Early Learning: Supporting Infants and Toddlers in Child Care Settings,* 295–355. Ypsilanti, MI: High/Scope Press

Schweinhart, Lawrence J. 1996. "An Effective Tool for Developmentally Appropriate Assessment." In *Supporting Young Learners 2: Ideas for Child Care Providers and Teachers,* Nancy A. Brickman, ed., 277–82. Ypsilanti, MI: High/Scope Press.

Slack, Sandy. 1996. "Rethinking the IEP Process." In *Supporting Young Learners 2: Ideas for Child Care Providers and Teachers,* Nancy A. Brickman, ed., 293–302. Ypsilanti, MI: High/Scope Press.

Tompkins, Mark. 1991. "Assessment: A System That Works for You, Not Against You." "Child-Oriented Lesson Plans: A Change of 'Theme.'" In *Supporting Young Learners: Ideas for Preschool and Day Care Providers,* Nancy A. Brickman and Lynn S. Taylor, eds., 205–19. Ypsilanti, MI: High/Scope Press.

Weikel, Linda. 1997. "Mentoring in the High/Scope Preschool Classroom." *High/Scope Extensions* (May/June): 1–3.

Answers to Exercise 6C

Sample anecdotes for EYC photos:

P. 33, Markie: In the block area at work time, Markie built a tall "window" tower using cardboard brick blocks and thin boards. He said, "One for you . . . One for you" as he placed one small block in each window. He stood on two big wooden blocks stacked on a small chair to reach the top.

P. 249, Tasha: At small-group time, Tasha added food coloring to the dough she mixed in her bowl.

P. 292, Trevor: At work time, Trevor stood in front of the mirror and drew on his face, hands, and arms with colored markers. He spent cleanup time in the bathroom, scrubbing himself with water, soap, and towels!

Part 2

The Active Learning Environment

Young children need space to use materials, explore, create, and solve problems; space to spread out, move around in, talk freely about what they are doing; space to work alone and with others; space to store their belongings and display their inventions; and space for adults to join them in support of their intentions and interests.

—**Educating Young Children**, *p. 111*

5

Arranging and Equipping Spaces for Active Learners

An Ideal Place to Be

▶ A. With a partner, discuss and design your "ideal personal place," a place where the two of you can do all the things both indoors and outdoors that are most interesting and important to you as individuals. Together, make a sketch or layout of this ideal environment.

▶ B. Share your sketch and ideas with another pair of partners who have also done this exercise. As a foursome, describe how this exercise relates to planning and setting up environments for young children.

Exercise 2

Childhood Memories of Play

Our own childhood play may remind us of some important features of environments for active learners. With a partner or group, discuss and record answers to A–D.

▶ A. What did you like to do as a young child?

▶ B. Where did you enjoy playing? Do you tend to remember indoor places, outdoor places, or both? Why?

▶ C. What materials did you use and enjoy? Did your favorite playthings tend to be "found" (natural or scrap) materials, or were they usually commercial or purchased materials? Why?

▶ D. How do your recollections bear on the task of arranging and equipping spaces for active learners? To what extent can and should an early childhood setting include space and materials for the kinds of play you remember enjoying as a young child?

Exercise 3

Making Play Space Inviting

People in general respond favorably to places that are comfortable, homelike, and welcoming, and preschool children are no exception! With a partner, do the following.

▶ A. Think about places that you find inviting, where you feel welcome. What particular features make them so?

▶ B. Look at the play spaces shown in the photographs in *EYC* Chapter 5 and throughout the rest of the book. What makes these play spaces inviting to children?

▶ C. What makes the house area homelike for Miguel in "Miguel Seeks the Comfort of Familiar Things in the House Area" on *EYC* p. 130? What makes it homelike for the children in "House Area Flexibility in Action" on *EYC* p. 130?

▶ D. How do your ideas about comfort correspond to the bulleted list of guidelines on *EYC* p. 113? What additional elements of comfort would you consider?

▶ E. Imagine that your current living space (house, apartment, dorm, co-op, condo, houseboat, trailer) is about to be converted into an early childhood center. What architectural changes (see *EYC* p. 114) would you make to accommodate active learners? Sketch the overall floor plan, including your modifications.

Exercise 4

Providing Pleasant Spaces for Eating, Napping, and Personal Storage

In some Northern European countries, children in early childhood settings nap on birch bunk beds (with low sides) built into the wall. Each child snuggles under a quilt. At mealtimes, tables are often set with low candles (similar to votive candles) or with flowering plants placed on woven cloth table runners. Some materials are stored in baskets. With a partner, consider the following.

▶ A. Think of your own favorite places to eat, sleep, and store your belongings. What characterizes these places?

▶ B. How might some of the elements you enjoy be included in early childhood centers where children regularly eat, nap, and store their coats, boots, pictures, toys, and so forth?

▶ C. Often in institutional settings, the focus is on efficiency rather than on comfort and aesthetics. Why? Are comfort and aesthetics qualities we value and wish to provide for our children? Why or why not?

▶ D. How might you make eating and napping comfortable and pleasing in the center you sketched for exercise 3E?

Exercise 5

Arranging Play Spaces to Meet Particular Needs

The same space can be arranged in many ways, depending on the needs of the program and the particular children in it. Pages 51–52 of this study guide provide four copies of a diagram to use with each of exercises A–D. The diagram shows a rectangular room that opens onto an outdoor play yard and also has stairs leading up to another room of similar size with a small kitchen. With a partner, use the diagrams to plan and sketch the way you would arrange the lower room, given the set of program needs described in each exercise.

▶ A. Arrange the space for a full-day program for 3-year-olds.

- Program children eat breakfast and lunch and take a nap after lunch.
- Interest areas should include a sand and water area, block area, house area, art area, toy area, and book area.

▶ B. Arrange the space for a half-day program for 3- and 4-year-olds (16 children in the morning, 16 children in the afternoon).

- Program children have a snack but no meals or nap.
- Include room for a block area, house area, art area, toy area, and book area, and also room for sand and water, computers, and music and movement activities.

- On arrival, after hanging up their coats, the children go straight to the book area for greeting circle.

▶ C. Arrange the space for a summer half-day program for 4-year-olds.

- Program children have a snack but no meals or nap.
- Interest areas should include a sand and water area, block area, house area, art area, computer area, toy area, and book area, and also room for music and movement.
- When it does not rain, some of the areas are set up on the blacktop outside the sliding glass doors.

▶ D. Arrange the space for a full-day program for 4-year-olds.

- Program children eat breakfast and lunch, and some of them nap.
- Include room for sand and water, computers, and movement and music, as well as a block area, house area, art area, toy area, and book area.
- On Sunday mornings the space is used for teen and adult Sunday school classes.

Exercise 6

Materials With Meaning for Children

Children are drawn to materials they see adults using. For examples of such materials, read "Identifying Children's Family Cultures" (*EYC* p. 120) and "Family Experiences Classroom Checklist" (*EYC* p. 121).

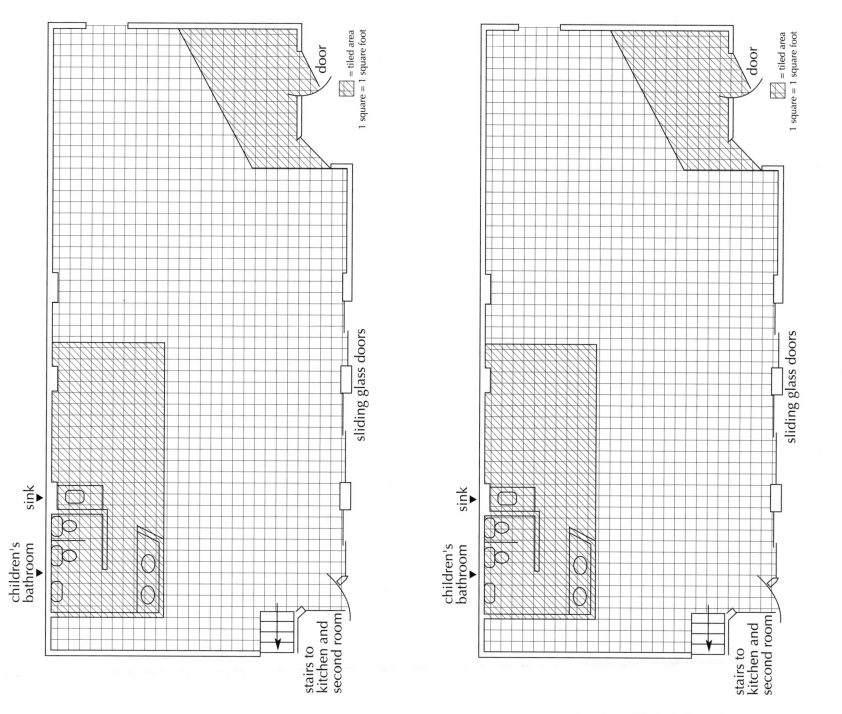

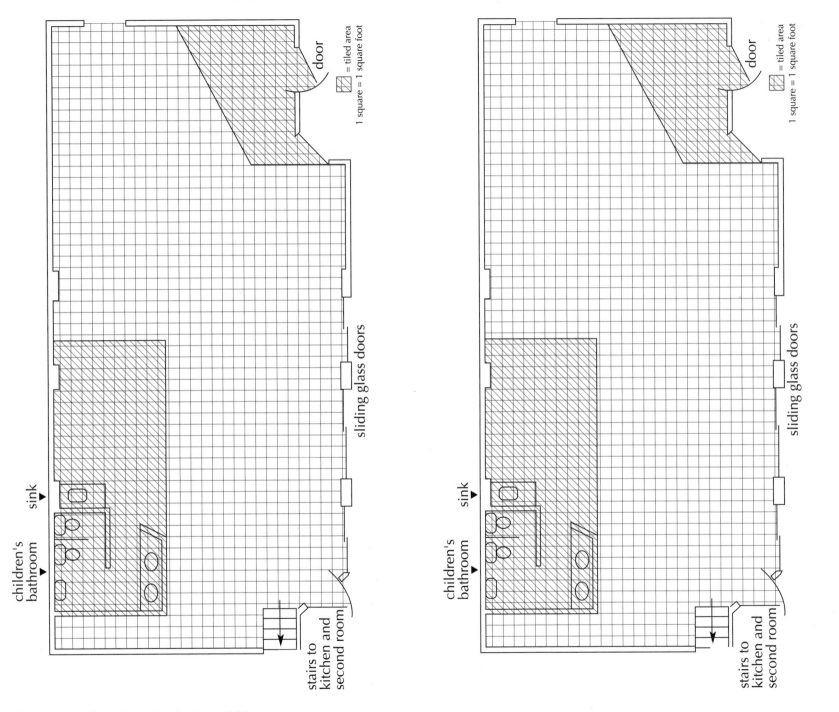

Person	Materials Reflecting Family Life	Materials Reflecting Community Life	Materials Reflecting Personal Interests

▶ A. Name some materials that have particular meaning to each person listed in (1)–(4). Arrange your answers in a chart like the one above.

❶ Yourself as a child

❷ Your sibling, cousin, niece/nephew, child, neighbor (select one)

❸ Your mother (or father) as a child

❹ Child in your class (or study child from earlier chapters)

▶ B. Imagine that the children in your chart are all in one preschool program. How and/or where would you include their materials in a preschool setting?

Exercise 7

Scrap, Natural, and "Real" Materials

Children explore and play with a wide variety of materials, many of which are not sold through child-supply catalogs or toy stores. Natural materials, such as sand, water, sticks, and stones, and interesting kinds of scrap materials are as fascinating to children now as they were to children generations ago. With a partner, do the following exercises.

▶ A. Read "Realness" (EYC p. 129). Why are "real" objects and materials—the ones that adults actually use—so important to young children?

▶ B. How might this need for "realness" relate to children's development of trust, autonomy, initiative, empathy, and self-confidence (discussed in EYC Chapter 2)?

▶ C. Look through the photographs in EYC, and use a chart like the following to list the natural, scrap, and "real" materials you see.

Natural Materials	Scrap Materials	"Real" Materials

▶ D. Take a walk outside through a natural area (park, woods, beach, meadow, field, pasture). Collect things that catch your eye, things you think children might like to explore and play with. After your walk, record what you collected, and explain why these materials are appealing and where you might include these materials in an early childhood play space.

▶ E. Take a walk through the commercial area(s) of your community, and think about what surplus materials business owners might be willing to

donate to an early childhood program. For example, a car dealership may donate steering wheels; a printer, envelopes and paper samples; a grocery store, Styrofoam trays and grocery bags; a beauty shop, empty shampoo bottles. Make a list of businesses, and list the materials each might donate.

▶ F. Approach a business owner and make a request for materials for your study child's program or for the program in which you arc currently teaching. What materials were you able to obtain?

▶ G. Visit the secondhand and thrift stores in your area—for example, the Salvation Army store, the Goodwill store, the St. Vincent De Paul store. What inexpensive real materials do you see that children might enjoy having in the house area?

Exercise 8

Materials Lists

For exercises A–D, look over all of the materials lists in EYC (these are listed in the insert on p. 54).

▶ A. What strikes you about the EYC lists of materials? How might they be useful to you?

▶ B. How do the key experiences help teaching teams think about materials to include in the interest areas?

▶ C. What are open-ended materials? Taken as a whole, what do the EYC materials lists say about providing open-ended materials for children?

▶ D. Suppose a child wants to "make a long, long necklace." What are some things from the EYC lists that the child could use to carry out this plan?

Materials Lists in *EYC*

Child Study:
Favorite Materials

▶ A. Review the child studies you completed in earlier chapters. Based on your observations, list some materials that your study child likes to use. (If you have observed more than one child, list materials for one or more of them.)

▶ B. Observe a preschool child at play for 10–20 minutes. As you watch and listen, write down what **materials** you see the child using, **how** the child is using them, and what in particular the child is **doing or attempting to accomplish** with them. Use a form like the following.

Child's Name_____ Date_____
Location_____
Time of Day_____
Time Observed _____

Materials	How Child Uses Materials	Intentions

Materials Expert

Think about a particular kind of early childhood play material that you find especially interesting or enjoyable. For example, maybe you really like blocks, paints, computer software, picture books, vehicles, baby dolls, or dress-up clothes. Choose whatever type of material appeals to you, and then do exercises A–D to become an expert on that material.

▶ A. Go to the Internet or library to find and read books or articles about the type of material you have selected. List the references you use, and briefly summarize what you learn from each one.

▶ B. If you are researching material that can be purchased, look at a variety of sales catalogs to find the scope and price range of these materials. Use a chart like the following to organize your findings.

Catalog	Material Description	Price

▶ C. Would it be possible to make the material you are researching? If yes, list resources that provide instructions for doing so, or describe your own plans for doing so. Estimate the cost of the needed materials.

▶ D. Suppose you are submitting a proposal to a funding source (perhaps to the director of your program) for purchasing or making the materials on which you have become an expert. In presenting the proposal, you need to give a rationale for this expenditure. Why are the materials you have chosen to research important to have in an active learning early childhood center? What types of play and what key experiences do they support?

Materials That Worry Adults and Satisfy Children

Throughout *EYC* you will see photographs of children using materials that may cause some adults to be concerned, usually about health and safety issues. For example, some adults believe that young children should not use computers, because they may become physically unfit or asocial from spending too much time in front of the screen (see *EYC* pp. 142–143 for a response to this concern). Do exercises A–B with a partner.

▶ A. For each of the potentially worrisome materials listed in (1)–(12), list typical adult concerns about the material. Then describe what children actually do with the material, why they enjoy it, and what they might be

learning from using it. Organize your answers in a chart like the following.

Material	Adult Concern	Child Use and Learning

① Anatomically correct dolls

② Cookie cutters

③ Food (to string, paint, etc.)

④ Glue in bottles

⑤ Hats for dress-up

⑥ Make-up/face paint

⑦ Pacifiers, other comfort objects

⑧ Saws and hammers

⑨ Scissors

⑩ Staplers

⑪ Stencils

⑫ Water, squirt bottles

▶ B. Which of the materials listed in exercises A(1)–(12) would you include in your early childhood setting? Why?

Storing and Labeling Materials

Storing and labeling materials promotes the find-use-return cycle in early childhood classrooms. (For a discussion of this process, see *EYC* pp. 121–123.)

▶ A. How does accessible storage of materials promote children's autonomy, initiative, and independence?

▶ B. Look at the photographs of labels on *EYC* pp. 122, 457, and 464, and read "A Label for David's Tub" (*EYC* p. 116). How are labels related to children's development of language and literacy?

▶ C. Consider the material on which you have become an expert (from exercise 10 on p. 55). How could you store and label these materials? List a variety of possibilities.

▶ D. Labeling the materials in an early childhood center takes time and energy. Who could help you in this process?

Examining Interest Areas

▶ A. Spend time in an early childhood center when the children are not present, and play in each one of the interest areas. Record which materials you found most compelling, and explain how the arrangement of space affected your choice of materials and your play with them.

▶ B. Return to the center while the children are engaged in the interest areas at work time (choice time, free play). For the duration of work time, rotate in observing the interest areas, observing each area for one minute at a time (you will need a stopwatch or a watch with a second hand). For each one-minute observation, record the **number of children** in the area and what **materials** they are using. Continue this rotational observation process until work time ends, and record your findings in a chart like the following.

Area	Minute #	Number of Children	Materials Used

▶ C. Based on the data you have collected, what conclusions can you draw about the use of interest areas and materials? For example, which areas and materials were used the most, used moderately, used very little or not at all? Why? Based on your observations, what changes might you make in the way the room is arranged and equipped?

▶ D. What, if any, is the correlation between your own experiences playing in the interest areas in exercise A and the way you observed children using the interest areas in exercise B?

Dividing Space Into Interest Areas

With a partner, read "Organizing Space" and "Establishing Interest Areas," the first two sections of the checklist on *EYC* p. 147. Using these two sections of the checklist as a guide, do exercises A–C. After completing A–C, discuss your three space arrangements with another pair who have also done these exercises.

▶ A. Arrange an *indoor-outdoor room in a warm climate* (use Diagram A on p. 57) so it is an active learning space for 16 preschool children.

▶ B. Arrange a *room in a public building* (use Diagram B on p. 57) so it is an active learning space for 16 preschool children.

▶ C. Arrange the *first floor of a house* (use Diagram C on p. 58) so it is an active learning space for 16 preschool children.

Arranging an Outdoor Play Space

After reviewing pp. 144–145 of *EYC*, design an outdoor play space that would transform an outdoor space you are familiar with (for example, the yard attached to your current dwelling, the open space around a public building) into a child-centered play space for active learners. You have unlimited funds for this

A. Indoor-Outdoor Room in Warm Climate

B. Room in a Public Building

outdoor sink

door to outside court

outdoor court

coat hooks

door to hallway

sink

sink

door

C. First Floor of a House

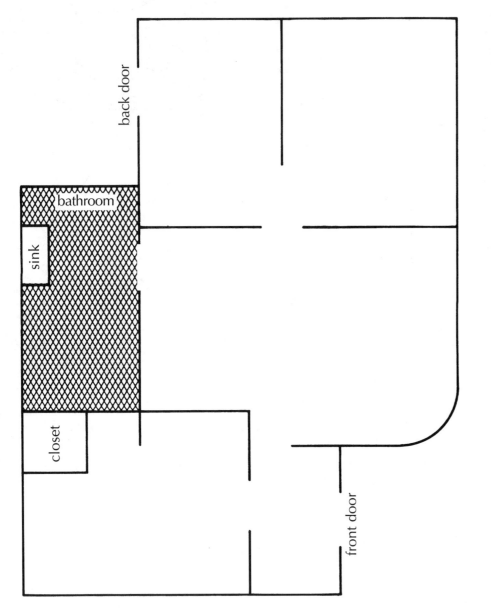

project, so do not be afraid to use your imagination! As you work, consider the following play area features:

- An enclosure around the perimeter
- Defined areas for various types of play— for example, sand and water play, gardening, riding wheeled toys, swinging, sliding, climbing, woodworking, pretend play, running, building, rolling, hiding, painting, playing ball
- Bushes, shrubs, and other landscaping features for quiet retreat
- A variety of textures—for example, sand, grass, rocks, water, wood, pea gravel
- A mound or hill for climbing and sliding
- Water accessible to the sand area
- A flat work surface in the sand area
- Shade

Exercise 16

Equipping an Outdoor Play Area[13]

It takes time and thoughtful use of available resources to establish an inviting outdoor play area.

▶ A. For each piece of play equipment in exercises (1) and (2), determine the **cost,** and list the **play options** it provides (climbing, sliding,

---

[13]This exercise was created by High/Scope educational consultant Vincent Harris. It first appeared in a slightly different version in the **High/Scope Extensions** curriculum newsletter, May/June 1991, p. 6.

carrying, filling, emptying, pouring, pretending, digging, and so on).

❶ A climbing structure

❷ Two wagons

▶ B. Balancing the cost against the play options, and taking into account the equipment's durability, which would you recommend purchasing, the climbing structure or the two wagons? Explain your reasoning.

Exercise 17

Children's Role in Room Arrangement

Arranging, equipping, and labeling an active learning play space is an ongoing task that takes time and effort. Adults do not have to do all the work themselves, however. Children can contribute to the process.

▶ A. In *EYC,* read "House Area Flexibility in Action," p. 130; "Creative Display Space," p. 134; "Toy Figures Attract Children," p. 136; and "A Book Area at Home," p. 138. What room arrangement role did children play in these scenarios?

▶ B. Suppose you are teaching in an early childhood center, and one morning, a parent arrives with a large refrigerator box. How might you involve children in deciding how to use and where to put this box?

▶ C. In two weeks, your early childhood program is moving next door, into a new building. Why would or wouldn't you involve

the children in this move? If you would involve them, what might their involvement entail?

Exercise 18

Self-Assessment: Physical Learning Environment

Items in section I of the High/Scope Program Quality Assessment (PQA): Preschool Version provide one way to assess the arrangement of an early childhood setting for its active learning potential. If you are currently teaching, use these items (four sample items appear on the next two pages) to make notes and rate your own classroom on a scale of 1–5. If you are not teaching, you might rate the classroom in which you did exercise 13 on pp. 56.

Exercise 19

Space Arrangement and Equipment Issues to Ponder and Write About

▶ A. Why is or isn't it important to provide young children with baby dolls that represent a variety of races?

▶ B. What are the **pros** and **cons** of using found space (such as a church basement or a gymnasium), shared space, and space designed specifically for young children?

▶ C. How might ideas about interest areas and materials be useful to parents?

▶ D. What public space would you particularly like to rearrange? Why?

▶ E. Do young children need a science area in which to pursue the scientific processes of observation, classification, experimentation, and drawing conclusions? Why or why not?

▶ F. Would it be possible to provide an active learning environment for preschool children that is entirely outdoors? Why or why not?

▶ G. How does an organized active learning space promote or inhibit children's spontaneity?

PQA Item I-B. The space is divided into interest areas (for example, building or block area, house area, art area, toy area, book area, sand and water area) that address basic aspects of children's play and development.

Supporting evidence/anecdotes:

☐ The space is not divided into interest areas.

☐ No interest areas are defined or apparent.

☐ Interest areas are not named and/or all areas have abstract names not easily understood by children (e.g., manipulative area, science area).

☐ Teachers and children do not refer to interest areas by area names.

☐ Some of the space is divided into interest areas (e.g., block and house).

☐ Some interest areas are clearly defined (e.g., by high and low shelves; large furniture).

☐ Some interest areas have names that are easily understood by children.

☐ Teachers and children sometimes refer to interest areas by area names.

☐ The space is divided into interest areas (block, house, art, books, toys, and so on).

☐ All of the interest areas are defined and clearly marked (e.g., by low shelves and furniture; carpeting).

☐ All interest areas have names that are easily understood by children (e.g, toy area, house area, book area).

☐ Teachers and children often refer to interest areas by area names.

| 1 | 2 | 3 | 4 | 5 |

PQA Item I-C. The location of the interest areas is carefully planned to provide for adequate space in each area, easy access between areas, and compatible activities in adjacent areas. [NOTE: If I-B is rated "1" for "space not divided" or "no interest areas defined," then I-C must also be rated "1."]

Supporting evidence/anecdotes:

☐ The location of interest areas inhibits the flow of traffic and play.

☐ Large furniture and shelves or room dividers block the view from one area to another.

☐ Inadequate space limits the number of children who can play in each interest area.

☐ Interest areas are not adjacent for compatible activities (e.g., art area is across the room from a sink or bathroom).

☐ The location of some interest areas allows children to move freely from one area to another.

☐ Some low furniture, shelves, and room dividers allow children and adults to see into some interest areas.

☐ Some interest areas have enough space for many children to play at once.

☐ Some interest areas are adjacent for compatible activities (e.g., block area is near house area).

☐ The location of all interest areas allows children to move freely from one area to another.

☐ Low furniture, shelves, and room dividers allow children and adults to see from one area to another.

☐ Each interest area has enough space for many children to play at once.

☐ Interest areas for compatible activities are adjacent (e.g., block area is near house area; art area is near sink or bathroom).

| 1 | 2 | 3 | 4 | 5 |

PQA Item I-D. An outdoor play area (at or near the program site) has adequate space, equipment, and materials to support various types of play. [Note: Where extreme weather conditions or safety considerations prevent the regular use of outdoor play space, a large and open indoor space, such as a gymnasium, may be used as a substitute.]

Supporting evidence/anecdotes:

☐ There is no outdoor play area.

☐ There is an outdoor play area nearby (e.g., local playground).

☐ The outdoor play area is easily accessible from the indoor space.

☐ The outdoor play area (or substitute large and open indoor area) is never used.

☐ The outdoor play area (or substitute large and open indoor area) is sometimes used; the indoor area is sometimes used when the outdoor area could be used.

☐ The outdoor play area (or substitute large and open indoor area) is always used; the indoor area is never used when the outdoor area could be used.

☐ The outdoor play area provides limited space, less than 35 square feet per child.

☐ The outdoor play area provides some space, between 36 and 99 square feet per child.

☐ The outdoor play area provides ample space, at least 100 square feet per child.

☐ There are no outdoor play equipment and materials.

☐ The space, equipment, and materials in the outdoor play area allow for some types of outdoor play (e.g., climbing, swinging, running).

☐ The outdoor play area includes both stationary and portable equipment and materials for various types of play (e.g., tricycles, sleds, balls, climbers, stones, boxes, buckets, chalk, scarves, brushes).

| 1 | 2 | 3 | 4 | 5 |

PQA Item I-F. Classroom materials are varied, manipulative, open-ended, and authentic and appeal to multiple senses (sight, hearing, touch, smell, taste).

Supporting evidence/anecdotes:

☐ Most of the materials in most of the interest areas lead to prescribed outcomes (e.g., art cutouts, lotto games, worksheets, coloring books, commercial toys—McDonald's figures).

☐ Some open-ended materials are available in some interest areas (e.g., boxes, paper, beads, paints).

☐ Most of the available materials in all interest areas are open-ended (e.g., blocks, books, sand, water, corks, dolls, scarves, toy vehicles, paints, shells).

☐ The classroom does not provide manipulative materials in any of the areas.

☐ The classroom provides some manipulative materials in some areas.

☐ The classroom provides many manipulative materials in all areas.

☐ Materials include many toy replicas in place of "real" items (i.e., toy plates and cups in place of real dishes, small plastic tools).

☐ Materials include some toy replicas in place of "real" items (e.g., toy register, toy broom).

☐ Materials include many "real" items in place of toy replicas (e.g., dog dish, firefighter boots, steering wheel, gardening tools, suitcases, briefcases, pots and pans, hammer and saw, telephone).

☐ Many materials do not appeal to all the senses (seeing, hearing, tasting, touching, and smelling).

☐ Some materials appeal to multiple senses (e.g., stuffed animals, instruments, play dough).

☐ Many materials appeal to multiple senses and include both natural and manufactured materials (e.g., materials include items with hard and soft textures; snacks with many smells and tastes; objects made of wood, fabric, metal, paper, liquid).

| 1 | 2 | 3 | 4 | 5 |

Related Publications

"Arranging Environments for Children." 1996. Ch. 3 in *Supporting Young Learners 2: Ideas for Child Care Providers and Teachers,* Nancy A. Brickman, ed., 115–144. Ypsilanti, MI: High/Scope Press.

Buckleitner, Warren, and Charles Hohmann. 1991. "Blocks, Sand, Paint . . . and Computers." In *Supporting Young Learners: Ideas for Preschool and Day Care Providers,* Nancy A. Brickman and Lynn S. Taylor, eds., 174–83. Ypsilanti, MI: High/Scope Press.

Esbensen, Steen B. 1987. *The Early Childhood Playground: An Outdoor Classroom.* Ypsilanti, MI: High/Scope Press.

Freeman, Bonnie Lash, and Ruby Brunson. 1991. "Home Day Care and High/Scope: A Natural Combination." In *Supporting Young Learners: Ideas for Preschool and Day Care Providers,* Nancy A. Brickman and Lynn S. Taylor, eds., 158–66. Ypsilanti, MI: High/Scope Press.

Gerecke, Katie. 1998. "Classroom Adaptations for Children With Special Needs." *High/Scope Extensions* (October): 1–3.

Harris, Vincent. 1991. "The Playground: An Outdoor Setting for Learning." In *Supporting Young Learners: Ideas for Preschool and Day Care Providers,* Nancy A. Brickman and Lynn S. Taylor, eds., 167–73. Ypsilanti, MI: High/Scope Press.

Harris, Vincent. 1996. "Open-Air Learning Experiences." In *Supporting Young Learners 2: Ideas for Child Care Providers and Teachers,* Nancy A. Brickman, ed., 119–74. Ypsilanti, MI: High/Scope Press.

High/Scope Program Quality Assessment (PQA): Preschool Version (Field-Test Edition). 2001. Ypsilanti, MI: High/Scope Press.

Hohmann, Charles. 1990. *Young Children & Computers.* Ypsilanti, MI: High/Scope Press.

Hohmann, Charles. 1996. "In the Elementary School— A New Activity Area Develops." In *Supporting Young Learners 2: Ideas for Child Care Providers and Teachers,* Nancy A. Brickman, ed., 135–36. Ypsilanti, MI: High/Scope Press.

Marshall, Beth. 1996. "Classrooms That Reflect Family Experiences." "Family Diversity Classroom Checklist." In *Supporting Young Learners 2: Ideas for Child Care Providers and Teachers,* Nancy A. Brickman, ed., 137– 44. Ypsilanti, MI: High/Scope Press.

Marshall, Beth. 1996. "'My Way'—Children at the Computer Area." In *High/Scope Extensions* (October): 1–3.

Post, Jacalyn. 1996. "Science: Here, There, and Everywhere." In *Supporting Young Learners 2: Ideas for Child Care Providers and Teachers,* Nancy A. Brickman, ed., 193–200. Ypsilanti, MI: High/Scope Press.

Post, Jacalyn, and Mary Hohmann. 2000. *Tender Care and Early Learning: Supporting Infants and Toddlers in Child Care Settings.* Ypsilanti, MI: High/Scope Press.

Rogers, Ann. 1991. "Settings for Active Learning." "Toward Culturally Diverse Settings." In *Supporting Young Learners: Ideas for Preschool and Day Care Providers,* Nancy A. Brickman and Lynn S. Taylor, eds., 151–57, 184–86. Ypsilanti, MI: High/Scope Press.

Terdan, Susan M. 1996. "The Book Area: From Beginning to End." In *Supporting Young Learners 2: Ideas for Child Care Providers and Teachers,* Nancy A. Brickman, ed., 133–34. Ypsilanti, MI: High/Scope Press.

Theemes, Tracy. 1999. *Let's Go Outside! Designing the Early Childhood Playground.* Ypsilanti, MI: High/Scope Press.

Tompkins, Mark. 1996. "Developing a Creative Art Area." In *Supporting Young Learners 2: Ideas for Child Care Providers and Teachers,* Nancy A. Brickman, ed., 127–32. Ypsilanti, MI: High/Scope Press.

Vogel, Nancy. 1997. *Getting Started: Materials and Equipment for Active Learning Preschools.* Ypsilanti, MI: High/Scope Press.

Related Videos

Computer Learning for Young Children. 1989. Color videotape, 13 min. Ypsilanti, MI: High/Scope Press.

The High/Scope Approach for Under Threes, U.S. Edition. 1999. Color videotape, part 2, "The Learning Environment," 13 min. London, England: High/Scope Institute U.K. (Available from High/Scope Press, Ypsilanti, MI.)

The High/Scope Curriculum: Its Implementation in Family Child Care Homes. 1989. Color videotape, 19 min. Ypsilanti, MI: High/Scope Press.

High/Scope K–3 Curriculum Series: Classroom Environment. 1991. Color videotape, 17 min. Ypsilanti, MI: High/Scope Press.

Setting Up the Learning Environment. 1992. Color videotape, 20 min. Ypsilanti, MI: High/Scope Press.

T he parts of the daily routine are like steppingstones on a path. Along this path children engage in a variety of adventures and experiences that interest them and suit their playful, inventive natures. A consistent daily routine allows enough time for children to pursue their interests, make choices and decisions, and solve "child-sized" problems in the context of ongoing events.

—*Educating Young Children, p. 151*

6

The High/Scope Daily Routine— A Framework for Active Learning

Defining an Active Learning Daily Routine

Do exercises A–H with a partner.

▶ A. What do you remember about your own early childhood routines?

▶ B. List some particular routines you have participated in sometime during your life, for example, school routines, work routines, or social routines. What characterized your routines?

▶ C. Exercises (1)–(4) list the distinguishing characteristics of an early childhood active learning daily routine (see *EYC* pp. 151–154 and 164). Evaluate each of the routines you listed in exercises A and B in terms of the characteristic given in each of exercises (1)–(4).

❶ Supports initiative

❷ Provides a social framework

❸ Provides a flexible structure

❹ Supports underlying values

▶ D. In the quotation on *EYC* p. 151, what is Urie Bronfenbrenner saying about reciprocity and balance of power? What do these ideas have to do with the philosophy guiding an active learning daily routine?

▶ E. In "John Dewey on Community Life" (*EYC* p. 153), what is John Dewey saying about community life, socialization, and activities in which everyone participates being the "chief carrier of control"? What does this mean? If "the activities in which all participate are the chief carrier of control," what is the role of adults?

▶ F. What would be the distinguishing characteristics of a daily routine in an authoritarian/directive setting? In a laissez faire/permissive setting? (See exercises C(1)–(4) for the characteristics of a daily routine in a supportive active learning setting.)

▶ G. How does a daily routine in a supportive setting serve as a framework for active learning?

▶ H. What are the benefits of such a routine to children? To teaching teams?

Parts of the Daily Routine

▶ A. Recall an early childhood program that you have observed or one that you have worked in or are currently working in. List all the parts of the program's daily routine.

▶ B. Exercises (1)–(7) list the periods of an active learning daily routine (described on *EYC* pp. 154–157). For each period, indicate which part of your routine (from exercise A) might correspond to it.

❶ Plan-work-recall ❺ Transition times
❷ Small-group time ❻ Eating and resting
❸ Large-group time ❼ Other
❹ Outside time

▶ C. Read "When Can I Do . . . ?" (*EYC* p. 157). When incorporating ballet into their daily routine, how did the teaching team take into account the need for child initiative, social community, flexibility, and the philosophy of active learning?

▶ D. In "Building Blocks of the Daily Routine" (*EYC* p. 159) Mrs. Ballou and Mr. Andrews use another approach to including movement experiences in their daily routine. How do they consider children's initiative, social community, flexibility, and active learning?

▶ E. Read "Parents and Children Together" (*EYC* p. 158). If you were to include parents regularly in one segment of the daily routine, which one would it be? Why?

Exercise 3

Program Length and Predictability

▶ A. Make a chart like the one below to list the **pros and cons of a full-day program** and the **pros and cons of a half-day program** for children, for teachers, and for parents.

(List children, teachers, parents in this column.)	Full-Day Program		Half-Day Program	
	Pros	Cons	Pros	Cons

▶ B. What has Swedish researcher Gunni Karrby (*EYC* p. 159) found about the impact of program length in full-day and half-day programs? How do her findings relate to the discussion of social climates (laissez-faire, supportive, directive) in *EYC* Chapter 2?

▶ C. For children, for teachers, and for parents, what are the pros and cons of a common child-arrival time (for example, all the children arrive on the bus at 8:30 a.m.)? Of staggered child-arrival times (for example, some children arrive at 8:30 a.m., some at 8:45 a.m., some at 9:00 a.m., and so forth)? Organize your answers in a chart, as you did for exercise A.

▶ D. Recall a time or situation in your life when you had no idea what was going to happen next. Based on that experience, do you think a consistent and predictable daily routine is or is not important for young children? Why?

Exercise 4

Sequencing the Daily Routine

▶ A. Elaine and Philip are a teaching team at the Scoville Junction Preschool. The scenario in each of exercises (1)–(8) describes some element of their half-day program's daily routine. For each exercise, name the part of the day described, using the terms *planning time, work time, recall time, small-group time, large-group time, outside time, transition,* and *snack time.*

❶ *It is a bright autumn day, and the children are all outdoors climbing, swinging, sliding, playing in the sand, playing ball, and riding wheel toys. Elaine is climbing on the climber with some children. Philip is helping another group of children dig a "big, deep hole" in the sandbox.*

❷ *Several children in the art area are making collages out of Styrofoam bits, fabric scraps, paper, wood scraps, foil, and glue. They call Philip over, because they can't get the foil to*

stick. *"So the glue won't work," he comments. "I wonder what else you could try." Elaine is a "patient" with a broken arm, which "doctors" are attending to in the "doctor's office." Children building in the block area stop their play momentarily to supply some "splints." In the music area, some children are playing tambourines and making up a dance; other children are playing store in the toy area using dominos, checkers, and puzzle pieces for props.*

❸ *Philip and the children at his table are finishing snack. Elaine and most of her children have gathered in the block area and are playing "Run, run, run around the circle." Gradually, as they finish eating, Philip and the rest of the children join the game.*

❹ *In the art area, Philip and half of the children are working with Play-Doh, toothpicks, and pipe cleaners. Some of the children are making people, some are making cakes, and some are squeezing, rolling, and flattening their Play-Doh. Philip tries out the children's ideas with his Play-Doh. In the toy area, Elaine and the rest of the children are finding things with holes and stringing them.*

❺ *"What would you like to do today?" Elaine and Philip each ask the children in their respective groups. Some children respond by pointing to an area. Others get a toy they would like to use. Others talk about what they will be doing.*

❻ *Children select shakers from a basket of shakers. "I wonder how we could move our shakers to the loud and soft music," Elaine says to the children. After a brief discussion in which the children suggest ways to move, Philip puts on the "loud and soft" music, and everyone—children and adults—plays shakers, moving with great energy during the loud parts of the music and moving with some restraint during the quiet parts.*

❼ At each table, children take turns passing out napkins and glasses, helping themselves to carrot sticks and peanut butter, and pouring their own juice. As they eat, they talk together among themselves and with Elaine or Philip about a variety of subjects, including the parade they saw over the weekend, grandparents, what they had for dinner the night before, and how many carrot sticks they have.

❽ The children in Elaine's group draw pictures of what they have done. Some talk about their pictures with Elaine. The children in Philip's group bring to their table the materials they have used at work time, so they can show how they used them.

▶ B. Make a list to show how you would sequence the elements of Elaine's and Philip's daily routine. Why did you select this particular sequence?

▶ C. What is another sequence they might use for their daily routine? Why?

Exercise 5

How Do Adults Support Children Throughout the Daily Routine?

Look at the photographs in *EYC* Chapter 6 (pp. 150–165). What are the adults in the photos doing? How are they supporting children? Record your observations in a chart like the following:

(List photo page numbers in this column.)	Time of Day	Adult Action/ Adult Support

Exercise 6

Child Study: Active Learning Within a Supportive Climate Throughout the Daily Routine

Observe a preschool child in an early childhood program setting for at least two hours during the heart of the program's daily routine (rather than for an hour of napping, for example). Record the parts of the daily routine you observe, and indicate how the child is engaged in active learning and receives adult support during each part. Use a child-study format like the following to record your answers.

Child's Name_____ Date_____
Location_____
Time Observed _____

Period of Day	Child's Actions/Language/ Choice/Materials	Adult Support

Exercise 7

Self-Assessment: Daily Routine

One way to assess the overall consistency of an early childhood daily routine and the time allotted to each segment is to look at it in terms of the High/Scope Program Quality Assessment (PQA): Preschool Version item II-A. If you are currently teaching, make notes and assess your own classroom by rating it on a scale of 1–5 on this item (shown on the next page of this study guide). If you are not teaching, you might look at the classroom in which you did the child study for exercise 6.

Exercise 8

Daily Routine Issues to Ponder and Write About

▶ A. Throughout the day in an early childhood setting, how much time do you spend interacting with girls? With boys? What kinds of activities do you prefer to support? To what extent do you support both vigorous and quiet play?

▶ B. How does the arrangement and equipment of the play space influence the way children experience the daily routine?

▶ C. Why is it necessary for adults to support children's active learning *throughout* the daily routine?

▶ D. What is the impact of an active learning daily routine on children who do not speak the predominant language of the early childhood setting?

▶ E. How do young children learn the daily routine?

PQA Item II-A. Adults establish a consistent daily routine. Children are aware of the routine.

Supporting evidence/anecdotes:

☐ Adults and children do not follow a consistent routine or sequence of events.	☐ Adults and children sometimes follow a consistent routine or sequence of events.	☐ Adults and children always follow a consistent daily routine or sequence of events. Adults let children know ahead of time about changes in the routine (e.g. field trips, a visiting artist).
☐ Adults and children do not refer to names for parts of the day.	☐ Adults and children sometimes refer to names for parts of the day.	☐ Adults and children often refer to names for parts of the day.
☐ Children are not aware of the sequence or nature of activities and depend on adults telling them what to do next.	☐ Children are somewhat aware that there is a fairly consistent daily routine (e.g., children know they will go outside at some point during the day and have lunch).	☐ Children are fully aware that there is a routine and can anticipate what activities come next (e.g., children name parts of the day, move on their own to the next activity, talk about what activity comes next).
1	2	3	4	5

Related Publications

Buckleitner, Warren, and Sue Terdan. 1991. "Day One: What We Did When the Children Arrived." In *Supporting Young Learners: Ideas for Preschool and Day Care Providers,* Nancy A. Brickman and Lynn S. Taylor, eds., 143–47. Ypsilanti, MI: High/Scope Press.

Evans, Betsy. 2000. "'Bye Mommy!' 'Bye Daddy!' Easing Separations for Preschoolers." *High/Scope Extensions* (September): 1–3.

Freeman, Bonnie Lash, Mary Hohmann, and Susan M. Terdan. 1991. "Planning a Daily Routine for Day Care Settings." In *Supporting Young Learners: Ideas for Preschool and Day Care Providers,* Nancy A. Brickman and Lynn S. Taylor, eds., 137–39. Ypsilanti, MI: High/Scope Press.

High/Scope Program Quality Assessment (PQA): Preschool Version (Field-Test Edition). 2001. Ypsilanti, MI: High/Scope Press.

Hohmann, Charles. 1991. "Planning the Kindergarten Day." In *Supporting Young Learners : Ideas for Preschool and Day Care Providers,* Nancy A. Brickman and Lynn S. Taylor, eds., 140–42. Ypsilanti, MI: High/Scope Press.

Hohmann, Charles, and Warren Buckleitner. 1992. *High/Scope K–3 Curriculum Series: Learning Environment.* Ypsilanti, MI: High/Scope Press.

Post, Jacalyn, and Mary Hohmann. 2000. "Establishing Schedules and Routines for Infants and Toddlers." In *Tender Care and Early Learning: Supporting Infants and Toddlers in Child Care Settings,* 191–294. Ypsilanti, MI: High/Scope Press.

Post, Jacalyn, and Mary Hohmann. 1996. "Planning the Day in Infant and Toddler Programs." "Child-Focused Caregiving Routines for Infants and Toddlers." In *Supporting Young Learners 2: Ideas for Child Providers and Teachers,* Nancy A. Brickman, ed., 103–14. Ypsilanti, MI: High/Scope Press.

Related Videos

The High/Scope Curriculum: The Daily Routine. 1990. Color videotape, 17 min. Ypsilanti, MI: High/Scope Press.

The High/Scope Curriculum: Its Implementation in Family Child Care Homes. 1989. Color videotape, 19 min. Ypsilanti, MI: High/Scope Press.

High/Scope K–3 Curriculum Series: Classroom Environment. 1991. Color videotape, 17 min. Ypsilanti, MI: High/Scope Press.

Answer to Exercise 4A

❶ outside time

❷ work time

❸ transition (from snack to large-group time)

❹ small-group time

❺ planning time

❻ large-group time

❼ snack time

❽ recall time

*B*y making daily plans, following through on them, and then recalling what they have done, young children learn to articulate their intentions and reflect on their actions. They also begin to realize they are competent thinkers, decision-makers, and problem-solvers.

—*Educating Young Children, p. 167*

Planning Time

7

The High/Scope Plan-Do-Review Process

Exercise 1

Intentions You Have Expressed, Plans You Have Made

With a partner or several friends, discuss and record your answers to exercises A–D.

▶ A. What are your earliest memories of expressing intent? What are some specific intentions or desires that you recall expressing, and how did you act on them?

▶ B. What plans do you remember making with friends or on your own?

▶ C. What role does planning play in your daily life?

▶ D. How is making and carrying out your own plans different from carrying out plans someone else has made for you?

Exercise 2

Child Study: Planning

Observe a preschool child in an early childhood program setting for 30–90 minutes. Do your observations during the heart of the program's daily routine (rather than during napping, for example). Watch and listen carefully. Record the way the child indicates intentions and plans at planning time and at other periods of the day—for example, at work time, outside time, small- and large-group times. On another day, repeat this observation process by observing and col-

lecting planning data on another child. For each child, use a child-study format like the following.

| Child's Name_____ Date_____ |
| Location_____ |
| Time Observed _____ |

Period of Day	How Child Indicates Plans (Child's Actions and Words)

Exercise 3

Self-Study: Planning

▶ A. For a week, keep a log of the intentions you express and the plans you make throughout the day. Describe how you indicate or express each intention and plan.

▶ B. At the end of the week, look over your entries. What strikes you about your personal planning process? What similarities and what differences do you see between your planning process and the planning process of the children you observed for exercise 2?

Exercise 4

Planning: Theories Behind the Practice

▶ A. Read about what Erik Erikson calls the stage of "initiative versus guilt" (*EYC* p. 168) and David Elkind's statement "Planning Supports Initiative" (*EYC* p. 169).

❶ What can you recall about times you have taken the initiative and felt pleased or satisfied about doing so?

❷ What can you recall about times you have taken the initiative and felt guilty about it?

❸ What can you recall about times you have decided not to take the initiative because you had learned that your ideas and initiatives were not welcome in that particular setting?

▶ B. Recall a situation in your childhood (or later life) in which you were chastised or punished in some way for your initiatives. How might you rewrite the script for that situation so your initiatives would have been supported?

▶ C. Read about Robbie Case's executive control structures on *EYC* p. 168–169 and about "Planning Mirrors Development" on *EYC* p. 172. How do Case's control structures relate to the child planning process?

▶ D. Recall an everyday problem you have encountered, and break it down to fit into Case's model of human thinking, which is shown below.

PROBLEM SITUATION ⟶ OBJECTIVE

STRATEGY

▶ E. John Dewey presents the view that education revolves around *goal-directed activity* and the *child's participation* "in the formation of the purposes which direct his or her activities in the learning process."[14] Dewey also says that "a purpose differs from an original impulse and desire through its translation into a plan and method of action based

[14]*Dewey, John, Experience and Education (New York: Macmillan, 1938, reprint 1963), p. 67.*

upon foresight of the consequences of acting under given observed conditions in a certain way. . . . The crucial educational problem is that of procuring the postponement of immediate action upon desire until observation and judgment have intervened" (p. 69). He goes on to say that "the occurrence of a desire and impulse is not the final end. It is an occasion and a demand for the formation of a plan and a method of activity" (p. 71).

❶ What is Dewey saying about the similarities and differences between impulses (desires) and plans?

❷ Describe an occasion in your life when you acted on an impulse. Describe an occasion when you had an impulse, or desire, that you shaped through observation, thought, and judgment before acting on it. What were the qualities and the outcomes of these two occasions?

▶ F. To expand your understanding of the theories that support the child planning process, go to the library and examine one or more of the books listed below. Record your findings and insights about the planning process.

- *Intellectual Development: Birth to Adulthood* by Robbie Case (1985)

- *Experience and Education* by John Dewey (1938, reprint 1963)

- *Childhood and Society* by Erik Erikson (1950)

Exercise 5

Elements of the Planning Process

▶ A. Recall a plan you have made. (This may be a plan from exercise 1 on p. 71 but doesn't have to be.) Analyze your plan by explaining

how it contained each of the following planning elements (discussed on *EYC* pp. 168–170).

❶ Establishing a problem or goal

❷ Imagining and anticipating actions

❸ Expressing personal intentions and interests

❹ Shaping intentions into purposes

❺ Deliberating

❻ Making ongoing modifications

▶ B. Go back to a study child from exercise 2 on p. 71 (or observe some other child at planning and work time who is making a plan and carrying it out). Analyze the child's plan, explaining how it contained each of the following planning elements (discussed on *EYC* pp. 168–170).

❶ Establishing a problem or goal

❷ Imagining and anticipating actions

❸ Expressing personal intentions and interests

❹ Shaping intentions into purposes

❺ Deliberating

❻ Making ongoing modifications

▶ C. Read the chart "The Impact of Planning on Children's Actions" on *EYC* p. 171.

❶ What strikes you about this information?

❷ What ideas does this chart convey to you about the planning process?

❸ What do you see as the difference between planning (expressing intentions) and not planning?

Why We Encourage Young Children to Plan

Educating Young Children (pp. 170–172) gives four reasons why children's planning is important:

- Planning encourages children to articulate their ideas, choices, and decisions.
- Planning promotes children's self-confidence and sense of control.
- Planning leads to involvement and concentration on play.
- Planning supports the development of increasingly complex play.

▶ A. Which of these abilities do you want to encourage in young children? Why?

▶ B. Which of these abilities does society encourage or fail to encourage in young children? If it fails to encourage, why?

▶ C. Read the definitions Kathy Sylva, Carolyn Roy, and Marjorie Painter developed for "simple play" and "complex play" (*EYC* p. 171).

❶ What observations, questions, concerns, and/or insights do you have about these definitions of play?

❷ To expand your understanding of simple and complex play, go to the library and examine *Childwatching at Playgroup & Nursery School* by Sylva, Roy, and Painter (1980). Summarize your findings.

Child Study: The Development of Planning

▶ A. Find a 1-year-old, a 2-year-old, a 3-year-old, a 4-year-old, and a 5-year-old. Observe each child at play for 20–30 minutes. Watch, listen, and record the way each child expresses intentions and acts on them.

❶ 1-Year-old   ❹ 4-Year-Old

❷ 2-Year-Old   ❺ 5-Year-Old

❸ 3-Year-Old

▶ B. How do your findings about planning by children of different ages (in exercise A) compare with the discussion on the development of children's planning on *EYC* pp. 172–173?

▶ C. Discuss your findings with those of someone else who has also done exercise A. What similarities or differences are there in your findings?

How Children Indicate Their Plans

▶ A. Think about the kinds of gestures and actions (nonverbal expressions of intent) and the verbal expressions you saw as you observed children for exercise 2 on p. 71 and for exercise 7A. From your observations, give one or more specific examples of each of the planning strategies listed in exercises (1)–(7).

❶ Pointing to an object, place, person

❷ Looking at an object, place, person

❸ Touching an object

❹ Bringing a toy or object to the adult

❺ Taking an adult to a place or thing

❻ Acting out the intended action

❼ Talking about intended actions in own words, phrases, sentences

▶ B. Many preschool teaching teams are surprised to find that they are biased toward children who indicate their plans verbally, yet anyone who has lived or worked with infants and toddlers learns to understand and respond to *their* nonverbal communications. Why is it important to support preschool children's nonverbal plans and expressions of intent?

Types of Plans Children Make

▶ A. The discussion on *EYC* pp. 175–176 reviews the kinds of plans preschool children typically make. In the chart below, give examples of *vague, routine, detailed, perfunctory,* and *real* plans **you** have made, as well as examples of each of these that you have seen **young children** make. Use a chart like the following to organize your answers.

Kind of Plan	Examples From My Life	Examples From Children

B. Why is it important to understand the types of plans people (including young children) make?

C. Why is it important for adults to support whatever type of plan children make rather than to expect, for example, that each child make a detailed plan?

D. In "Planning Is a Real Opportunity" (*EYC* p. 176), what distinction do Carla Berry and Kathy Sylva make between planning as "a promise to do something acceptable" and planning as "a mental model to guide future action"?

Exercise 10

The Development of Children's Planning Over Time

A. Read "Teri: Planning Theme and Variations" (*EYC* p. 177). How did Teri's plans actually change over time?

B. How did William's plans (described on that same *EYC* page) actually change over time?

C. Why do you think that, often, young children who participate in the planning process in an active learning program setting also engage in a planning process at home?

Exercise 11

Supporting the Planning Process: Photographs of Adults

The following questions are based on a close examination of the photographs on *EYC* pp. 166–193.

A. In these photographs, where are the adults physically positioned in relation to the children? Why? What does their physical location have to do with supporting the child's planning process?

B. What are the adults focusing their attention on? Why?

C. Which photograph is your favorite among this group of photographs? Why?

D. How are the support strategies adults are using in these photographs of planning time related to the adult support strategies listed on *EYC* pp. 40 and 66?

Exercise 12

Identifying Support Strategies in Ruth's Planning Time

With a partner or several friends, read aloud the transcript of preschool teacher Ruth's planning time on *EYC* pp. 178–179.

A. What materials does Ruth use to focus the children's interest at planning time?

B. For each statement Ruth makes in the planning dialogue, list the support strategy (or strategies) Ruth is using from the list on *EYC* p. 195. Use a chart like the following to organize your answers. (For brevity and easy identification, you might number Ruth's statements from 1 to 15.)

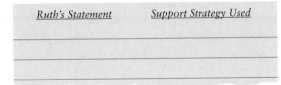

Ruth's Statement	*Support Strategy Used*

C. From your analysis of Ruth's statements, what conclusions can you draw about the conversational strategies Ruth uses to support children's planning?

D. Which child in Ruth's planning group makes the shortest statements? Why? What distinguishes the conversational moves Ruth makes in her dialogue with him? (See *EYC* p. 218 for a description of five conversational moves—*enforced repetition, closed question, open question, contribution, acknowledgment*—and their effects on children's language.)

Exercise 13

Adult Attitudes About Children's Planning

Adults approach the child planning process with a variety of attitudes—"I can't even decide what to have for lunch, so how can 3- and 4-year-olds possibly make plans?" "I'll just do planning time and get it over with." "Maybe I can steer children toward activities they are having difficulty with." "What a great life skill to support in young children!" "I wonder what kinds of ideas children *do* have about what they want to do." "I'm really going to have to trust children to make decisions about how they are going to spend their work time!" With a partner or several friends, discuss the following.

A. What are your own worst fears about planning time and the process of child planning? (See also "Common Adult Concerns About Planning Time" on *EYC* p. 194.)

B. What do you find exciting about the process of child planning?

C. Which personal attitudes and tendencies of yours might impede children's planning? Which ones might support children's planning?

Exercise 14

Focusing on Children at Planning Time

The discussion in *EYC* (pp. 180–181) indicates the importance of striving to have *intimate planning conversations, stable planning groups,* and *visible people and materials to choose from.* **Why** is each of these characteristics—**intimacy, stability,** and **visibility**—important to the child planning process, and **how** might you provide for each one in your current or prospective early childhood setting? Record your ideas in a chart like the following.

Characteristic	Why?	How?

Exercise 15

Trying Out Planning Games and Experiences

Exercises A–D are based on the planning games and experiences described on *EYC* pp. 182–183.

A. Pick out a game or experience from each of the **four categories** that *EYC* lists—**visibility games, group games, props and partnerships,** and **representations.** On four different days in an early childhood program setting, try out the selected game or experience with a small group of children at planning time. If planning time has not been formally instituted in the setting where you are working, try out the game or experience just before free play or activity time. Listen and watch to see **what children do and say** during each situation. Use a chart like the following to record your findings.

Category	Game/Experience	Children's Actions & Words

B. If you were to construct a planning box containing the props and materials needed to carry out the games and experiences described on *EYC* pp. 182–183, what would you put into it?

C. Why might such a planning box be useful? How might you use it at planning time?

D. If you are currently teaching or student-teaching or can work in an early childhood program setting over a period of time, collect representations children make at planning time. (Include the child's name and date on the back of each representation.) At the end of the collection period, examine the representations you have gathered. What can you conclude about the changes you see in each child's representations and planning process over time?

Exercise 16

Ways of Conversing With Children About Their Plans

Exercises A–G are based on the discussion of planning time conversations on *EYC* pp. 184–190.

A. At planning time, what is the difference between asking children "what" questions and asking them "where" questions?

B. In the conversation between Barry and the adult (*EYC* pp. 184–185), how does the adult respond to Barry's story about his dog? Why?

C. What does the dialogue between Barry and the adult illustrate about following a child's lead at planning time?

D. What characterizes "talking story" (*EYC* p. 185)? What conversational moves does it depend on? (See *EYC* p. 218 for a description of conversational moves—*enforced repetition, closed question, open question, contribution, acknowledgment.*)

E. What is the role of *listening* in the process of supporting children's planning? Why is adult listening important to the child's learning process?

F. With a partner, read through the 12 italicized planning conversations on *EYC* pp. 186–190. After reading each conversation once, reread it to identify and record which **type of conversational move** (see exercise D) the adult makes each time he or she addresses the child. **Tally your findings** in a chart like the one shown here. Which conversational moves are most prevalent in these planning time conversations? Why?

Type of Conversational Move	Tally of Times Move Is Used

▶ G. How would you describe the traits these adults display in their planning conversations with children? (For example, one trait might be patience.)

Exercise 17

Self-Study: Recording and Analyzing Planning Time Conversations

(This exercise involves a tape recorder.)

▶ A. If you are currently teaching or student teaching or can work in an early childhood setting over a period of time, tape-record some of the conversations you have with children at planning time. Later, listen to your recording and make a written or typed transcript of it. Read the transcript of your conversation and identify the conversational **support strategies** you used (*EYC* p. 195) and the **conversational moves** you made (*EYC* p. 218).

▶ B. Based on your analysis of your conversations with children, what conclusions can you make about children's planning abilities and your strengths as a supporter of children's planning?

Exercise 18

Keeping a Planning Time Journal

(This exercise may be repeated periodically.)

▶ A. If you are currently teaching or student-teaching, choose one child in your planning group and keep a log of anecdotal observations on that child's daily approach to planning—that is, note the child's words and actions at planning time. If you are not teaching, but your study child from earlier chapters is involved in a program that includes child planning, observe and record that child's actions and words at planning time on a regular basis.

▶ B. Periodically review the anecdotal data you have collected, and draw some conclusions about how your child is planning and how his or her plans have changed or evolved.

Exercise 19

Valuing Children's Plans

Exercises A–I list the strategies for valuing children's plans that are discussed on *EYC* pp. 190–191 under the heading "Adults value children's plans." Give one or more specific examples of how, at planning time, you have used (or how some other adult has used) each of the strategies listed in A–I.

▶ A. Setting aside time each day for planning

▶ B. Asking children open-ended questions that call for actions

▶ C. Listening attentively to children's responses

▶ D. Conversing with children about their plans

▶ E. Building on children's ideas and intentions

▶ F. Giving children time to respond, then following children's cues

▶ G. Accepting children's unique responses

▶ H. Encouraging rather than praising children's ideas

▶ I. Writing down children's plans

Exercise 20

Planning Scenarios: What Would You Do?

Given everything you know about *what* planning is, *why* it is important, *how* children indicate their plans, and *how* adults can support and value children's nonverbal and verbal plans, decide how, at planning time, you might support each of the specific children described in the scenarios in exercises A–G.

▶ A. *The children in your early childhood program have been planning for work time for several months. Today, **Denise**, a new child, joins your planning group on her first day in your active learning program. She has just turned 3 years old and appears to be quite shy.*

▶ B. *At planning time **Timmy** begins by telling you about a fishing experience he had with his dad. "I caught three fish, big ones! We dug worms. They eat 'em, and I felt tugs on my line. We couldn't stand up, because then the boat might tip. We skinned 'em and cut off their heads, and you could see what they ate! One just ate a crayfish. We opened him up and saw it!"*

▶ C. ***Raymond** and **Elise** plan to make a farm together in the block area. They leave the planning group to get started on their farm. As you are planning with another child, you see that Raymond and Elise are dressing up in the house area.*

▶ D. *At the beginning of the day, **Clarice** comes through the door, saying "I don't wanna make a plan! I don't wanna make a plan!"*

▶ E. *Every day, **Devone** and a certain friend plan to play together. Today as usual, Devone plans to play with that same child but discovers that he is at home with the flu.*

▶ F. *At planning time, **Rachel** is so eager to get started on her plan that she can barely stay with her planning group. When it is her turn to plan, she says, "Play there!" (pointing to the block area) and leaves before you can ask her what she plans to do.*

▶ G. *At planning time, when you ask children to bring to the table something they plan to use at work time, **Josh** goes to the block area and watches other children gather materials. He returns to the table empty-handed.*

Exercise 21

Self-Assessment: Planning Time

Item II-D of the High/Scope Program Quality Assessment (PQA): Preschool Version provides one way to assess planning time in an early childhood program. If you are currently teaching, use this item (shown at the right) to make notes and to rank on a scale of 1–5 your own planning time. If you are not teaching, you might use the classroom in which you did your child study for exercise 2 on p. 71.

PQA Item II-D. The program has time each day during which children make plans and indicate their plans to adults. [Note: If time to plan is set aside but not observed, score at level 1.]

Supporting evidence/anecdotes:

☐ There is no time set aside for children to make plans or indicate their plans to adults.	☐ Sometimes there is time set aside for children to make plans or indicate their plans to adults.	☐ There is a daily time set aside for children to make plans or indicate their plans to adults.
☐ Adults plan and direct the day's activities (e.g., adults tell children where to play, what materials to use, or what activities to complete; adults close certain areas).	☐ Adults use rote or routine strategies for planning (e.g., children always make one- or two-word plans or adults always write down children's plans).	☐ Adults use a range of strategies to support children's planning (e.g., props, area signs, tape recorder, singing; planning individually, in pairs, in work groups).
☐ Adults do not encourage children to plan or recognize when children are indicating plans in ways consistent with their developmental levels.	☐ Adults sometimes encourage children to plan in ways that are consistent with their developmental levels.	☐ Adults encourage children to plan in ways that are consistent with their developmental levels (e.g., by pointing, bringing objects to the planning table, moving toward the chosen area, acting out what they want to do, making drawings, making verbal plans).
☐ Adults assign children areas to play in and/or materials are chosen and/or set out by the adult.	☐ Some areas and some materials are available to some children for making their plans (e.g., a specific number of children are allowed in each area, "the block area is closed today," only play dough is available in the art area).	☐ All areas and materials are available to children for making their plans.
1	2	3	4	5

Work Time

Why We Have Work Time

Exercises A–D are based on the work time scenarios and discussion on *EYC* pp. 196–199 and on the photographs of work time on *EYC* pp. 196–224.

▶ A. For each work time feature listed in exercises (1)–(6), give specific examples from the *EYC* work time photographs and scenarios.

❶ Children carry out intentions.

❷ Children play with purpose.

❸ Children participate in a social setting.

❹ Children solve problems.

❺ Children construct knowledge as they engage in the High/Scope key experiences.

❻ Adults observe, learn from, and support children's play.

▶ B. Select four *EYC* work time photographs. Explain what **kind of knowledge** the child might be constructing in each photo situation. Also identify what **key experiences** the child might be involved in. (See the key experience list in *EYC* on p. 22.) Organize your answers in a chart like the following:

Photo Page #	What Children Are Doing	Knowledge Children Might Be Constructing/ Related Key Experiences

▶ C. From the photographs and work time scenarios, how might you describe the spirit of work time?

▶ D. Select two work time features from exercises A(1)–(6). Explain why each one of them is important in an active learning early childhood setting.

Identifying Types of Play[15]

The following exercises are based on the definitions of play types discussed on *EYC* pp. 201–203.

▶ A. For each of the play types listed in exercises (1)–(4), find four photographs anywhere in *EYC* to illustrate the type of play. Record the page number of each photo, and describe what the children are doing in each of the photos.

❶ Exploratory play

❷ Constructive play

❸ Pretend play

❹ Games

▶ B. Which kind(s) of play are you particularly drawn to? Why? Which are you least attracted to? Why? How might these biases affect the kinds of play you are apt to join when supporting young children at work time?

▶ C. Why is it important for adults to value and support each of the four types of play

---

[15]*For related study guide exercises on play types, see Chapter 2, exercise 11 on p. 20 and exercise 12 on p. 20.*

instead of expecting all children to be involved in the same type or level of play?

▶ D. Think for a moment about how these four play types are related to active learning and the key experiences. Then construct a statement that describes the relationship between play types, active learning, and the key experiences.

Child Study: Work Time

In an active learning early childhood setting during work time, observe 5 or 6 children for 10 minutes each (observing the first child for the first 10 minutes, the second child for the second 10 minutes, and so forth). As you watch and listen, once each minute write down what each child says and does. For each 10-minute observation, use a chart like the one on p. 79 to record your observations of the **status of the child's plan** (initiating, working on, modifying, completing, beginning a new plan), the **social context** of the child's play (onlooking, solitary, parallel, group), and the **type of play** the child is engaged in (exploratory, constructive, pretend, games). (For a discussion of these terms, see "What Children Do at Work Time" on *EYC* pp. 199–203.)[16]

---

[16]*For a complete discussion of "target child" observation, see* **Childwatching at Playgroup & Nursery School** *by Kathy Sylva, Carolyn Roy, and Marjorie Painter.*

(List minutes #1–#10 in this column)	Actions	Words	Plan Status	Social Context	Play Type

Adult Attitudes Toward Work Time

Exercises A–D are based on the eight statements on *EYC* pp. 203–204 that describe some of the contrasting attitudes that often shape adults' approach to young children at work time. With a partner, discuss and record your answers to exercises A–D.

➤ A. What are your personal beliefs about how adults support young children's learning? How did you form these beliefs, or where do they come from?

➤ B. Select one of the eight *EYC* statements. Give examples of yourself or other adults exhibiting the attitudes described in the statement you have chosen.

➤ C. How do these eight statements relate to the support strategies listed in the checklists on *EYC* pp. 40 and 66?

➤ D. High/Scope consultant Beth Marshall[17] describes three adult interaction styles based on three different approaches to work time:

---

[17]*"Interacting Effectively With Children,"* **High/Scope Extensions,** October 1993, p. 6.

- *Bystanders* watch children's play but are not really part of it. Bystanders often can be found sitting in chairs, or standing and looking down on children as children play on the floor. Though bystanders may help children get started with an activity or may make an occasional comment about what children are doing, they are otherwise uninvolved in children's play.

- *Managers* move rapidly from situation to situation, overseeing the use of materials and solving problems for children. In calm moments, they may do paperwork or lesson plans as children play. Managers are generally on the go and rarely take time to tune in to individual children long enough to find out their thoughts or feelings. When there is a problem to solve or a job to do, they are task oriented, focusing on getting the job done as efficiently as possible.

- *Co-players* play with children. First they observe children and imitate their actions. Then they join in children's play in a supporting role, making sure that *children* maintain control of the play situation. Co-players are usually seen sitting on the floor actively participating in play.

❶ How are these work time roles related to the social climates discussed in *EYC* Chapter 2, on pp. 47–50?

❷ Which of the roles—*bystander, manager,* or *co-player*—would be most appropriate in an active learning early childhood setting? Why?

Effects of Room Arrangement on Children's Work Time Interactions

➤ A. From the photographs on *EYC* pp. 110–149, select four photographs of children at work time. Identify each photograph by its page number, and for the setting shown in that photo, describe how room arrangement and equipment affect the children's work time play.

➤ B. How might you support a child who makes a work time plan for which no specific materials are available—for example, a plan to make a squirrel's nest or a giant metal monster?

➤ C. How might you support a child whose work time plan involves materials from all parts of the room—for example, a child who plans to look at things with a flashlight all around the room?

Scanning the Interest Areas to Gain the Child's Perspective on Play

Exercises A–D are based on the discussion of scanning on *EYC* pp. 204–208.

➤ A. What strategies do you use at work time (free play, choice time) to decide which child or group of children you will join?

B. Assume that you are scanning the play space at work time to decide which child or group you will join. Your attention is drawn to these children—Kiku and Maria (photo on *EYC* p. 153), Brianna (left-hand photo on *EYC* p. 201), Jamison (upper-left corner of photo on *EYC* p. 205), Audie and James (photo on *EYC* p. 207), and Kirsten (photo on *EYC* p. 219). In a chart like the following, describe what you observe from each photograph about the **plan status, social interactions, play types,** and **key experiences** the children are engaging in. (For descriptors, refer to the insert on *EYC* p. 206.)

Child(ren)	Plan Status	Social Context	Play Type	Key Experience(s)

C. From your charts, choose one child (or pair of children), and formulate a plan for an on-the-spot interaction with that child.

D. With one or two others who also did exercise C, discuss your interaction plan and their interaction plan. Which child or children did they focus on and why?

Exercise 28

Offering Comfort and Contact to Children at Work Time

A. Describe how children are gaining comfort and contact in each *EYC* photograph listed in (1)–(7).

❶ The three photos at the top of p. 51

❷ The photo on p. 113

❸ The photo on p. 186

❹ The photo on p. 208

❺ The photo on p. 209

❻ The photo on p. 224

❼ The two photos on p. 358

B. Read "Nobody Paid Attention to Me When I Pouted!" (*EYC* p. 209).

❶ To what extent and how did you receive comfort and contact as a child?

❷ How do you think your early experiences with comfort and contact might affect your approach to young children who are in need of comfort and contact?

C. Young children indicate their need for comfort and contact in a wide variety of ways, some more winsome and engaging than others. For example, children may ask for comfort and contact by calling your name, sitting on your lap, stroking your hand, leaning against you, clinging to you, looking sad, crying, hitting, throwing a tantrum.

❶ Describe the way you generally interpret and respond to each of these types of behavior in a young child.

❷ Is there any response that you described for exercise (1) that you would alter if you interpreted the particular child behavior (however unengaging it might be) as a request for comfort and contact?

D. What concerns do you have about specific ways of offering young children comfort and contact? (For example, "Children won't be ready for kindergarten if I let them sit on my lap." "What if a parent accuses me of 'bad touching'?" "I don't like children hanging on me!")

E. Why do or don't you believe it is important for a preschool teacher or caregiver to provide young children with comfort and contact?

Exercise 29

Adult Attitudes Toward Play

Whereas some adults play enthusiastically with young children, others have mixed feelings about being children's play partners. For examples of adult ambivalence about play, read "What? **Me** Play! You've **Got** to Be Kidding!" (*EYC* p. 213).

A. What is your personal attitude about playing with children?

B. What do you recall about adults playing with you as a child?

C. How are you even now playful in your everyday life?

Exercise 30

Playing With Children at Work Time

The following exercises are based on the discussion of adult play strategies on *EYC* pp. 210–213.

A. Joining children's play begins by looking for a natural opening. This is similar to the openings you look for when joining peers who are already engaged in activity or conversation.

❶ Think of a situation in which, while you were doing something, another person joined you. What made the other person's entrance into your activity pleasant or disruptive?

❷ Describe some natural play openings you have seen in children's play. (You might refer to exercises 24 on p. 78 and 27B on p. 80.)

❸ Think of a situation in which, when you joined a child's play, the play stopped. What was the child doing, and how might your actions have disrupted the play? What might you do differently next time, in a similar situation?

❹ Think of a situation in which, when you joined a child's play, the play continued. What was the child doing, and how did you enter the play in a supportive manner?

❺ Whose needs might you be fulfilling when you enter a child's play—yours, the child's, or both? Why?

▶ B. Joining children's play means putting yourself on their physical level. This is similar to what you often do when you want to be sure you are communicating person-to-person with another adult.

❶ Examine the work time photos on *EYC* pp. 203–224. Where are the adults positioned in relation to the children? What physical positions do adults assume?

❷ What impact does it have on children when an adult assumes their physical level? What impact does assuming the child's physical level have on the adult?

❸ How does putting yourself on the child's physical level relate to the elements of adult support for children discussed in *EYC* Chapter 2— *sharing of control, focusing on strengths, forming*

authentic relationships, supporting children's play, and *encouraging problem solving?*

❹ In your experience, can an adult who plays with children also convey being "in charge," so as to give children a sense of safety and security? Why or why not?

▶ C. Once you have joined children's play, one strategy is to *play in parallel* with children. This might be similar to what you do when a friend is washing the car and you pick up a sponge and work alongside.

❶ What is parallel play with children? How is parallel play related to taking cues from children? To following children's leads?

❷ In the interaction involving filling containers with sand, which is described on *EYC* p. 211 at the top of the third column, neither the adult nor the child speaks. How *does* the adult interact with the child?

❸ Is language a necessary part of all play? Why or why not? Why might many adults find it particularly difficult to refrain from talking when playing with children?

❹ A possible conversation at the sand table is given at the end of the third column on *EYC* p. 211. Which conversational moves—*enforced repetition, closed question, open question, contribution, acknowledgment*—is the adult using in this conversation?

▶ D. *Playing as a partner* is another way to support children's play. This might be similar to joining a friend who is planting a garden, talking together about where to plant the beans and the corn, and then one of you digging the holes for the seeds and the other following behind to drop the seeds into the holes.

❶ How are the adults playing as partners with children in the scenarios on *EYC* pp. 212–213?

❷ Adults often have a tendency to try to move children's play toward an adult-set learning goal (for example, they want children who are playing with clay to talk about shapes). Why might this be so? What strategies can adults use to help themselves attend to *children's* goals, thoughts, ideas, and feelings rather than to their own? Based on what you know about active learning, why is it important to attend to children's goals?

Exercise 31

Conversing With Children at Work Time

(Exercise A involves a tape recorder.)

To refresh your memory about sharing control in conversations, turn to exercise 7 of Chapter 2, on p. 18. If you have not yet done exercise 7, find a partner and do it at this time before proceeding with A and B below.

▶ A. Tape-record a conversation you have with a preschool child at play. Later, listen to your conversation, and create a typed or written transcript of it. Then analyze your conversation for two things: Describe **your responsiveness to the child's cues and leads,** and **identify the conversational moves you make** (enforced repetition, closed question, open question, contribution, acknowledgment), **and the effect of each conversational move** on the child's response.

B. We know that questions can actually inhibit conversation and therefore must be used sparingly with children. (See the discussion on *EYC* pp. 216–218.) At the same time, most adults have been schooled to believe that questioning children lies at the heart of the educational process.

❶ In a teaching/learning setting, whose questions are more important, the teacher's or the child's? Why?

❷ Read the four *italicized* work time conversations between adults and children on *EYC* pp. 216–218. How many questions does the adult ask in each conversation? What is the nature of each question? What other conversational moves does the adult make?

Exercise 32

Practicing for Play Step-by-Step

For exercises A–D, you will need a partner and a variety of play materials that are open-ended, such as blocks, vehicles, clay, marbles, pipe cleaners, stones, or shells.

A. Together, choose some materials to play with, and assume the role of an adult (or teacher) while your partner assumes the role of a child (or player). Then follow steps 1–3.

- *Step 1, watch and listen:* As the child plays, position yourself on the child's physical level. Watch and listen to the child to determine what kind of play the child is engaged in. After several minutes, stop to discuss with your partner and record what you have observed and how your partner feels about your attention.

- *Step 2, enter nonverbally:* The child continues play from step 1. You, as the adult, enter the child's play *nonverbally* by following the child's cues and using the materials in the same way the child is using them. After several minutes, stop to discuss with your partner and record what you have observed and how your partner feels about your entry into the play.

- *Step 3, converse:* The child continues the play begun in steps 1 and 2. You, the adult, continue to play with the materials, following the child's leads and ideas. Look for an opportunity for conversation. When one arises, converse using comments, observations, and acknowledgments (rather than questions). After several minutes, stop to discuss with your partner and record what you have observed and how your partner feels about conversing in this manner.

B. Switch roles, with you taking the role of the child and your partner taking the role of the adult. Choose a new set of play materials, and repeat steps 1–3 from exercise A.

C. Switch roles so you are once again the adult and your partner is the child. Choose a new set of play materials, and follow step 4 below.

- *Step 4, watch and listen, enter nonverbally, converse.* This step calls for again following steps 1–3 from exercise A, but this time do not stop for any discussion after steps 1 and 2. After completing all three steps, stop to discuss your experiences together. How did the child feel about your support? What did you learn about the child through her play?

D. Switch roles for the last time. Choose a new set of materials. Repeat step 4 from exercise C, and reflect on and record your findings from this exercise.

Exercise 33

Encouraging Children's Problem Solving at Work Time

As you work through the following exercises, keep in mind the steps for conflict resolution (listed in this study guide on p. 21 and described in *Supporting Young Learners 2* on pp. 30–34) and the problem-solving discussion in *EYC* on pp. 218–221.[18]

A. How do you feel when you encounter a snag or problem—for example, when you lock your keys in your car, drop a contact lens on the floor, or discover that your bike has a flat tire? What is your immediate response?

B. The first steps in the problem-solving approach to conflict are to approach the situation calmly and to acknowledge the child's feelings of frustration, discouragement, anger. In the *"Darn! I can't get this open"* conversation (*EYC* p. 220, first column) and the conversation in the first two columns of *EYC* p. 221, how might the children involved be feeling? How might you enlarge the first conversation to acknowledge the child's feelings?

---

[18]*For more about this important topic, read "Acknowledging Children's Feelings" by Betsy Evans in* **High/Scope Extensions** *March/April 1995, p. 6, "Helping Children Resolve Disputes and Conflicts" by Betsy Evans in* **Supporting Young Learners 2**, *pp. 27–30, and* **You Can't Come to My Birthday Party! Conflict Resolution With Young Children** *by Betsy Evans.*

C. For exercises (1)–(4), consider these two work time scenarios:

Eli is pounding the role of masking tape and then stamping on it, because he can't find the free end of the tape.

Tashonna cries as she tries unsuccessfully to fit her baby doll's arms into a sweater.

❶ List all the feelings Eli might be experiencing.

❷ Imagine and record (and possibly act out with a partner) the problem-solving conversation you might have with Eli. Be sure to acknowledge Eli's feelings.

❸ List all the feelings Tashonna might be experiencing.

❹ Imagine and record (and possibly act out with a partner) the problem-solving conversation you might have with Tashonna. Be sure to acknowledge Tashonna's feelings.

Exercise 34

Gathering Work Time Anecdotes

One aspect of the adult's role at work time is observing children and recording the observations in some way. (See the first column of *EYC* p. 222 for recording suggestions.) Team members turn their observations into anecdotes in the course of daily team planning, as they discuss what they observed, interpret their observations, and plan what to do the next day to support children's interests and development. (See *EYC* Chapter 4 for a review of this process.)

▶ A. Go back and look at the work time observations of children that you made for exercise 24

on p. 78. From these observations, write at least two anecdotes per child observed. Then, turn to the list of key experiences (*EYC* p. 22). Decide which key experience each of your anecdotes is most closely related to, and record all your anecdotes for the various children on the single Key Experience Notes form[19] included on the next two pages. (In an actual classroom situation, teachers would use one form per child when recording anecdotes.)

▶ B. Based on your observations and anecdotes, describe ways you might plan to support these children if you were going to be in their classroom the next day.

Exercise 35

Child Study: Adult Support at Work Time

In an active learning early childhood setting during work time, observe 5 or 6 children for 10 minutes each—observe the first child for the first 10 minutes, the second child for the second 10 minutes, and so forth. As you watch and listen, write down once each minute what each child **says** and **does**. For each 10-minute observation, use a chart like the following to record your observations of **how adults join or support** that child's play—how they offer comfort and contact, and how they play, converse, and support problem solving. (Some of the children you observe may not interact with adults in the time you observe them. In some observations, the adult may already have joined the child's play by the

---

[19]*The Key Experience Notes forms are used with the **High/Scope Child Observation Record (COR)** described on EYC p. 98.*

time you begin to observe.) At the end of your observation, if no adult interacted with a particular child you observed, make a note of how *you* might have supported that child's play during the time you observed it.

(List minutes #1–#10 in this column)	Child's Actions	Child's Words	Adult Support

Exercise 36

Work Time Scenarios: What Would You Do?

Assume that the following work time scenarios are unfolding before you in your early childhood setting. As you read the scenario in exercise A, look at the indicated *EYC* photographs.

▶ A. *Brendan and Mark have dressed up in Batman and Robin capes and are driving their Batmobile, complete with leg protectors and a steering wheel, to "rescue people from the fire in the burning building" [EYC p. 196]. Brianna and Megan are using glue, paper, and glitter at the art table. Kacey and Francis are under the art table, pretending to be kitties [EYC p. 200]. In the*

Key Experience Notes

High/Scope
Child Observation
Record (COR)
For Ages 2½–6

CHILD COR OBSERVATION RECORD

Observer's name: _____

Child's name: _____

Creative Representation	Language and Literacy	Initiative and Social Relations	Movement	Music

Key Experience Notes

High/Scope
Child Observation
Record (COR)
For Ages 2½–6

Observer's name: _____

Child's name: _____

Classification	Seriation	Number	Space	Time

music area, Lena, Patrice, Julia, and Kelly are using streamers and playing CD music as they play a "stop-and-start" game they have made up [EYC p. 202]. Eli, Chris, and Troy are building roads and tunnels with blocks while Alex and Matt are looking for fires to put out. "Wait, we're not having any fires," Troy says, as the two fire fighters douse the area with "water" from their "hoses" [EYC p. 202]. At the computer area, Jamison and Trey have just started working with an interactive computer program called "The Playroom"(by Broderbund Software) while Andrew is engrossed in an interactive story program [EYC p. 166, top right].

❶ Which child or group of children would you join? Why?

❷ What strategies would you use to support their play? (Use the work time support strategies on EYC p. 224 as a guide.)

❸ Discuss your planned interactions with one or two other people who are also doing this exercise. How do your plans compare with theirs?

▶ B. At work time, Jessa and Anna are in the block area, pretending to be bees. They have constructed a "beehive" out of large hollow blocks and are "buzzing" around it. Carla, their teacher, watches them for a few minutes and then comes over to play with them. "BZZZZZ, BZZZZZ, BZZZZZ," she says, pretending to fly around the hive with them. "Anna, bees are yellow. Why don't you go and get the yellow scarves to wrap around us, then the other children will know we are bees." Anna nods and goes to get the scarves. "Jessa, help me make some honey," Carla says. "Bees make honey from nectar that they get

from flowers. What could we use for our honey?" Carla asks. Jessa brings over the cylinder blocks and gives them to Carla.[20]

❶ How does Carla enter Anna's and Jessa's play?

❷ After Carla enters, who is in charge of the play, Carla or the children? Why?

❸ How might you play as a partner with Anna and Jessa?

▶ C. At work time, Brian uses the wooden train tracks to construct an elaborate connecting track system all around the toy area. Ellen, his teacher, comes over to Brian and tells him that he'll have to move his track because it's right in front of the toy shelf where the other children need to stand to reach the toys. She offers to help him take apart his track and then gives him a carpet square, telling him that he can build his track on that instead.

❶ How would you describe the role Ellen has assumed in this situation? What might be her attitude toward work time?

❷ How might you interact with Brian as a partner in play?

▶ D. Everyday for the past three weeks, Matthew, Emily, and Tal have planned to make a "fire truck." At work time, they each put on a red hat and go to the block area, where they lay out all the red cardboard blocks in a large rectangle on the floor. They then dump other smaller blocks and toys into their "fire truck" (the large rectangle

of cardboard blocks), saying it's their "food." Sometimes they take the long wooden blocks and, pretending they are hoses, they run around the classroom "squirting" the other children. Often, this bothers the other children. Unless she is needed to intervene in a conflict, Wendy, their teacher, usually uses work time to catch up on her attendance and meal counts and other paperwork.

❶ How would you describe Wendy's approach to work time?

❷ How might you join Matthew, Emily, and Tal as a play partner?

▶ E. At work time, Jalessa is in the house area making "ice cream." She uses an ice cream scoop to form balls of play dough. Brenda, her teacher, walks over to the house area, picks up a baby doll, and sitting down on the floor next to Jalessa, begins to rock her baby. Brenda says to Jalessa, "Oh, my baby is really hungry. Do you have any baby food for her?"

❶ What assumptions does Brenda seem to make about Jalessa's play?

❷ What might you do if you were to enter Jalessa's play as a parallel player? What might you find out from Jalessa?

[20]Work time scenarios B–E were contributed by High/Scope teacher and consultant Beth Marshall.

Exercise 37

Self-Study: Supporting Children at Work Time

(This exercise, which involves a video camera, may be repeated periodically.)

If you are currently teaching or student teaching or can work in an early childhood setting over a period of time, videotape some of your work time interactions with children. Later, watch each video clip one time through, just to see what you look and sound like and what, in general, happened. Then watch each video clip again, this time looking for the **type of play** you joined, the **support strategies** you used, and the **children's response** to your actions and words.

▶ A. What did you learn about the children involved in each interaction?

▶ B. As a supporter of children's play, what strengths did you exhibit in each work time interaction? What, if anything, might you do differently in a similar situation?

Exercise 38

Self-Assessment: Work Time

Item II-E of the High/Scope Program Quality Assessment (PQA): Preschool Version provides one way to assess work time in an early childhood program. If you are currently teaching, use PQA item II-E (given at the right) to make notes and assess your own classroom by rating it on a scale of 1–5. If you are not teaching, you might look at the classroom you observed for exercise 24 on p. 78.

PQA Item II-E. The program has time each day (e.g., work time, choice time, center time, free play) during which children initiate activities and carry out their intentions. [Note: If time for child initiation and choice is set aside but not observed, score at level 1.]

Supporting evidence/anecdotes:

☐ There is no daily time set aside when children can initiate activities and carry out their intentions.

☐ There is a daily choice time during which children sometimes can initiate activities and carry out their own intentions (e.g., only 4 children allowed in the block area, some areas have preset activities).

☐ There is a daily choice time in which children always initiate activities and carry out their intentions.

☐ During choice time, children do preset activities (e.g., the adult sets out materials in each area for children to play with, such as blocks, Legos, crayons and worksheets, puzzles, books).

☐ During choice time, children sometimes do preset activities (e.g., children participate in an art activity set up in the art area or leave an activity to brush their teeth).

☐ Throughout choice time, children carry out their own initiatives and activities (i.e., children choose areas, people, and materials; children are free to invent activities and use materials creatively; children are free to change activities).

☐ Adults direct how children use materials and/or carry out activities (e.g., all children are expected to make the same products, all children are expected to respond to adults with the same words and actions).

☐ Children make some choices about where and how to use materials and/or carry out activities (e.g., children can decide what to do with the construction paper that the adult set out for an art activity).

☐ Throughout choice time, children make many choices about where and how to use materials and carry out activities (e.g., children can choose from a variety of art materials on the shelves to support their activities, children are free to bring materials from one area to another).

| 1 | 2 | 3 | 4 | 5 |

Recall Time

Understanding the Elements of Recall

Recalling is a reflective process through which people strive to make sense of experiences. With a partner, do the following exercises, which are based on the discussion of what recall is and why it is important on *EYC* pp. 225–228.

▶ A. Recalling involves remembering and reflecting on actions and experiences.

❶ Read and discuss the quotation about storytelling and remembering by psychologist Roger Schank on *EYC* p. 225. What does he mean by "talking is remembering"?

❷ Think of some creative human work that is particularly meaningful to you. It might be a drawing, painting, sculpture, or weaving; a piece of music; a book, poem, play, or movie; a mathematical proof or formula; a scientific finding, structure, machine, or invention. How did the creator of this work represent or make sense of what he or she knows?

❸ What does psychologist Edmond Bolles mean when he describes memory (on *EYC* p. 225) as "a living product of desire, insight, and consciousness"?

❹ Recall some incident from life, and talk with someone else (one or more people) who can recall the same incident. To what extent do your respective memories of the incident coincide? To what extent do they diverge? If they diverge,

what does this tell you about the *construction of memory*?

❺ What is meant by the quotation from Edmond Bolles in the insert on *EYC* p. 232?

▶ B. Recalling involves associating plans, actions, and outcomes.

❶ Describe a plan you made and carried out in which the outcome was clearly connected to your original plan.

❷ Describe a plan you made and carried out in which the outcome was quite different from what you imagined in your original plan.

❸ At recall time will young children always be able to make the connection between their plans, actions, and outcomes? Why or why not?

▶ C. Recalling involves talking with others about personally meaningful experiences.

❶ Read and discuss educator Elliot Eisner's statement about language in the first column of *EYC* p. 227. What is the role of playful social interchange in the recall process?

❷ What does Eisner mean when (in the second column of *EYC* p. 227) he says that "without representation, culture itself would not be possible"?

▶ D. Recalling involves forming and then talking about mental images. Recall a dream or an incident from your own life, examining the mental images that form in your mind as you relive this dream or situation. Then select and try out two ways to convey or represent the sense and feelings of the mental images you see. For example, you might use words,

drawing, sculpture, music, or dance to communicate the images in your mind.

❶ From your two forms of representation, what did you discover about recalling?

❷ Is language necessary for recall, or will other forms of communication work? Why or why not?

▶ E. Recalling involves expanding consciousness beyond the present.

❶ What does educator Anthony Pellegrini mean by the "language of absence" (in the first column of *EYC* p. 228)?

❷ How might recalling stretch children's sense of time?

❸ Why is it important for young children (and other people) to be able to reflect on experience? List as many reasons as you can think of.

Child Study: Recall

Observe a preschool child in an early childhood program setting for 30–90 minutes during the heart of the program's daily routine (rather than during napping, for example). Watch and listen carefully, and record the way the child reflects on experiences at recall time and at others times of the day (work time, outside time, small- and large-group times). On another day, repeat this observation process, observing and collecting recall data on another child. For the observations of each child, use a form like the one at the top of the next column.

Child's Name_____ Date_____
Location_____
Time Observed _____

Time of Day	How Child Recalls Experiences (Child's Actions and Words)

How Children Recall

With a partner, do the following exercises, which are based on the discussion of what children do as they recall on *EYC* pp. 228–231:

- Children grow in their capacity to recount past events.
- Children select experiences to recall.
- Children construct their own understanding of what they have just done.
- Children recall experiences in a variety of ways.

▶ A. From your own experiences and observations, give examples of how you have seen and heard a 2-year-old, a 3-year-old, a 4-year-old, and a 5-year-old recall. If you do not have experience with a wide range of children, talk with someone who has or, better yet, observe some children between ages 2 and 5 years. Use a chart like the following.

Child's Age	How Child Recalls, Recounts Past Events

▶ B. Children select experiences to recall.

❶ If a trusted friend asks you to tell about your own childhood, what are several stories you might select to tell? (Instead of recounting each story, simply write a descriptive title or phrase for each story.)

❷ Recall yourself as a teenager. Did you tell your parents everything you did at school or with your friends, or did you select only parts of that life to share? Why?

❸ Think of a preschool child you have seen at work time and recall time. What parts of work time did the child select to recall?

❹ What is the role of selectivity in recalling experiences?

❺ At recall time, would you expect a child to tell about *everything* he or she did at work time? Why or why not?

▶ C. Children construct their own understanding of what they have just done.

❶ What does Bolles mean when he says, "We remember things according to our own understanding of what happened, not according to the way something really occurred" (first column of *EYC* p. 230)?

❷ Give an example of how your understanding of a particular situation or event has been different from what actually happened.

❸ Give an example of a preschooler's recall that is shaped by his or her understanding of the world. If you do not have an example from your own observation of preschoolers, find an example in *EYC*.

▶ D. Children recall experiences in a variety of ways.

❶ How does 3-year-old Tara recall in the scenario on *EYC* pp. 230–231?

❷ Some preschoolers comprehend spoken language but for various reasons do not talk. They can, however, recall. How might they do this?

Self-Study: Recall

For a week, keep a log of all the ways you recall events, situations, feelings, ideas; all the stories you tell; all the ways you indicate what has happened to you and what you have noticed and discovered. At the end of the week, look over your entries. What strikes you about your personal recall process? Do you see any similarities or differences between your recall process and the recall process of the children you observed in exercise 40? Record your thoughts and insights.

Examining Becki's Recall Time

With a partner or several friends, read aloud the transcript of preschool teacher Becki's recall time on *EYC* pp. 231–232. Then discuss the following:

▶ A. What strikes you about this recall dialogue?

▶ B. Identify which conversational move Becki makes each time she speaks. (See *EYC* p. 218 for a description of five conversational moves—*enforced repetition, closed question, open question, contribution, acknowledgment*—and their effects on children's language.)

► C. What recall support strategies does Becki use? Refer to the list of strategies on *EYC* p. 241.

► D. Who appears to be the least experienced recaller in this group of children? On what observations did you base your conclusions?

Exercise 44

Supporting the Recall Process: Photos of Adults at Recall

► A. What do the photos on pp. 226–241 of *EYC* tell you about the adult's role at recall time?

► B. Of these photos of recall time, which one is your favorite? Why? In this photo, what support strategies does the adult appear to be using? (See support strategies listed in *EYC* on pp. 40, 66, and 241.)

► C. How might the adults in each of the *EYC* photographs listed in exercises (1)–(10) be supporting children's recall as it occurs throughout the day?

❶ Photo on p. 55

❷ Photo on p. 217

❸ Photo on p. 288

❹ Photo on p. 344

❺ Photo on p. 373

❻ Left photo on p. 450

❼ Bottom photo on p. 474

❽ Photo on p. 476

❾ Photo on p. 484

❿ Photo on p. 522

Exercise 45

Adult Attitudes Toward Recall, Storytelling, and Reflection

In today's world, many adults are extremely busy with school, work, meetings, child care, church, volunteer commitments, and so forth. They are involved in scheduling their days and doing what needs to be done, which leaves little time for reflection. Sometimes, this "too busy" tendency is also reflected in the early childhood setting, where adult teams support children through planning and carrying out their plans but then find it difficult to make time for recalling.

► A. Why is or isn't reflection, recall, or storytelling important?

► B. Examine your recall log from exercise 42 on p. 89. What effect did recalling have on your daily life? How did you feel when someone listened attentively to your reflections?

► C. Because preschool children are just learning to reflect on their experiences, recalling with them takes particular patience on the part of adults. In spite of the time it takes for children to construct and communicate their reflections, why is it important for adults to support children's recall and storytelling on a daily basis?

► D. When adults listen attentively to children and follow their leads and ideas, recall and reflection are apt to creep into children's conversations throughout the day. Give examples you have observed of children recalling at times other than recall time.

Exercise 46

Making Recall Time Comfortable and Inviting

The discussion on *EYC* pp. 232–233 indicates the importance of recalling *in intimate groups and places*, and doing so *with those who shared the experience* being recalled. Why is each of these two conditions important to children's recall and reflection? How might you provide for each of these two conditions in your current or prospective early childhood setting?

Exercise 47

Trying Out Games and Experiences for Recall Time

This exercise is based on the recall games and experiences described on *EYC* p. 235.

► A. Pick out a game or experience from each of the four categories listed—*tours, group games, props and partnerships,* and *representations.* On four different days, in an early childhood program setting, try out the selected game or experience with a small group of children at recall time. If the program does not have a specific recall time, try out your game experience just after free play or activity time. Use a chart like the following to record your observations of what children do and say during each game experience that you try.

Game/Experience Category	Name of Game/ Experience	Children's Actions & Words

B. If you are currently teaching or student teaching or can work in an early childhood program setting over a period of time, collect or photograph representations children make at recall time. (Include the child's name and date on each representation.) At the end of your collection period, examine the representations you have gathered. What strikes you about these representations? What do they suggest to you about children's ability to recall?

Exercise 48

Supporting Children's Recall Conversations, Reflections, and Stories

The following exercises are based on the discussion of ways adults converse with children about their work time experiences on *EYC* pp. 234–241.

▶ A. By its very nature, reflection takes time. It cannot be rushed, especially in young children who are just learning to use language to recount their experiences. What kind of inner dialogue might have to take place in an adult's head to provide time for children to communicate their thoughts and feelings? That is, what might you say to yourself to keep yourself from rushing a child's recall or from supplying the words you think the child might need?

▶ B. Asking an open-ended question (such as "What did you do at work time?") is a common way to initiate recall with a child. Give several examples of how you might begin a recall conversation *without* using a question.

▶ C. Exercises (1)–(8) give the opening line of dialogue in each of the eight recall conversations on *EYC* pp. 236–239. Explain how adults follow children's leads and cues in each conversation.

❶ "What did you do, Naaman?"

❷ "I saw you with lots of stuffed animals, Bethany."

❸ "I'm not telling what I did."

❹ "Chris, you've been waiting to talk on the TV."

❺ "I worked on the computer."

❻ "I maked it real, real tall."

❼ "I saw you with lots of stuffed animals, Bethany."

❽ "We put that big board up and . . ."

Exercise 49

Recall Time Scenarios: What Would You Do?

Using everything you know about the way young children recall and how adults support them, describe how you might support each child's recall in the following recall scenarios. You may wish to refer to the support strategies listed on *EYC* pp. 40, 66, and 241.

▶ A. *You planned to use the telephones as recall props. Lynette, however, comes to your recall group bringing a big painting she has made. The other children express interest in the monsters she has painted. It is clear that Lynette's recall has already begun **without** the telephones.*

▶ B. *When it is Niko's turn to recall, he glances at the big blocks, then looks down at his hands and says nothing.*

▶ C. *With the flashlight beam, Sasha is pointing to a puzzle she did at work time. Instead of talking about her puzzle making at that point, she puts the flashlight down, gets up, and brings the puzzle back to the recall group.*

▶ D. *Alphonse is telling a very long recall story about the Batman Ranger play he and another child were involved in, and others are occasionally adding to the story.*

▶ E. *When it is Malek's turn to recall, she says, "You have to guess!"*

▶ F. *After Kevin shows the construction he made with pipe cleaners, wire, toothpicks, and glue, he says, "I want to show it to Rue'Nette" (the teacher at the other recall group).*

▶ G. *While the other children in your recall group are finding and bringing back something they used at work time, Ethan returns empty-handed, saying "I brought back something inbisible!"*

▶ H. *The children in your program have never recalled before. On the table, you have gathered materials that each child in your group played with at work time, including the Legos that Rafael has played with.*

▶ I. *Yerchenik speaks fluent Armenian and comprehends some English. When it is her turn to recall, she talks animatedly in Armenian.*

▶ J. *Caleb has built an elaborate cardboard-tube structure that is resting on the top of the block shelf. He wants all the children in his recall group to go to the shelf to look at his creation.*

Exercise 50

Keeping a Recall Journal

If you are currently teaching or student-teaching, choose one child in your recall group and keep a log of anecdotal observations on that child's daily approach to recall—that is, note the child's words and actions at recall time. If you are not teaching, but your study child from earlier exercises in this study guide is involved in a program that includes recall time, observe that child's actions and words at recall time on a regular basis. Periodically review the anecdotal data you have collected, and draw some conclusions about how the child is recalling.

Exercise 51

Self-Study: Videotaping Planning and Recall Times

(This exercise, which involves a video camera, may be repeated periodically.)

If you are currently teaching or student-teaching or can work in an early childhood setting over a period of time, periodically videotape your planning and recall times. After each taping session, first watch the video footage to see what you look and sound like, and what in general happened. Then watch the planning and recall times again, observing individual children to see how they plan and recall. Also look for the support strategies you use and the types of conversational moves you include in your dialogue with children. What conclusions can you draw about children's planning and recall abilities and about your own strengths as a supporter of child planners and recallers?

Exercise 52

Self-Assessment: Recall Time

Item II-F of the High/Scope Program Quality Assessment (PQA): Preschool Version provides one way to assess recall time in an early childhood program. If you are currently teaching, use PQA item II-F (on the next page) to make notes and assess your own classroom by rating it on a scale of 1–5. (If you are not teaching, you might look at the classroom in which you did exercise 2 on p. 71.)

Exercise 53

Planning, Work, and Recall Issues to Ponder and Write About

➤ A. In an early childhood setting, is children's planning limited to planning time? Why or why not?

➤ B. Do children who do not talk nevertheless have and express intentions? If not, why not? If so, how?

➤ C. What is the relationship between making one's own choices, plans, and decisions and following someone else's directions?

➤ D. How can adults who have not been encouraged to make choices and decisions support children's planning?

➤ E. In your life, what is the adult equivalent of work time?

➤ F. At work time, what is the role of play by children and adults?

➤ G. Why and how will preschoolers tend to modify their plans during work time?

➤ H. How is recalling related to the process of creative representation? To early literacy?

➤ I. How does the process of recalling help children construct memory?

➤ J. How does recalling contribute to a child's "sense of self"?

➤ K. Is recalling limited to recall time? Why or why not?

Related Publications

Evans, Betsy. 1995. "Acknowledging Children's Feelings." *High/Scope Extensions* (March/April): 6.

Evans, Betsy. 1996. "Helping Children Resolve Disputes and Conflicts." In *Supporting Young Learners 2: Ideas for Child Care Poroviders and Teachers*, Nancy A. Brickman, ed., 27–34. Ypsilanti, MI: High/Scope Press.

Evans, Betsy. 2002. *You Can't Come to My Birthday Party! Conflict Resolution With Young Children.* Ypsilanti, MI: High/Scope Press.

Graves, Michelle. 1991. "Child Planning: Why It's Important, How to Get Started." In *Supporting Young Learners: Ideas for Preschool and Day Care Providers*, Nancy A. Brickman and Lynn S. Taylor, eds., 115–19. Ypsilanti, MI: High/Scope Press.

Graves, Michelle. 1996. *The Teacher's Idea Book 2: Planning Around Children's Interests.* Ypsilanti, MI: High/Scope Press.

Graves, Michelle. 1996. "Work Time: Teacher Habits That Are Hard to Break." In *Supporting Young Learners 2: Ideas for Child Care Poroviders and Teachers*, Nancy A. Brickman, ed., 61–68. Ypsilanti, MI: High/Scope Press.

High/Scope Program Quality Assessment (PQA): Preschool Version (Field-Test Edition). 2001. Ypsilanti, MI: High/Scope Press.

Hohmann, Charles, and Warren Buckleitner. 1992. *High/Scope K–3 Curriculum Series: Learning Environment.* Ypsilanti, MI: High/Scope Press.

PQA Item II-F. The program has time each day during which children remember and review their activities and share with adults and peers what they have done. [Note: If time to review is set aside but not observed, score at level 1.]

Supporting evidence/anecdotes:

1	2	3
☐ There is no time set aside for children to recall or reflect on what they have done.	☐ Sometimes there is time set aside for children to recall or reflect on what they have done.	☐ There is a daily time set aside for children to recall and reflect on their activities.
☐ Children never share what they have done with others.	☐ Adults use rote or routine strategies for recalling (e.g., adults always ask children "Where did you go?" or "What did you do today?").	☐ Adults use a variety of strategies to encourage children to share and recall their experiences (e.g., props, area signs, pillowcases, Hula-Hoop, tape recorder; recalling individually, in pairs, in work groups).
☐ Adults do not encourage children to recall or recognize when children are sharing experiences in ways consistent with their developmental levels.	☐ Adults sometimes encourage children to recall in ways that are consistent with their developmental levels.	☐ Adults encourage children to recall in ways that are consistent with their developmental levels (e.g., by showing, re-enacting, describing in words, or making drawings of their activities).

| 1 | 2 | 3 | 4 | 5 |

Hohmann, Mary. 1991. "The Many Faces of Child Planning." In *Supporting Young Learners: Ideas for Preschool and Day Care Providers,* Nancy A. Brickman and Lynn S. Taylor, eds., 120–28. Ypsilanti, MI: High/Scope Press.

Marshall, Beth. 1993. "Interacting Effectively With Children." *High/Scope Extensions* (October): 6.

Marshall, Beth. 2001. "TRUST in Children's Play." *High/Scope Extensions* (January/February): 1–3.

Post, Jacalyn, and Mary Hohmann. 2000. "Establishing Schedules and Routines for Infants and Toddlers." In *Tender Care and Early Learning: Supporting Infants and Toddlers in Child Care Settings,* 190–293. Ypsilanti, MI: High/Scope Press.

Sylva, Kathy, Carolyn Roy, and Marjorie Painter. 1980. *Childwatching at Playgroup & Nursery School.* Ypsilanti, MI: High/Scope Press.

Tompkins, Mark. 1991. "A Look at Looking Back: Helping Children Recall." In *Supporting Young Learners: Ideas for Preschool and Day Care Providers,* Nancy A. Brickman and Lynn S. Taylor, eds., 129–36. Ypsilanti, MI: High/Scope Press.

Vogel, Nancy. 2001. The *Teacher's Idea Book 5: Making the Most of Plan-Do-Review.* Ypsilanti, MI: High/Scope Press.

Related Videos

Adult-Child Interactions: Forming Partnerships With Children. 1996. Color videotape, 60 min. Ypsilanti, MI: High/Scope Press.

The High/Scope Curriculum: The Daily Routine. 1990. Color videotape, 17 min. Ypsilanti, MI: High/Scope Press.

The High/Scope Curriculum: Its Implementation in Family Child Care Homes. 1989. Color videotape, 19 min. Ypsilanti, MI: High/Scope Press.

The High/Scope Curriculum: The Plan-Do-Review Process. 1989. Color videotape, 20 min. Ypsilanti, MI: High/Scope Press.

High/Scope K–3 Curriculum Series: Classroom Environment. 1991. Color videotape, 17 min. Ypsilanti, MI: High/Scope Press.

How Adults Support Children at Planning Time in High/Scope's Demonstration Preschool. 1997. Color videotape, 19 min. Ypsilanti, MI: High/Scope Press.

How Adults Support Children at Recall Time. 1997. Color videotape, 19 min. Ypsilanti, MI: High/Scope Press.

How Adults Support Children at Work Time in High/Scope's Demonstration Preschool. 1997. Color videotape, 25 min. Ypsilanti, MI: High/Scope Press.

Supporting Children in Resolving Conflicts. 1998. Color videotape, 24 min. Ypsilanti, MI: High/Scope Press.

hough these special times have special features, they share a common goal: to encourage children's active involvement with materials, people, ideas, and events. During group times, outside time, and transition times, active learning is the guiding philosophy, just as it is during the plan-work-recall sequence. Throughout these activities, children make choices and decisions, learn through direct experience, and talk about what they are doing.

—*Educating Young Children*, p. 245

Small-Group Time

Exerxise 1

Experiencing Small-Group Time

For this exercise, gather together four or five friends and any set of materials you would particularly like to explore or use—for example, tools and wood; paints, brushes, and paper; computers and computer software; balls; string and macrame instructions; marbles and tubes; clay; photographs; travel books, brochures, and maps. Whatever you select, make sure there are enough materials for everyone to work with at once. Spend 15 minutes (or more) exploring, experimenting, trying out ideas with these materials. Enjoy yourselves.

▶ A. What struck you about this small-group experience?

▶ B. What made it enjoyable?

▶ C. How was it different from working with these materials by yourself?

▶ D. What did you learn?

Exercise 2

Examining Three Small-Group Times in Early Childhood Settings

Read the following small-group-time scenarios in *EYC:* "The 'Pineapple Connection'" (p. 246), "All the Colors of the Rainbow" (pp. 246–248), Catherine's egg-coloring experience (pp. 251–252).

Also read "One Teacher's Thoughts About a Small-Group Time Using Found Materials" (p. 254).

▶ A. What in particular strikes you about each of the small-group experiences?

▶ B. What did you learn about Catherine?

▶ C. In the egg-coloring small group, why were the children talking so much about colors, even though no adult ever asked, "What color is that"?

▶ D. Teacher Ruth Strubank describes discussing and reflecting on small-group time at the end of the day, during daily team planning. What role does this discussion and reflection play?

Exercise 3

Active Learning at Small-Group Time

▶ A. Re-read the small-group-time (SGT) scenarios cited in exercise 2, and identify which of the five active learning ingredients (materials, manipulation, choice, language from children, support from adults) occur in each one. Use a chart like the following to organize your answers.

Active Learning Ingredient	Pineapple SGT (p. 246)	Egg-Coloring SGT (pp. 246–248, 251–252)	Found Materials SGT (p. 254)

B. As active learners, what are the children learning in each of the small-group times listed in your chart?

C. Select a photograph of small-group time from *EYC* pp. 244–264. What does the photograph tell you about active learning at small-group time?

D. Why is active learning in a supportive climate important at small-group time?

Exercise 4

Balancing Adult Initiative With Adult Support at Small-Group Time

A. What do adults initiate at small-group time?

B. From reading the small-group-time scenarios involving pineapples, coloring eggs, and found materials (see exercise 2 on p. 95), what conclusions might you draw about adult initiative at small-group time?

C. How do adults initiate and maintain a supportive climate at small-group time? (Refer to the elements of support on *EYC* p. 66.)

D. Sometimes adults confuse teacher initiation with being directive, regarding small-group time as "my time to teach." Look at Becki's egg-coloring small-group time in terms of the elements of support (*EYC* p. 66). What did Becki initiate? How did she maintain a supportive climate? How did she support children's activities?

E. Read "Adults Examine Their Beliefs About How Children Learn at Small-Group Time" (*EYC* pp. 253–256). In the pineapple, egg-coloring, and found materials small groups, what conclusions can you draw about the adults' attitudes toward each of the child actions listed in (1)–(8)? Use a chart like the following to organize your answers.

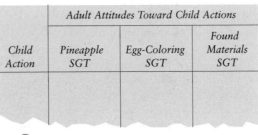

	Adult Attitudes Toward Child Actions		
Child Action	Pineapple SGT	Egg-Coloring SGT	Found Materials SGT

❶ Experiencing

❷ Drilling

❸ Conversing

❹ Listening to adults talk

❺ Solving problems

❻ Following adult directions

❼ Adding materials

❽ Waiting for adults to add materials

Exercise 5

Small-Group Time: Why Bother?

This exercise is based on the discussion on *EYC* pp. 248–250 about small-group time as an opportunity to build on children's strengths and interests, introduce interesting materials, and support positive interactions between children and peers and between children and adults. Discuss the following with a partner.

A. What things have you done as part of a small group of people? What small-group interactions in your life do you enjoy? Why?

B. From your own experiences, what kind of learning occurs for you in a small group in which you feel safe to explore and try out ideas? In a small group in which someone tells you exactly what to do?

C. Why are small-group experiences important to young children?

Exercise 6

Meeting Places for Small Groups

A. Look at the *EYC* photographs of small groups identified in (1)–(9), and identify *where* the small group shown in the photo(s) is occurring.

❶ Photos on pp. 56 and 359

❷ Photos on pp. 118 and 134

❸ Photo on top of p. 138

❹ Top right photo on p. 144

❺ Photo on p. 155 and photos on pp. 245–247

❻ Photos on p. 79 and on pp. 250, 252, 264

❼ Photo on p. 255

❽ Photo on p. 318

❾ Photos on p. 319

B. If you are currently teaching or student teaching, think of and list all the places in and around your setting where you could hold small-group times.

Observing Catherine at Small-Group Time

The following exercises are based on the scenario of Catherine at Becki's egg-coloring small-group time, *EYC* pp. 251–252.

▶ A. Answer exercises (1)–(5) to describe Catherine's participation in the small group:

1 What were her actions?

2 What language did she use?

3 What discoveries did she make?

4 What were her social interactions?

5 What problem solving did she do?

▶ B. Based on the descriptive notes you just made about Catherine in the egg-coloring scenario, write two or more anecdotes about Catherine. Using the list of key experiences (*EYC* p. 22), decide which key experience each of your anecdotes is most closely related to, and enter your anecdotes on the Key Experience Notes form[21] on the following two pages.

▶ C. What do adults gain by observing and listening to children at small-group time?

Child Study: Small-Group Time

▶ A. Find an active learning early childhood setting. During small-group time, observe a single child for the entire small-group time. As you

---

[21]*The Key Experience Notes forms are used with the **High/Scope Child Observation Record** (COR) described on EYC p. 98.*

watch and listen, once each minute write down what the child **says** and **does**. Also note the **social context** of the child's play (onlooking, solitary, parallel, group), and the **type of play** the child is engaged in (exploratory, constructive, pretend, games). Use a format like the following.

| Child's Name_____ Date_____ |
| Location_____ |
| Time Observed _____ |

Minutes	Actions	Words	Social Context	Play Type

▶ B. After your observation, write as many anecdotes as you can about the child you observed. Then, using the list of key experiences (*EYC* p. 22), decide which key experience each anecdote is most closely related to, and record your anecdotes on the Key Experience Notes form on pp. 98–99. (In an actual classroom situation, teachers use one Key Experience Notes form per child. In this case, however, you will be recording anecdotes about Catherine [exercise 7B] and your study child on a single form.)

Forming Small Groups

This exercise is based on the *EYC* discussions of group stability (first column of p. 248) and group balance (p. 256). With a partner, discuss and record your answers to A–E.

▶ A. Assume that you and your teaching teammate have sixteen 3-and 4-year-old children in your early childhood setting. List the criteria you might consider when you divide your children into two well-balanced small groups.

▶ B. Which criteria would you take into account to create two small groups at the beginning of the program year?

▶ C. What circumstances might cause you to consider changing the makeup of these two small groups?

▶ D. Suppose that you are just initiating small-group times. In what concrete ways might you use photographs or symbols to let children know which small group they are in?

▶ E. Suppose that you and your teaching partner decide to change small groups after winter break. What concrete ways might you use to inform children of this change on their first day back from vacation?

Planning Active Learning Small-Group Times

This exercise examines four beginning points for planning small-group time:

- Children's interests
- Materials
- Key experiences
- Local traditions

Key Experience Notes

High/Scope
Child Observation
Record (COR)
For Ages 2½–6

CHILD COR OBSERVATION RECORD

Observer's name: _____

Child's name: _____

Creative Representation	Language and Literacy	Initiative and Social Relations	Movement	Music

Key Experience Notes

High/Scope
Child Observation
Record (COR)
For Ages 2½–6

Observer's name: _____

Child's name: _____

Classification	Seriation	Number	Space	Time

A. Exercises (1)–(5) concern planning small-group time around the *interests of individual children*.

❶ Read the discussion "Plan around the interests of individual children" (*EYC* p. 257) and "A Sample Small-Group-Time Plan: Jumping" (*EYC* p. 255). For each of the five bulleted examples in the discussion on p. 257 and for the "Jumping" plan, list the **child's interest** and the **small-group experience** that originated from it. An example from the first paragraph of the p. 257 reading appears in the sample chart.

Child's Interest	Resulting Small-Group Experience
p. 257 Brianna and Audie are interested in Band-Aids.	Adult provided Band-Aids for children to explore and use at SGT.

❷ Read the anecdotes about Jonah in the "Key Experience Notes" on *EYC* pp. 306–307. Describe two interests of Jonah's and two small-group-time experiences you might plan based on these interests.

❸ Look through the photographs of work time on *EYC* pp. 196–224. Choose two of the photos, and identify the interest the child or children are showing in each one of them. What is a small-group experience you might plan based on each of these interests?

❹ Review the observations of your study child(ren) in Chapter 1, exercise 6, page 8; Chapter 2, exercise 9, page 19; and Chapter 7, exercise 24, page 78. For each exercise, list **two**

of the child's interests and a possible **small-group experience** based on each of these interests. Use a chart like the following to organize your answers.

Chap #/ Exercise #	Child's Interest	Possible Small-Group Experience Based on Child's Interest

❺ Think of a particular child or children you know in your own early childhood setting or elsewhere. What are some of the child(ren)'s interests, and what small-group experience might you plan based on each of those interests?

B. Exercises (1)–(5) concern planning small-group time around *new and unexplored materials*.

❶ Read the discussion "Plan around new and unexplored materials" (*EYC* p. 257) and "A Sample Small-Group-Time Plan: Exploring Coconuts" (*EYC* p. 255). For each of the five bulleted examples in the discussion on p. 257 and for the "Exploring Coconuts" plan, list the **adult's observations** about materials and the resulting **small-group experience**. An example from the first paragraph of the p. 257 reading appears in the sample chart.

Adult's Observations About Materials	Resulting Small-Group Experience
p. 257 Four children have been using tempera paints but not watercolors.	Provided children with watercolors, brushes, and large sheets of paper at SGT.

❷ Return to the anecdotes about Jonah on *EYC* pp. 306–307. Name some new or overlooked materials Jonah might enjoy, and describe small-group experiences you might plan around these materials.

❸ Look through the work time photographs on *EYC* pp. 196–224, and list all the materials you see children using. Based on this information, what small-group time might you plan around a related new material, an overlooked material, or a new combination of materials?

❹ Review the observations of your study child(ren) in Chapter 1, exercise 6, page 8; Chapter 2, exercise 9, page 19; and Chapter 7, exercise 24, page 78. List all the materials these children used, and think of a possible small-group experience based on related new materials, overlooked materials, or a new combination of materials. Use a chart like the following to organize your answers.

Chapter #/ Exercise #	Materials Study Children Used	Possible Small-Group Experience

❺ If you are currently teaching, student-teaching, or in some way associated with an early childhood setting, list the materials the children have been using, and think of a possible small-group time featuring new materials, overlooked materials, or a new combinations of materials.

C. Exercises (1)–(5) concern planning small-group time around *key experiences*.

❶ Read the discussion "Plan around the High/Scope key experiences" (*EYC* pp. 257–259) and "A Sample Small-Group-Time Plan: Making Play-Doh Models" (*EYC* p. 254). For each of the five bulleted examples in the discussion on pp. 257–259 and for the "Making Play-Doh Models" plan, list the **key experience the adult selected** and the **small-group experience** he or she planned around it. An example from the first paragraph of the pp. 257–259 reading appears in the sample chart below.

Key Experience	Resulting Small-Group Experience
p. 258 Space: Fitting things together and taking them apart.	Provided children with stacking pegs and pegboards at SGT.

❷ Return to the anecdotes about Jonah on *EYC* pp. 306–307. List two specific key experiences Jonah is experiencing (see the list on *EYC* p. 22). Describe a small-group-time experience you might provide based on each of the two key experiences you have selected.

❸ Assume the role of one of Jonah's teachers. Although you have gathered some anecdotes about Jonah related to the space key experiences, you find that you have *not* recorded any space-related anecdotes about several of the other children in your class. Select two space key experiences (see the list on *EYC* p. 490). Think of two interesting small-group experiences you might provide around these two key experiences.

❹ Review the list of key experiences (*EYC* p. 22). Select two key experiences that really interest you or that you would like to know more about. Describe two small-group experiences children might enjoy in which they would experience these key experiences.

❺ Think about children in your early childhood setting or children you know well. List two key experiences you see in their play. What small-group experiences might you plan around these key experiences?

▶ D. Exercises (1)–(3) concern planning small-group time around *local traditions*.

❶ Read the discussion "Plan around local traditions" (*EYC* p. 259) and "A Sample Small-Group-Time Plan: 'Writing' Thank-You Cards" (*EYC* p. 254). For each of the five bulleted examples in the p. 259 discussion and for the "'Writing' Thank-You Cards" plan, list the **local tradition** the adults focused on and the **small-group experience** they planned around it. An example from the first paragraph of the p. 259 reading appears in the sample chart below.

Local Tradition	Resulting Small-Group Experience
p. 259 Children see the high school marching band during outside time.	Provided children with musical instruments and had a parade at SGT.

❷ List local traditions that occur in your community. Select one tradition and think of an active learning small-group time you might plan around it.

❸ Think of the children and families you know. List the local traditions and celebrations that are of particular importance to them. Select one tradition, and think of an active learning small-group experience you might plan around it.

▶ E. Now that you have considered the origins of small-group-time plans, record your thoughts about the following relationships:

❶ What is the relationship between children's interests and the key experiences?

❷ When planning a small-group time around children's interests, key experiences, or local traditions, what role do materials play?

❸ If you plan a small-group time around a specific key experience, is it still important to consider children's interests and materials? Why or why not?

Exercise 11

Exploring Potential Small-Group-Time Materials[22]

With a partner or with a group of friends, gather and explore two or more of the following sets of materials:

- Dried beans (lima, kidney, navy), playing cards, plastic lids
- Biodegradable packing "peanuts," colored paper, containers of water, paper towels

---

[22]*This exercise was created by High/Scope educational consultant Linda Weikel. It first appeared in a slightly different form in a 1996 High/Scope Registry Conference session entitled "Developing Small-Group Experiences: What Shall We Do Tomorrow?"*

- Storybooks, stuffed animals
- Cardboard boxes, paint, brushes
- Cardboard tubes, marbles
- Eyedroppers, colored water, clear cups, ice cube trays, coffee filters
- Dirt, stones, pebbles, foil pans, water
- Moist clay
- Plastic worms and lizards (from bait shop or discount store), clear plastic cups, water
- Empty plastic 2-liter bottles, tennis balls
- Shells, sand, box lids or trays
- Sponge letters, numbers, shapes, animals; paint, paper, newspaper

Upon completing your exploration of the sets of materials, use a form like the one below to record your thoughts about the potential of each of these sets of materials for small-group time.

Materials:

SGT possibly planned around—

- *Children's interest in_____*

- *New/unexplored material_____*

- *Key experience_____*

- *Local traditions_____*

Key experiences I might observe at SGT:

Notes:

Looking at Becki's Egg-Coloring Small-Group Time

For this exercise, read about Becki's egg-coloring small-group time (*EYC* pp. 246–248, 251–252). Think about it in terms of the discussion about the beginning, middle, and end of small-group time on *EYC* pp. 260–263 and the checklist on *EYC* p. 264.

▶ A. What might Becki's *originating idea* for this small-group time have been?

▶ B. What *materials* did Becki have ready for each child?

▶ C. How did Becki *begin* small-group time? What were her actions and words?

▶ D. What *support strategies* did Becki use?

▶ E. What *key experiences* occurred as children colored eggs?

▶ F. How did Becki bring this small-group time to a *close*?

Observing a Small-Group Time

▶ A. Watch an entire active learning small-group time from beginning to end. As you watch and listen, look for and make notes about the items on the small-group-time checklist from *EYC* p. 264, which is reproduced on the facing page.

▶ B. Based on your notes and checklist, what were the strengths of this small-group time?

▶ C. What, if anything, might you do differently if you were to carry out a similar small-group time? Why?

Self-Study: Plan, Do, and Review a Small-Group Time

(Exercise B involves a tape recorder or video camera.)

▶ A. Plan a small-group time for a group of children you know. Complete exercises (1)–(6) to describe your plan.

   ❶ Originating idea:

   ❷ Materials:

   ❸ Beginning:

   ❹ Middle—ways to support children:

   ❺ Key experiences you might see:

   ❻ End:

▶ B. Prepare for and carry out your small-group time. Videotape or audiotape the small group, and later look at or listen to your tape.

   ❶ What did you find out about the children in your small group?

   ❷ What key experiences occurred?

   ❸ What support strategies worked? Why?

   ❹ What might you do differently another time? Why?

How Adults Support Children at Small-Group Time: A Summary

Adults examine their beliefs about how children learn at small-group time.

Adults form well-balanced small groups.

Adults plan small-group experiences ahead of time.

_____Plan around the interests of individual children.

_____Plan around new and unexplored materials.

_____Plan around key experiences.

_____Plan around local traditions.

Adults prepare for small groups before children arrive.

_____Gather materials for each child.

_____Have materials ready.

Adults set small groups in motion: the beginning.

_____Give children materials as they arrive.

_____Make a brief introductory statement.

Adults support each child's ideas and use of materials: the middle.

_____Move to children's physical level.

_____Watch what children do with materials.

_____Listen to what children say.

_____Move from child to child so all children receive attention.

_____Imitate children's actions.

_____Converse with children, following their leads.

_____Encourage children to do things for themselves.

_____Refer children to each other for ideas and assistance.

_____Ask questions sparingly.

Adults bring small-group time to a close: the end.

_____Realize that children finish at different times.

_____Give children a warning near the session's end.

_____Support children's concluding observations.

_____Tell children that materials will be available at work time.

_____Ask children to put away materials.

Small-Group Scenarios: What Would You Do?

Using everything you know about active learning at small-group time and the ways adults support active learners, decide how you might support children in the following small-group scenarios. You may wish to refer to the support strategies listed on *EYC* pp. 40, 66, and 264.

▶ A. *During a small-group time in which children are decorating boxes and cardboard tubes, Saul leaves to go to the bathroom. On his way back to your small group, he stops to see what his friend Jamison is decorating at the other small group.*

How might you support Saul's interest in Jamison's work?

▶ B. *The children in your small group are exploring and molding clay. Although Clarice has a lump of clay in front of her, she holds her dolly, sucks her thumb, and watches the other children work with clay.*

How might you support Clarice?

▶ C. *After reading the story **Ferdinand** by Robert Lawson, you encourage the children in your small group to make drawings of the part of the story that they particularly enjoyed. From the materials you have provided, they select paper, paints, and crayons and get started. Ben, however, goes to the art shelf, finds a small box and some crepe paper, and says, "I'm going to make a bullfighter hat!"*

How might you support Ben's idea for illustrating part of the story?

▶ D. *For your small-group time, the children are gathered around the water table, which is filled with warm soapy water. They are washing dishes, pots, pans, and silverware from the house area. "Uh, oh," says Karina, "we need to rinse these." "Yeh, and they need a place to dry!" adds Rubin.*

How might you support Karina's and Rubin's ideas?

▶ E. *You and your small group of children are sitting among the pillows in the book area, reading **Caps for Sale** by Esphyr Slobodkina. When you come to the sentence "When he woke up he was refreshed and rested," Tareella says, "My mama tells me, 'Don't be fresh.' He in trouble?"*

How might you support Tareella's observation?

▶ F. *You have noticed that a number of children in your small group are writing their names, so today at small-group time, you provide each child with a set of wooden letters including the letters in the child's name, along with paper, pencils, and markers. While several children find, talk about, arrange, and trace the letters in their names, Tristram uses his letters as vehicles, "driving" them around on his paper and making motor-like noises.*

How might you support Tristram's choice?

Small-Group-Time Issues to Ponder and Write About

▶ A. What is the role of materials in small-group time?

▶ B. What if you plan a small-group time around a seriation key experience and, instead of seriating the materials, the children use them to create representations?

▶ C. What is the dynamic between adult initiative and child initiative at small-group time?

▶ D. What is the difference between small-group time and work time from a child's perspective? From an adult's perspective?

▶ E. Might children plan, work, and recall at small-group time? Why or why not?

▶ F. What distinguishes small-group time from other parts of the daily routine?

▶ G. Why might story reading be more effective at small-group time than at large-group time?

▶ H. How can you tell what children are learning at small-group time?

Large-Group Time

Recalling Large-Group Experiences

With a partner or several friends, recall large-group experiences you have had as a child or in later life. As you discuss your experiences, consider where large-group gatherings took place, the make-up of the group, what brought the group together, to what extent group members participated, and the formality or informality of the group.

▶ A. What made your large-group experiences memorable?

▶ B. Ask your parents, grandparents, or friends from an earlier generation about large-group experiences they had as children or in later life. What kinds of communal experiences do they remember?

▶ C. Do you spend as much time in communal groups as did your parents, grandparents, or older friends? Why or why not?

▶ D. Why do people seek out (or avoid) large-group experiences?

Exercise 18

Examining Three Large-Group Times in Early Childhood Settings

Read the following large-group-time scenarios in *EYC*: "The Information Exchange" (pp. 265–266), "Moving and Singing Together" (p. 266), Kenneth's

experience of moving and singing together (pp. 269–270), and "One Teacher's Thoughts About Large-Group Time" (p. 273).

▶ A. Based on these scenarios, how would you define large-group time from a child's point of view? From an adult's point of view?

▶ B. Even though the activity did not involve materials for each child, what drew and held the children's attention during "The Information Exchange"? What was the role of children's language?

▶ C. During "Moving and Singing Together," what role did choice-making play? What choices did the children make?

▶ D. How is the way Beth thinks about large-group time similar to the way you think about it? How is her thinking different from yours?

Exercise 19

A Rationale for Large-Group Time

Read the discussion of what large-group time is and why it is important on *EYC* pp. 267–269. Then do exercises A–F with a partner.

▶ A. Traditionally, many adults have viewed large-group time (or circle time) as a time for children to learn to listen and follow directions. What are other reasons adults have traditionally given for having large-group time in early childhood programs?

▶ B. For what reasons do adults in a High/Scope active learning setting engage children in large-group experiences?

▶ C. What is the role of *active learning* (materials, manipulation, choice, language from children, support from adults) in a High/Scope large-group time?

▶ D. Why is community-building an important aspect of large-group time in a supportive early childhood setting?

▶ E. What choices do children make as they do the "Five Little Monkeys" chant at Becki's large-group time (*EYC* pp. 267–268)?

▶ F. Why is Becki unconcerned about whether the children count backwards as they chant "Five Little Monkeys"?

Exercise 20

Sharing Control With Children at Large-Group Time

▶ A. Read the John Dewey quote on *EYC* p. 23 (top of second column of insert). How might you interpret this quote in terms of large-group time?

▶ B. Describe how each of Dewey's ideas, listed in (1)–(5), is manifested in Beth's and Sam's large-group time (LGT) "Moving and Singing Together" (*EYC* pp. 266, 269–270).

❶ Knowledge of individuals

❷ Knowledge of subject matter

❸ Selection of activities that lend themselves to social organization

❹ Providing all individuals with the opportunity to contribute something

⑤ Activities in which all participate being the chief carrier of control

▶ C. Look at the photographs of large-group time in *EYC* (pp. 26, 49, 57, 65, 88, 105, 156, 265–281, 380, 410, 414, 422, 425, 428, 431, 432, 441, 445, 460–461). What do these photos suggest to you about children's and adult's enjoyment and control at large-group time?

▶ D. In an early childhood setting, how might one balance an adult's need for control and children's need for action at large-group time?

Exercise 21

Large-Group Time From a Child's Point of View

In *EYC* read "What Children Do at Large-Group Time" (pp. 269–270). Also recall children you know and what they do at large-group time.

▶ A. Describe Kenneth's large-group-time experience in terms of each of the elements in (1)–(5).

   ❶ Actions

   ❷ Language

   ❸ Discoveries

   ❹ Social interactions

   ❺ Problem solving

▶ B. What needs and desires do preschool children have at large-group time?

▶ C. How might the ingredients of active learning help meet children's needs at large-group time?

Exercise 22

Child Study: Large-Group Time

▶ A. During large-group time in an active learning early childhood setting, observe a single child for the entire large-group time. As you watch and listen, once each minute write down what the child **says** and **does**. Also note the **social context** of the child's play (onlooking, solitary, parallel, group), and the **type of play** the child is engaged in (exploratory, constructive, pretend, games). Use a child observation format like the following.

| Child's Name_____ Date_____ |
| Location_____ |
| Time Observed _____ |

Minutes	Actions	Words	Social Context	Play Type

▶ B. After your observation, write as many anecdotes as you can about the child you observed. Then, turn to the list of key experiences (*EYC* p. 22), decide which key experience each anecdote is most closely related to, and record your anecdotes on the Key Experience Notes form included on the next two pages.

Exercise 23

Planning Active Learning Large-Group Times

This exercise examines four beginning points for planning large-group times:

   • Children's interests

   • Music and movement key experiences

   • Cooperative play and projects

   • Currently meaningful events

▶ A. Exercises (1)–(4) concern planning large-group times around *children's interests*.

❶ Read the discussion "Plan around children's interests" (*EYC* pp. 271–272) and "A Sample Large-Group-Time Plan: Playing Horses" (*EYC* p. 274). For each bulleted example in the pp. 271–272 discussion and for the "Playing Horses" plan, list the **child's interest** and the **large-group experience** that originated from it. An example from the first paragraph of the p. 271 discussion appears in the following sample chart.

Child's Interest	Resulting Large-Group Experience
p. 271 Linda, David, and Kerry often dance with scarves at work time.	Adult provided children with scarves. Played the song "Oh How Lovely Is the Evening" at LGT as children danced with scarves.

❷ Read the anecdotes about Jonah on *EYC* pp. 306–307. List two interests of Jonah's and two large-group-time experiences you might plan based on these interests.

❸ From the photographs of work time on *EYC* pp. 196–224, choose two photos, identify the interest the child or children are showing in each one, and record a possible large-group experience you might plan based on each interest.

❹ Review the observations of your study child(ren) in Chapter 1, exercise 6, page 8; Chapter 2, exercise 9, page 19; and Chapter 7, exercise 24, page 78. For each exercise, list one of the child's interests and a possible large-group experience based on that interest.

High/Scope
Child Observation
Record (COR)
For Ages 2½–6

Observer's name: _____

Child's name: _____

Creative Representation	Language and Literacy	Initiative and Social Relations	Movement	Music

Key Experience Notes

High/Scope
Child Observation
Record (COR)
For Ages 2½–6

Observer's name: _____

Child's name: _____

Classification	Seriation	Number	Space	Time

© HIGH/SCOPE EDUCATIONAL RESEARCH FOUNDATION

B. Exercises (1)–(5) concern planning large-group time around *music and movement key experiences*.

❶ Read the discussion "Plan around music and movement key experiences" (*EYC* pp. 272 and 276) and "A Sample Large-Group-Time Plan: Singing Favorite Songs" (*EYC* p. 274). For each bulleted example in the discussion and for the "Singing Favorite Songs" plan, list the **music or movement key experience** the adult selected and the **large-group experience** he or she planned around it. An example from the first paragraph of the p. 272 discussion appears in the following sample chart.

Music or Movement Key Experience	Resulting Large-Group Key Experience
p. 272 Music KE: Developing melody. (Deola and Corrin sang the phrase "We all live in a yellow submarine" repeatedly at work time.)	Adults added an ending to the "Yellow Submarine" phrase to create a melody and sang it with the children at LGT. Children added new words.

❷ Look through *EYC* Chapter 13, Movement (pp. 411–431). For each movement key experience, list a large-group experience suggested in the text. Use a chart like the following.

Movement Key Experience	Large-Group Experience Suggested in EYC

❸ Look through *EYC* Chapter 14, "Music" (pp. 433–445). For each music key experience, list a large-group experience suggested in the text. Use a chart like the following.

Music Key Experience	Large-Group Experience Suggested in EYC

❹ Assume the role of one of Jonah's teachers. Although you have gathered some music and movement anecdotes about Jonah, you find that you have *not* recorded any music and movement anecdotes about several of the other children in your class. Select one music key experience and one movement key experience. Describe an interesting large-group experience you might provide around each of these key experiences.

❺ Select one music key experience and one movement key experience that interest you or that you would like to learn more about. Then describe a large-group experience children might enjoy in which they would take part in each of these key experiences.

▶ C. Exercises (1)–(3) concern planning large-group times around *cooperative play and projects*.

❶ Read the discussion "Plan around cooperative play and projects" (*EYC* pp. 276–277) and "A Sample Large-Group-Time Plan: Moving Sand" (*EYC* p. 275). For each bulleted example in the pp. 276–277 discussion and for the "Moving Sand" plan, list the **type of cooperative play or project** the adults selected and the **large-group experience** they planned. An example from the first paragraph of the p. 276 discussion appears in the following sample chart.

Cooperative Play or Project	Resulting Large-Group Experience
p. 276 Since children were telling stories, adults decided to try cooperative storytelling.	Provided children with red and grey puppet cloths and rubber bands to represent Little Red Riding Hood and the wolf. Told story of LRRH while children acted out story with puppets.

❷ Think of the children you know. Then, describe a story, game, or group project they might enjoy and how you might build this into an active learning large-group experience.

❸ What are some things you liked to do as a child that helped adults or older children accomplish a task? For example, you might recall washing windows, picking up windfall apples, pulling weeds, moving lumber, hanging laundry to dry. How might you provide a similar experience for young children at large-group time?

▶ D. Exercises (1)–(4) concern planning around *events currently meaningful to your children*.

❶ Read the discussion "Plan around events currently meaningful to your children" (*EYC* pp. 277–278) and "A Sample Large-Group-Time Plan: Helium Balloons" (*EYC* p. 275). For each bulleted example in the pp. 277–278 discussion and for the "Helium Balloons" plan, list the **event or celebration** adults selected and the **large-group experience** they planned for it. An example from the first paragraph of the p. 277 discussion appears in the following sample chart.

Event	Resulting Large-Group Experience
p. 277 Children sing "Jingle Bells" as they play.	Provided children with bells and sang "Jingle Bells" at LGT.

❷ The children in your early childhood setting have had a number of experiences with fire engines. (See *EYC* p. 315 for photographs of some of these experiences.) What large-group experience might you plan based on the children's trip to the fire station?

❸ The children in your center have been watching construction workers put in a new parking lot for the neighboring building. What large-group experience might you plan around this local event?

❹ Think of the young children you know. What event is currently meaningful to them? What large-group experience might you plan based on that event?

Exercise 24

Looking Closely at a Large-Group Time

For this exercise, select either Beth and Becki's large-group time (*EYC* p. 273) *or* Beth and Sam's large-group time (*EYC* pp. 266, 269–270). Look at the large-group time you have selected in terms of the discussion of the beginning, middle, and end of large-group time on *EYC* pp. 279–280 and the checklist on *EYC* p. 281.

▶ A. What might have been the teaching team's *originating idea* for this large-group time?

▶ B. What *materials* did this large-group experience rely on?

▶ C. How did the teaching team *draw children into* large-group time?

▶ D. What did the children do in the *middle* of large-group time?

▶ E. How did adults *support children* at large-group time?

▶ F. How did the *end* of large-group time lead into the next part of the day?

Exercise 25

Drawing Children Into Large-Group Time[23]

Rather than wait for all of the children to assemble for large-group time and then begin, it is important in an active learning setting to begin large-group time with an activity children will find interesting, will want to join, and can easily join even after it has begun.

▶ A. Look through the section on large-group time in *EYC* (pp. 265–281). List all of the activities *EYC* mentions that adults use to draw children into large-group time.

▶ B. What characterizes these opening activities? Why are they easy to join?

---

[23]*The ideas for exercises 25 and 26 came from High/Scope educational consultants Susan Terdan and Linda Weikel and the participants in Linda's 1996 Lead Teacher Training Projects in Anderson, SC, and Savannah, GA.*

▶ C. How effective would telling a story be as a way to begin large-group time? Why?

▶ D. List activities you currently know or do with children that might make good openers for large-group time, and explain why each one might serve to draw children in.

Exercise 26

Making Large-Group Experiences Participatory

Adults who work with young children often have a repertoire of activities they like to do with young children at large-group time. The purpose of this exercise is to find ways to make "old standby" activities as participatory as possible for children by considering the ingredients of active learning—*materials, manipulation, choice, language from children,* and *support from adults.*

▶ A. *Participatory songs:* One way to increase child choice and participation in the song "Old MacDonald Had a Farm," for example, is to pause at the beginning of each verse, ask a child to name an animal, and make the animal's sound *before* singing the verse, so children have all the information they need to sing through the new verse without stopping. List five children's songs you know, and for each one, describe how you could include children's choices and ideas.

▶ B. *Participation in turn-taking games:* One way to provide more turns more rapidly in the game "Duck, Duck, Goose," for example, is to divide the children into two or three circles, so four or six children can run and chase at a time. List three other children's games, and describe ways to make each of them more participatory.

C. *Participation in learning new songs:* Learn new songs from recordings on your own; then sing these songs with children without the recording. This gives children control over the song-learning process by giving them the opportunity to control the tempo, add verses and motions, and so forth. List two songs you might learn from a recording, and describe ways you might introduce each of them to children without the recording.

Exercise 27

Observing a Large-Group Time

A. Watch an active learning large-group time from beginning to end. As you watch and listen, make notes and check the applicable items on the large-group-time checklist from *EYC* p. 281, which is reproduced at the right.

B. Based on your notes and checklist, what were the strengths of this large-group time?

C. What, if anything, might you do differently if you were to carry out a similar large-group time? Why?

Exercise 28

Self-Study: Plan, Do, and Review a Large-Group Time

(Exercise B involves a tape recorder or video camera.)

A. Plan a large-group time for a group of children you know. Describe your plan in terms of each of the elements in (1)–(6) on the next page.

How Adults Support Children at Large-Group Time: A Summary

Adults examine their beliefs about how children learn at large-group times.

Adults plan large-group experiences ahead of time.

_____Plan around children's interests.

_____Plan around music and movement key experiences.

_____Plan around cooperative play and projects.

_____Plan around events currently meaningful to the children.

Adults prepare for large-group time before children arrive.

_____Modify songs and games to fit children's development and specific events.

_____Practice ahead of time.

_____Have materials ready.

Adults set large-group time in motion: the beginning.

_____Draw children to the group with an easy-to-join activity.

_____Start right away with the children who have gathered.

Adults support children's ideas and initiatives: the middle.

_____*Briefly* introduce the next experience.

_____Participate on children's physical level.

_____Turn props and materials over to children.

_____Watch and listen to children.

_____Follow up on children's suggestions and modifications.

_____Let children be the leaders.

Adults bring large-group time to a close: the end.

_____Make the final large-group experience a transition to the next part of the daily routine.

_____Put materials away as part of the transition activity.

❶ Originating idea

❷ Materials

❸ Easy-to-join beginning

❹ Active middle

❺ Support strategies

❻ Ending transition

▶ B. Prepare for and carry out your large-group time, recording it on videotape or audiotape. Then review your large-group time by viewing or listening to the tape.

❶ What did you find out about the children in your large group?

❷ How did you support children's choices and ideas?

❸ What might you do differently another time? Why?

Large-Group Scenarios: What Would You Do?

To decide how you might support the children in the following large-group scenarios, you may wish to refer to the support strategies listed on *EYC* pp. 40, 66, and 281.

▶ A. *The children are singing and making up new verses to the song "Here We Go Looby Loo" at large-group time—except for Raymond, who is finishing the painting he began at small-group time, and Stewie, who is taking all his paintings off the wall.*

How might you support Raymond's and Stewie's choices at large-group time?

▶ B. *It is the middle of large-group time. The children are moving to music, pretending to be "whales and fishes." Jareed's mom and little sister enter the room to pick him up, but they are a little bit early. Jareed's little sister goes to Jareed and stands next to him. "We're bein' fish!" he tells her. He continues to swim while she watches. "I know what! You can be a rock the fishes swim around," he tells her.*

How might you support Jareed's ideas for including his little sister in large-group time?

▶ C. *You, your teammate, and your children are singing "Five Little Ducks." During the singing, Albert, Craig, and Brandon get up and begin to dance as they sing. The rest of the children watch and continue to sing.*

How might you support Albert, Craig, and Brandon?

▶ D. *At large-group time, the children are re-enacting* The Tale of Peter Rabbit. *One "rabbit," Chris, bumps into another "rabbit," Pat. Pat hits Chris, and Chris begins to cry.*

How might you and your teammate support the children who are acting out the story and at the same time help Chris and Pat resolve their conflict?

▶ E. *At large-group time, you, your teammate, and the children are playing a game of magic carpet squares, hopping from one square to the next and freezing on a square when the music stops. During one stop, Mini gets off her carpet square and says, "I'm an alligator." She "swims" in the "water" between the squares. The other children follow her lead.*

How might you support Mini's new large-group-time idea?

▶ F. *At the end of large-group time, six children still have ideas for new verses to add to the "What We Saw on Our Walk" song. "We have time for Tina's, Joey's, and Rachel's ideas," you say, "before the bus comes for going home." As you sing Tina's verse, Anna cries. (Anna was one of the children who had a new verse idea but who didn't get chosen for lack of time.)*

How might you acknowledge Anna's feelings and come up with a strategy for singing her verse?

▶ G. *At large-group time, you, your teaching partner, and the children have been doing a movement game in which children take turns showing and leading a movement for everyone else to try. After the tenth child has a turn and suggests "wiggle your toes," Mack, Melissa, and Athi leave the group and go to the beanbag chairs in the book area, where they pretend to be "roller guys."*

How might you act on the cues Mack, Melissa, and Athi are providing you?

▶ H. *All the children are moving in different ways to the "boing, boing" music, a favorite recorded musical selection. Many children are saying "Look at me!" "Look what I'm doing!" as you and your teammate move among the children, watching and imitating their motions. One child, Tonnette, puts her fingers in her ears and loudly says, "Be quiet!" You realize that with the music playing and many children calling for your attention, it is very noisy.*

How might you turn Tonnette's call for quiet into an opportunity for problem solving?

Self-Assessment: Small-Group Time and Large-Group Time

Items II-G and II-H of the High/Scope Program Quality Assessment (PQA): Preschool Version provide one way to assess small- and large-group times in an early childhood program. If you are currently teaching, use PQA item II-G (given at the right) to make notes and assess your own classroom by rating it on a scale of 1–5. If you are not teaching, you might look at the classroom in which you did exercises 8, 13, 22, and 27 in this chapter.

Large-Group-Time Issues to Ponder and Write About

▶ A. What do adults fear most about large-group time? Why?

▶ B. What makes large-group experiences enjoyable for adults and children?

▶ C. In everyday life, what kinds of activities call for large groups (that is, they either cannot be done or are very difficult to do individually or in small groups)?

▶ D. What is the role of active learning in early childhood large-group times?

▶ E. At large-group time, why might *telling* stories be more effective than *reading* stories?

PQA Item II-G. The program has a time each day for small-group activities that reflect and extend children's interests and development. [Note: If time for small-group activities is set aside but not observed, score at level 1.]

Supporting evidence/anecdotes:

☐ There is no time set aside for small-group activities.

☐ Adults direct small-group times so that children do not contribute their own ideas or participate at their own developmental levels (e.g., children are expected to use materials in the same way, follow directions, answer questions or make the same product).

☐ Adults do not support or extend children's small-group activities.

☐ The children and adult(s) in each small group change each time.

☐ Sometimes there is time set aside for small-group activities.

☐ Sometimes children contribute their own ideas or participate at their own developmental levels at small-group times (e.g., children are asked to classify the nature materials, but can group them in their own ways).

☐ Adults use some strategies to support or extend children's small-group activities (e.g., after materials are given to children, adults help when needed).

☐ Children and adult(s) stay with the same small group for 1–2 months.

☐ There is a daily time set aside for small-group activities.

☐ Throughout small-group time, children contribute their own ideas and participate at their own developmental levels (e.g., individual children explore and use the same set of materials in their own ways).

☐ Adults use many strategies to support and extend children's small-group activities (e.g., they observe what children do, move from child to child, comment on what children are doing and saying, imitate and add to children's actions; use the materials themselves).

☐ Children and adult(s) always stay with the same small group for at least 2 months or more.

| 1 | 2 | 3 | 4 | 5 |

Outside Time and Transitions

Exercise 32

Remembering Outdoor Play

With a partner or several friends, recall your own outdoor play as a child.

▶ A. Where outdoors did you enjoy playing?

▶ B. What materials did you use?

▶ C. How was your outdoor play different from your indoor play?

▶ D. What made outdoor play memorable? What was the spirit of your outdoor play?

Exercise 33

Child Study: Outside Time

▶ A. During outside time at an active learning early childhood setting, observe as many children as you can for 10 minutes each—observe the first child for the first 10 minutes, the second child for the second 10 minutes, and so forth. As you watch and listen, once each minute write down what the child **says** and **does**. Also write down your observations of the **social context** of the child's play (onlooking, solitary, parallel, group), and the **type of play** the child is engaged in (exploratory, constructive, pretend, games).

Use a chart like the following for each child's 10-minute observation.

(In this column, list minutes #1–#10.)	Child's Actions	Child's Words	Social Setting	Play Type

▶ B. After your observation, write as many anecdotes as you can about the children you observed. Then, turn to the list of key experiences (*EYC* p. 22), decide which key experience each anecdote is most closely related to, and record your anecdotes for the various children on the single Key Experience Notes form included on the next two pages.

Exercise 34

Examining Children's Outdoor Play

▶ A. To get a picture of what young children do outdoors, look at the outdoor photographs from *EYC* that are listed by page number in (1)–(27). Describe the children's **actions** and the **materials** the children are using in each photo or group of photos.

❶ pp. 19, 244, 283, 402, 521 (right-hand photo)

❷ pp. 284, 436

❸ pp. 286 (left-hand photo), 427

❹ pp. 286 (right-hand photo), 488, 510

❺ pp. 287 (top photo), 410 (left-hand photo)

❻ pp. 13, 144 (left-hand photo), 287 (bottom photo), 300

❼ p. 288

❽ front cover

❾ p. 26

❿ pp. 29, 255, 410 (middle photo), 415

⓫ p. 31

⓬ pp. 52, 416

⓭ pp. 56, 75

⓮ pp. 83, 431

⓯ pp. 156, 499

⓰ pp. 110, 150, 374, 502

⓱ pp. 144 (right-hand photo), 500, 521 (left-hand photo)

⓲ pp. 152, 163, 490

⓳ p. 275

⓴ p. 301

㉑ p. 318

㉒ p. 395

㉓ p. 396

㉔ p. 410 (three bottom photos)

㉕ p. 419

㉖ p. 443

㉗ p. 489

▶ B. What are children **doing** and **using** in each of the outside-time scenarios described on these *EYC* pages?

❶ p. 282　　❸ p. 287

❷ p. 284　　❹ p. 288

Key Experience Notes

High/Scope
Child Observation
Record (COR)
For Ages 2½–6

Observer's name: _____

Child's name: _____

Creative Representation	Language and Literacy	Initiative and Social Relations	Movement	Music

High/Scope
Child Observation
Record (COR)
For Ages 2½–6

Observer's name: _____

Child's name: _____

Classification	Seriation	Number	Space	Time

C. What were the children you observed in exercise 33A on p. 114 doing and using at outside time?

D. What else have you seen young children doing and using outdoors?

E. From your observations, what distinguishes children's outside time from the other parts of their daily routine?

F. Why is outside time important for children?

Exercise 35

Adult Attitudes Toward Playing Outside With Children

With a partner, discuss and record your answers to exercises A–E.

A. Some people really enjoy being outdoors and doing outdoor things. What, if anything, do you currently enjoy about being outside? What in nature particularly attracts your attention?

B. Some people prefer not to spend much time outside. What, if anything, do you dislike about being outdoors?

C. What features of your local weather, climate, or environment are particularly agreeable? What can make going outside in your area unpleasant?

D. In your area, are there certain times of day when it is more pleasant to be outside? When it is less pleasant to be outside? Does your preschool daily routine (or some preschool daily

routine you know of) take these variations into account?

E. How might your attitude about being outdoors affect your interactions with children at outside time?

Exercise 36

Supporting Children's Outdoor Play

A. Look at the outdoor photographs on the *EYC* pages listed in (1)–(9), and record what you see adults doing in each photo or group of photos.

① p. 31
② p. 283
③ pp. 284, 295, 318 (center of photo)
④ pp. 287, 410
⑤ p. 288
⑥ p. 352
⑦ p. 406
⑧ p. 416
⑨ p. 443

B. Read the discussion of the adult's role at outside time on *EYC* pp. 285–288. Then, from exercise 34A on p. 114, choose two outside photographs that do *not* include adults. Explain how you might support the children in each of the two photographs.

C. In an active learning setting, how is the adult's role at outside time similar to the adult's role at work time?

Exercise 37

Child Study: Adult Support at Outside Time

During outside time in an active learning early childhood setting, observe as many children as you can for 10 minutes each—observe the first child for the first 10 minutes, the second child for the second 10 minutes, and so forth. As you watch and listen, once each minute write down what the child **says** and **does**. Also write down your observations of **how adults join and/or support** that child's play—how they offer the child comfort and contact, play, converse, and support problem solving. (Some of the children you observe may not interact with adults in the time you observe them. In some observations, the adult may already have joined the child's play by the time you begin to observe.) At the end of your observation, if no adult interacted with one or more of the children you observed, make a note of how *you* might have supported that child's play during the time you observed it. Use a chart like the following for each 10-minute observation.

(In this column, list minutes #1–#10.)	Child's Actions	Child's Words	Adult Support: C & C, Play, Converse, P–S

Outside Time Scenarios: What Would You Do?

Assume that each of the following outside time scenarios is occurring in your early childhood setting.

▶ A. *Kacey is running after Alex and Chris, calling "Stop! You're under arrest!" Meghan, Francis, and Kelly are talking and laughing as they swing together on the tire swing. Eli is pouring buckets of water down the bike-path slope and watching to see how far "the water goes down." He then rides his bike through the water while looking over his shoulder to see the wet tire tracks he makes on the dry part of the pavement. Mark and Jamison are gathering walnuts, climbing up the climber, and dropping the walnuts from the highest point. Brendan and Lena are climbing in a low bush next to the storage shed. "Ships ahoy," they call, "pirates!" Patrice and Julia add water to the sandbox, then fill cups with wet sand and turn the cups over to make a row of "cakes" of sand. Brianna is pushing Troy on the taxi. Andrew is lying on the grass watching something intently. Matt and Trey are gathering all the playground balls and rolling them down the slide, trying to get them to land inside a tire they have positioned at the end of the slide.*

❶ Which child or group of children might you join? Why?

❷ What strategies might you use to support their play? (Refer to the support strategies on *EYC* pp. 224 and 288 as a guide.)

❸ Discuss your planned outside time interactions with one or two other people who are also doing this exercise. What strikes you about your collective interaction plans?

▶ B. *In their game of "chase the bad guys," Kacey captures Alex next to the sandbox. As she "arrests" him, she steps on two of Julia's sand cakes. Julia cries and tells Kacey, "I hate you. You can't come to my birthday, not ever!" While Kacey takes Alex to jail, Julia comes to you and says, "Kacey broke my cakes."*

How might you respond to Julia, keeping in mind the steps in the problem-solving approach to conflict (listed on p. 21 of this study guide)?

▶ C. *"Teacher, teacher, we need a push," Kelly calls from the tire swing, just as Andrew comes up to you with a long worm in his hand and says, "Look what I found!"*

How might you support both Kelly's and Andrew's requests?

▶ D. *In the yard next to the playground, several workmen drive up in a truck and begin to dig a trench. A group of the children gather by the fence to watch. "Hey, what are you guys doing?" Jason calls to the men. The workmen keep digging.*

How might you support the children's interest in this situation?

▶ E. *Francis runs up to you, squirts water on you using a water bottle from the outdoor sand and water area, and then runs away giggling.*

How might you support Francis's outdoor play?

▶ F. *Troy is hanging by his knees from the top of the dome climber. Then he pulls himself up so he is sitting on top of the climber. "Teacher," he calls to you, "come here. Watch this!" When you come and stand next to the climber to watch, he says, "No, I mean come up here and watch!"*

How might you support Troy's idea?

▶ G. *At outside time, you, your teammate, and the children are playing on a very warm day, when it begins to rain very lightly. Some of the children notice the rain, but no one stops playing. Meghan and Lena notice that the rain is "making spots" on their sidewalk chalk drawings. When Brendan sees you looking up at the sky, he says, "The rain feels good! We don't want to go in!"*

How might you support Brendan's idea?

Self-Study: Supporting Children at Outside Time
(This exercise, which involves a video camera, may be repeated periodically.)

If you are currently teaching or student teaching or can work in an early childhood setting over a period of time, videotape some of your outside time interactions with children. Watch each video clip one time through just to see what you look and sound like and what, in general, happened. Then watch each video clip again, this time looking for the *type of play* you joined, the *support strategies* you used, and the *children's response* to your actions and words.

▶ A. What did you learn about children in each outside time?

▶ B. Describe what strengths you exhibit as a supporter of children's play in each outside time interaction. What, if anything, might you do differently another time in a similar situation?

A Personal Consideration of the Nature of Transitions

With a partner, discuss and record your answers to exercises A–E.

▶ A. In your own life, what transitions have you experienced (for example, moving, changing schools)? Which transitions have gone smoothly? Why? Which ones have been more difficult? Why?

▶ B. In a typical day in your life, what transitions do you experience? What makes them smooth, problematic, or somewhere in between?

▶ C. In general, how do you respond to change? Under what circumstances do you welcome change? Resist change? Both anticipate and fear change?

▶ D. How do you balance your need for stability and consistency with your need for change and new experiences?

▶ E. How do you respond to changes over which you have some control? Why? How do you respond to changes over which you have no control? Why?

Child Study: Transitions

▶ A. In an early childhood program setting, observe one child for at least two hours during the heart of the daily routine (rather than for an hour of napping, for example). As you watch and listen carefully, record what the child **does** and **says** during transition times (for example, as the child enters the early childhood setting, as the child moves from large-group time to outside time). On another day, repeat this observation process by observing and collecting transition data on another child. For each child's observation, use a child-study format like the following.

| Child's Name_____ Date_____ |
| Location_____ |
| Time Observed _____ |

Transition	Child's Actions	Child's Words

▶ B. After your observation, write as many anecdotes as you can about the children you observed. Then, from the list of key experiences (*EYC* p. 22), choose the key experience that each anecdote is most closely related to, and record all of the anecdotes on the single Key Experience Notes form included earlier, on pp. 115–116 of this chapter.

Children's Needs at Transition Times

▶ A. For each kind of transition listed in (1)–(7), describe what needs children may have at the time.

❶ From home to center

❷ From breakfast to planning time

❸ Cleanup time

❹ From large-group time to outside time

❺ From lunch to nap

❻ From nap to small-group time

❼ From center to home

▶ B. How can children's transition time needs for consistency, security, and control be served by each of the ingredients of active learning—materials, manipulation, choice, language from the child, support from adults?

The Adult's Role at Transition Times

The following exercise is based on the discussion of transition times on *EYC* pp. 288–293, 222–223, and 64–65.

▶ A. What support strategies did teachers Sam and Becki use in the two cleanup scenarios listed in (1)–(2), which are taken from "Responding to the Unexpected" on *EYC* pp. 291–292?

❶ Painting the bathroom

❷ Making the pile of toys

▶ B. In your early childhood setting (or in an early childhood setting you know), what transitions do the children currently experience?

▶ C. Which transition is the smoothest? Why?

D. Which transition is the most difficult? Why? What support strategies might you try? (See *EYC* p. 293 for reference.)

E. Read "'Ready or Not!' Cleanup Time Games" (*EYC* p. 292). What kind of cleanup games do you currently play with children? What other games might you try?

Self-Study: Supporting Children at Transition Times

(This exercise, which involves a video camera, may be repeated periodically.)

If you are currently teaching or student-teaching or can work in an early childhood setting over a period of time, videotape some of your interactions with children during transition times. Then watch each video clip one time through just to see what you look and sound like and what, in general, happened. Watch each video clip again, this time looking for the *type of play* involved in each transition, the *support strategies* you used, and the *children's response* to your actions and words.

A. What did you learn about the children in these transition times?

B. What strengths do you exhibit as a supporter of children's play at cleanup time? What, if anything, might you do differently in a similar situation?

Transition Scenarios: What Would You Do?

A. *Carleen arrives at your early childhood center with her "blankie" (a favorite comfort item) draped around her neck like a scarf. After she hangs up her sweater, says good-bye to her mom, and joins the book readers at the greeting circle, she sits on the floor, sucks her thumb, and strokes her blankie.*

How might you support Carleen's method of comforting herself during her transition from home to center?

B. *While the other children finish breakfast, Jason sits under the breakfast table, playing with some little cars.*

How might you support Jason during the transition from breakfast to planning time?

C. *During cleanup after work time, Vera sits in the beanbag chair reading a storybook.*

How might you support Vera's interest in books at cleanup time?

D. *Although Troy plays with materials in each interest area during work time, he focuses his cleanup efforts on putting away the fingerpaints and washing the art table.*

How might you support Troy at cleanup time?

E. *At the end of large-group time, the children are galloping like horses to their cubbies to get their jackets for outside time. Dree, however, is lying curled up in the middle of the block area, where large-group time took place. "Dree," you say, "you're lying down!" "I'm a horse with a broken leg," she replies.*

How might you support Dree's pretend play at this transition time?

F. *You, your teammate, and your children are coming in for lunch after outside time. Right outside the door, JT stops and says, "Look at the ants!" He squats down to get a better view of a line of ants carrying crumbs from one side of the sidewalk to the other. The rest of the children gather around to watch the ants at work.*

How might you support JT's discovery during this transition time?

G. *You are about to go outside when a sudden storm blows up. Rain pours down, thunder rolls, and lightning fills the air. Since it is too dangerous to go outside and you have no gym or large-motor room, you and your teammate decide to set up an obstacle course in the classroom.*

How might you support and involve your children in this unexpected transition?

Self-Assessment: Transitions

Item II-I of the High/Scope Program Quality Assessment (PQA): Preschool Version provides one way to assess transition times in an early childhood program. If you are currently teaching, use PQA item II-I (on the facing page) to make notes and assess your own classroom by rating it on a scale of 1–5. If you are not teaching, you might assess the classroom in which you did exercises 41 and 44 in this chapter.

Exercise 47

Outside Time and Transition Issues to Ponder and Write About

▶ A. How important is outside time and the observation of nature to young children in urban settings?

▶ B. At outside time, how can adults balance their need to keep children physically safe against children's need for physical challenge and adventure?

▶ C. If young children have access to a well-equipped gym or large-motor room, how important is outdoor play? Why?

▶ D. What outdoor elements and design features can make outside time inviting to adults?

▶ E. What do adults fear most about transition times? Why?

▶ F. How do the elements of support—sharing of control between adults and children, focusing on children's strengths, forming authentic relationships with children, making a commitment to supporting children's play, and adopting a problem-solving approach to social conflict—contribute to child-centered transition times?

PQA Item II-I. During transition times, children have reasonable choices about activities and timing as they move from one activity to the next.

Supporting evidence/anecdotes:

1	2	3
☐ Children do not have choices at transition times (e.g., children are assigned seats).	☐ Children sometimes have choices at transition times (e.g., children can choose to sit next to anyone for large group).	☐ Children make choices during transition times (e.g., how to move from one part of the room to another, which person to travel with, what materials to clean up).
☐ Adults do not let children know transitions are coming.	☐ Adults sometimes let children know transitions are coming.	☐ Adults let children know transitions are coming (e.g., announce "After recall time we will have snack"; "Five more minutes until we go inside").
☐ Parts of the day do not overlap; adults require children to stop what they are doing and wait as a group until everyone is ready for the next activity (e.g., everyone must clean up before starting large group; everyone must line up at the same time to go to the bathroom).	☐ Some parts of the day overlap; children sometimes have the option of finishing the previous activity or moving on to the next activity without the rest of the group.	☐ Parts of the day overlap; children have the option of finishing the previous activity or moving to the next activity without the rest of the group (e.g., not all children have to finish snack before the next activity begins).
☐ Adults do not plan ways for children to make transitions.	☐ Adults sometimes plan ways for children to make transitions (e.g., at the end of large group, the adult calls the children with shoes that tie to go to the bathroom).	☐ Adults plan ways for children to make transitions (e.g., choosing the next children to make the transition according to some characteristic of their clothing: "Now all children wearing sweat pants jump to the coat rack," encouraging children to move along the floor in their own way toward their cubbies at outside time).

| 1 | 2 | 3 | 4 | 5 |

Related Publications

Ansbach, Ursula. 2000. "Beyond the Blue Horizon—Promoting Outdoor Experiences." *High/Scope Extensions* (May/June): 1–4, 8.

Beardmore, Carol. 1996. "Greeting Time: A Smooth Transition for Children." In *Supporting Young Learners 2: Ideas for Child Care Providers and Teachers*, Nancy A. Brickman, ed., 97–102. Ypsilanti, MI: High/Scope Press.

"Designing Routines for Active Learners." 1996. In *Supporting Young Learners 2: Ideas for Child Care Providers and Teachers*, Nancy A. Brickman, ed., 57–114. Ypsilanti, MI: High/Scope Press.

Evans, Betsy. 2000. "'Bye Mommy!' 'Bye Daddy!' Easing Separations for Preschoolers." *High/Scope Extensions* (September): 1–3.

Graves, Michelle. 1996. *The Teacher's Idea Book 2: Planning Around Children's Interests*. Ypsilanti, MI: High/Scope Press.

Graves, Michelle. 1997. "A Planning Process for Active Small-Group Times." *High/Scope Extensions* (September): 1–3.

Graves, Michelle. 1997. *The Teacher's Idea Book 3: 100 Small-Group Experiences*. Ypsilanti, MI: High/Scope Press.

High/Scope Program Quality Assessment (PQA): Preschool Version (Field-Test Edition). 2001. Ypsilanti, MI: High/Scope Press.

Hohmann, Charles. 1996. "Small Groups in Elementary Classrooms." In *Supporting Young Learners 2: Ideas for Child Care Providers and Teachers*, Nancy A. Brickman, ed., 83–86. Ypsilanti, MI: High/Scope Press.

Hohmann, Charles, and Warren Buckleitner. 1992. *High/Scope K–3 Curriculum Series: Learning Environment*. Ypsilanti, MI: High/Scope Press.

Hohmann, Mary. 1996. "Small-Group Time: Active Children, Active Adults." In *Supporting Young Learners 2: Ideas for Child Care Providers and Teachers*, Nancy A. Brickman, ed., 77–82. Ypsilanti, MI: High/Scope Press.

Perrett, Becki. 1996. "Group Times: What Makes Them Work?" "Shifting Gears Smoothly: Making the Most of Transition Times." "Cleanup: The Toughest Transition." In *Supporting Young Learners 2: Ideas for Child Care Providers and Teachers*, Nancy A. Brickman, ed., 71–76, 87–96. Ypsilanti, MI: High/Scope Press.

Post, Jacalyn, and Mary Hohmann. 2000. "Establishing Schedules and Routines for Infants and Toddlers." In *Tender Care and Early Learning: Supporting Infants and Toddlers in Child Care Settings*, 190–293. Ypsilanti, MI: High/Scope Press.

Theemes, Tracy. 1999. *Let's Go Outside! Designing the Early Childhood Playground*. Ypsilanti, MI: High/Scope Press.

Related Videos

Adult-Child Interactions: Forming Partnerships With Children. 1996. Color videotape, 60 min. Ypsilanti, MI: High/Scope Press.

The High/Scope Curriculum: The Daily Routine. 1990. Color videotape, 17 min. Ypsilanti, MI: High/Scope Press.

The High/Scope Curriculum: Its Implementation in Family Child Care Homes. 1989. Color videotape, 19 min. Ypsilanti, MI: High/Scope Press.

High/Scope K–3 Curriculum Series: Classroom Environment. 1991. Color videotape, 17 min. Ypsilanti, MI: High/Scope Press.

Small-Group-Time Video Series. 1988. Five color videotapes, Ypsilanti, MI: High/Scope Press—
1. *Counting With Bears,* 17 min.
2. *Plan-Do-Review With Found Materials,* 25 min.
3. *Working With Staplers,* 12 min.
4. *Representing With Sticks & Balls,* 14 min.
5. *Exploring With Paint & Corks,* 12 min.

Part 3

Key Experiences in Early Childhood Development

The key experiences describe the kinds of discoveries young children make as they strive, through their own actions, to make sense of their world. Taken together, the key experiences provide adults with a framework for understanding young children; supporting their intellectual, physical, and social strengths; and planning experiences that are appropriate to each child's level of development.

—Educating Young Children, p. 298

9

Introduction to the High/Scope Key Experiences

Recognizing Key Experiences

Do exercises A–D with one or more partners.

▶ A. Use the list of key experiences on p. 126 of this study guide. For each of the 58 key experiences listed, find one photograph anywhere in *EYC* that might illustrate that key experience, and write the page number of the photograph after the key experience. For example, here are four *EYC* photographs that show children engaged in the **creative representation** key experience *recognizing objects by sight, sound, touch, taste, and smell:*

> p. 19 bottom-left photo *(children recognize applesauce by sight and smell)*
>
> p. 26 bottom photo *(child recognizes icicles by sight and touch)*
>
> p. 179 *(child recognizes things to play with through "spyglasses")*
>
> p. 237 *(child recognizes a covered block by touch alone)*

▶ B. Find or take 10 photographs of a preschool child in action. For each photograph, write an anecdote that describes what the child is doing and, if possible, what the child is saying. After the anecdotal caption, list the key experience(s) the child is engaged in.

▶ C. Turn again to the key experience list on the next page, and number the key experiences from 1–58. Then, turn to the Jonah anecdotes on *EYC* pp. 306–307. For each anecdote about Jonah, indicate (by number) the key experience(s) most clearly related to it. For example, the *1/8* **creative representation anecdote** is related to **KE #2** *(imitating actions and sounds)* and **KE #3** *(relating models, pictures, and photographs to real places and things).*

▶ D. Read the anecdotes in (1)–(11). For each anecdote, identify (by number, as in the previous exercise) the key experience(s) that is (are) most closely related to it.

❶ *2/12* At WT, James pushes a wooden train under a block tunnel, saying "I can go under here."

❷ *2/17* At WT, James looks at two sets of wooden trains and says, "I need more. I counted with my mouth closed."

❸ *2/17* At OT, James sings "The Monkey Swinging in the Tree" all the way through as he and Audie swing on the tire swing.

❹ *3/26* At WT, James says to Mikey, "Want to play with us?" while he and Audie are working at the computer.

❺ *3/26* At WT, James types "JAMES" at the computer.

❻ *4/6* At SGT, James makes a "people" out of Play-Doh, including two arms and two legs coming out of a head that has two eyes and a mouth.

❼ *4/20* At snack, James reads the helper chart and says, "Andrew's name is on top. Audie's is in the middle, and mine is on the bottom!"

❽ *4/21* At WT, James and Audie make a bed out of wooden blocks. It has "candles, so we won't have to sleep in the dark."

❾ *4/26* At WT, James paints paper towel tubes, then makes a cover for the tubes out of paper and masking tape "so my cubby won't get wet paint all over it."

High/Scope Preschool Key Experiences

Creative Representation

- Recognizing objects by sight, sound, touch, taste, and smell
- Imitating actions and sounds
- Relating models, pictures, and photographs to real places and things
- Pretending and role playing
- Making models out of clay, blocks, and other materials
- Drawing and painting

Language and Literacy

- Talking with others about personally meaningful experiences
- Describing objects, events, and relations
- Having fun with language: listening to stories and poems, making up stories and rhymes
- Writing in various ways: drawing, scribbling, letterlike forms, invented spelling, conventional forms
- Reading in various ways: reading storybooks, signs and symbols, one's own writing
- Dictating stories

Initiative and Social Relations

- Making and expressing choices, plans, and decisions
- Solving problems encountered in play
- Taking care of one's own needs
- Expressing feelings in words
- Participating in group routines
- Being sensitive to the feelings, interests, and needs of others
- Building relationships with children and adults
- Creating and experiencing collaborative play
- Dealing with social conflict

Movement

- Moving in nonlocomotor ways (anchored movement: bending, twisting, rocking, swinging one's arms)
- Moving in locomotor ways (nonanchored movement: running, jumping, hopping, skipping, marching, climbing)
- Moving with objects
- Expressing creativity in movement
- Describing movement
- Acting upon movement directions
- Feeling and expressing steady beat
- Moving in sequences to a common beat

Music

- Moving to music
- Exploring and identifying sounds
- Exploring the singing voice
- Developing melody
- Singing songs
- Playing simple musical instruments

Classification

- Exploring and describing similarities, differences, and the attributes of things
- Distinguishing and describing shapes
- Sorting and matching
- Using and describing something in several ways
- Holding more than one attribute in mind at a time
- Distinguishing between "some" and "all"
- Describing characteristics something does not possess or what class it does not belong to

Seriation

- Comparing attributes (longer/shorter, bigger/smaller)
- Arranging several things one after another in a series or pattern and describing the relationships (big/bigger/biggest, red/blue/red/blue)
- Fitting one ordered set of objects to another through trial and error (small cup–small saucer/medium cup–medium saucer/big cup–big saucer)

Number

- Comparing the number of things in two sets to determine "more," "fewer," "same number"
- Arranging two sets of objects in one-to-one correspondence
- Counting objects

Space

- Filling and emptying
- Fitting things together and taking them apart
- Changing the shape and arrangement of objects (wrapping, twisting, stretching, stacking, enclosing)
- Observing people, places, and things from different spatial viewpoints
- Experiencing and describing positions, directions, and distances in the play space, building, and neighborhood
- Interpreting spatial relations in drawings, pictures, and photographs

Time

- Starting and stopping an action on signal
- Experiencing and describing rates of movement
- Experiencing and comparing time intervals
- Anticipating, remembering, and describing sequences of events

⑩ *5/10* At WT, James asks Brianna if he can do the dinosaur puzzle with her. When she says no, he works on another puzzle until she is finished. Then he does the dinosaur puzzle by himself.

⑪ *5/19* At OT, James pushes Jalessa on the swing and says, "I'm pushing you with both hands 'cause that makes you go straight."

Exercise 2

Why Bother With Key Experiences?

Exercises A–F are based on the discussion of the significance of the key experiences on *EYC* pp. 302–304.

▶ A. *Key experiences can help focus adults' observations and interpretations of children's actions.* Look at the child-study exercises you did for Chapters 7 and 8 (observing a child during each part of the daily routine) and the anecdotes you created based on your observations (which you recorded on the Key Experience Notes form). To what extent has sorting your anecdotes about your study child according to the key experience categories helped you interpret your child's actions and language? Why?

▶ B. *Key experiences can serve as a cross-cultural reference for observing and interpreting a child's actions.* Imagine that you are in an early childhood setting where all the children speak sign language, Spanish, Chinese, or some other language you do not know. How might knowledge of the key experiences help you begin to understand children's interests and actions?

▶ C. *Key experiences can help adults maintain reasonable expectations for children.* In some early childhood settings, adults expect preschool children to spend large parts of the day not talking. Which key experiences support the idea that in an active learning setting, it is reasonable and developmentally appropriate to expect and encourage young children to talk freely throughout the day?

▶ D. *Key experiences can answer questions about the legitimacy of children's play.* Return to Chapter 8, exercise 3B on p. 96, in which you described what children are learning during three small-group times. Now, for (1)–(3) below, identify which *key experiences* describe what the children are learning in each of those small groups.

❶ Pineapple small-group time

❷ Egg-coloring small-group time

❸ Found materials small-group time

▶ E. *Key experiences can guide decisions about materials and the daily routine.*

❶ Return to Chapter 5, exercise 11A on p. 55. For each material listed in (1)–(12) of that exercise, identify the key experience the material might support. How might the key experiences help a teaching team decide whether or not to include these materials in their early childhood setting?

❷ Select one part of an active learning daily routine—planning time, work time, recall time, small-group time, large-group time, outside time, or transitions. Then, from Chapter 7 or Chapter 8, review the observations you made of your study child during that particular time of day. What key experiences was your study child engaged in? What does this tell you about that particular time of day?

▶ F. *Key experiences enable adults to recognize and support children's emerging abilities.* List the capacities you have seen emerging in your study child. Which key experiences do you associate with each capacity?

Exercise 3

Everyday Uses of Key Experiences

These exercises are based on a discussion of the uses of the key experiences on *EYC* pp. 304–308.

▶ A. *Key experiences can serve as a basis for assessing the materials available to children.* Read "Providing Materials That Support Key Experiences" on *EYC* p. 305. Then select a key experience of particular interest to you or your children, and fill out a chart like the one below based on your own early childhood setting or the setting where you observe your study child.

KE Category:		KE:
(List the room's interest areas in this column.)	*Current Materials*	*Materials to Add*

▶ B. *Key experiences can help you organize and interpret observations of children.* You have already begun this process, starting with Chapter 4, exercises 6, 7, and 8 on pp. 40 and 42. Now, return to Chapter 1, exercise 6 on p. 8, and Chapter 2, exercise 9 on p. 19. From these observations of your study child, collect anecdotes and record them on the Key Experience Notes form on the next two pages.

Key Experience Notes

**High/Scope
Child Observation
Record (COR)
For Ages 2½–6**

CHILD
COR
OBSERVATION
RECORD

Observer's name: _____

Child's name: _____

Creative Representation	Language and Literacy	Initiative and Social Relations	Movement	Music

High/Scope
Child Observation
Record (COR)
For Ages 2½–6

CHILD COR OBSERVATION RECORD

Observer's name: _____

Child's name: _____

Classification	Seriation	Number	Space	Time

C. *Key-experience-based child observations can be the basis for daily team planning.* Again, you have already begun this process. Turn to Chapter 4, exercise 8C on p. 42, and Chapter 7, exercise 34B on p. 83, to review the support strategies you planned based on your observations and interpretations of your study child's actions and language. With a partner who is also doing these exercises and has a study child, discuss and record in a chart like the following how you might support your study children during several parts of the day, based on the anecdotes you recorded for the previous exercise.

Time of Day	*Support Strategies We Might Try*

D. *Key experiences can be a guide to planning small-group and large-group times.* With a partner who also has a study child, review the anecdotes about your study children that you have recorded on the Key Experience Notes forms. Use forms like the ones below to record your ideas for a small-group and a large-group experience, based on what you know about your children.

Small-Group-Time Plan

Originating idea:

Materials:

Beginning:

Middle—*ways to support children:*

Key experiences we might see:

End:

Large-Group-Time Plan

Originating idea:

Materials:

Easy-to-join beginning:

Active middle:

Support strategies:

Ending transition:

E. *Key experiences can guide your on-the-spot interactions with children.* Look again at the video clips of your own interactions with children at work time (video clips gathered for Chapter 7, exercise 37 on p. 86). Identify a situation in which you did use or, in hindsight, you could have used a key experience to guide your interaction with a child.

F. *The **High/Scope Child Observation Record for Ages 2½–6 (COR)** is a key-experienced-based planning and assessment tool.* Interview a teaching team that is using the COR, and describe how they use it and what they think about it. If you cannot locate such a team, examine the contents of a COR kit, or the COR for the computer— COR for Windows or COR-Mac. What strikes you about the COR? How might it be useful to you as a teacher?

Exercise 4

Key Experience Card Game

For this exercise, which is a card game, you will need three other people—four players in all. Make a set of "key experience cards" by using 58 three-by-five index cards and writing a different key experience on each one. Also make 10 "category cards" by writing each of the key experience categories on an index card. Then play the "key experience card game" by following these steps:

- Line up the 10 category cards so everyone in your group can see them.

- Shuffle the 58 key experience cards, and deal them face down to the four players.

- Choose one player to begin. That player selects the card on the top of his or her pile and reads it aloud. Together, without consulting any list, decide which category this key experience belongs to, then place it below the agreed-upon category card. The second player then selects a card, reads it aloud, and so on, until you have categorized all the key experience cards.

When you have read and categorized all 58 cards, check the organization of your cards against the key experience list (on p. 126 of this book). What are your findings? Do not worry about cards you have incorrectly categorized, but do make sure you discuss and read about key experiences you have questions about.

Exercise 5

Creating an Illustrated Key Experience List

For this project, you will need a collection of photographs of young children, a camera, and a key experience list (See *EYC* p. 299). The idea is to create an illustrated key experience list made up of 58 photographs, each photograph showing a child (or children) engaged in a particular key experience. Begin by looking through the photographs you currently have of young children.

Select photographs that illustrate particular key experiences. Then, look for opportunities to take photographs of children engaged in the key experiences you have left to illustrate. Assemble and caption your photographs in a photo album or on a poster board. Share your illustrated list with your teaching teammates.

Exercise 6

Key Experience Issues to Ponder and Write About

▶ A. In your own words, how would you describe this collection of statements called the *key experiences?*

▶ B. Where do the key experiences come from?

▶ C. Is it necessary for adults in an active learning setting to be familiar with the key experiences? Why or why not?

▶ D. Are there things you have seen young children do or heard them say that do not seem to be associated with any of the key experiences? Describe them.

▶ E. What does educational psychologist Charles Hohmann mean when he says that "flexibility lies at the heart of the idea of the key experiences" in his statement on *EYC* p. 297?

▶ F. How are the key experiences related to active learning? Which came first, active learning or the key experiences? Why?

Related Publications

Graves, Michelle. 1989. *The Teacher's Idea Book: Daily Planning Around the Key Experiences.* Ypsilanti, MI: High/Scope Press.

Graves, Michelle. 1996. *The Teacher's Idea Book 2: Planning Around Children's Interests.* Ypsilanti, MI: High/Scope Press.

High/Scope Child Observation Record (COR) for Ages 2½–6. 1992. Ypsilanti, MI: High/Scope Press.

High/Scope Preschool Key Experience Poster. Easy-to-read wall chart, 22 × 34 inches. Ypsilanti, MI: High/Scope Press.

Hohmann, Charles. 1996. *Foundations in Elementary Education: Overview.* Ypsilanti, MI: High/Scope Press.

Hohmann, Mary. 1991. "Key Experiences: Keys to Supporting Preschool Children's Emerging Strengths and Abilities." In *Supporting Young Learners: Ideas for Preschool and Day Care Providers,* Nancy A. Brickman and Lynn S. Taylor, eds., 61–70. Ypsilanti, MI: High/Scope Press.

Post, Jacalyn, and Mary Hohmann. 2000. "Key Experiences: What Infants and Toddlers Learn." In *Tender Care and Early Learning: Supporting Infants and Toddlers in Child Care Settings,* 35–54. Ypsilanti, MI: High/Scope Press.

Wheel of Learning/Key Experience Card. Laminated card, 8½ × 11 inches. Ypsilanti, MI: High/Scope Press.

Preschoolers feel a powerful urge to construct their own symbols as substitutes for actual objects and experiences. Through pretending, model-making, painting, and drawing, preschoolers construct their own scripts and images and become conscious of themselves as players and image-makers.

—**Educating Young Children**, *pp. 311–312*

10

Creative Representation

Creative Representation

Creating Representations

This exercise contains two activities in creative representation. Together with a partner, do the following:

Representation: A Chair

- Explore a chair, using all your senses. For example, turn your chair over, stack it, push it, hit it, look at it from different viewpoints. Do whatever you can think of to discover things about your chair.

- Imitate your chair.

- Find a picture or photograph of a chair, and compare it to your chair.

- Pretend with your chair. For example, perhaps you are sitting in an elegant restaurant or in a dentist's chair. Perhaps your chair is a raft, a cave, a motorcycle.

- Make a model of your chair or some other chair.

- Draw a picture of your chair or some other chair.

Representation: Something of Importance

Using some medium that you prefer (for example, mime, dance, drama, sculpture, drawing, painting, weaving, photography, music), create a piece that represents something of importance to you. Share your creation with someone.

Based on what you did in the two activities above, write your own working definition of *creative representation.*

Experiencing and Recalling Representations

▶ A. Throughout your life, what representations have you created? What have you enjoyed about making them?

▶ B. What representations created by others do you particularly like to look at, watch, or listen to?

▶ C. Why do you think our early ancestors drew pictures on rocks and on the walls of caves; decorated their utensils, clothing, and bodies; told stories, sang songs, and beat on drums?

▶ D. Go to a museum, a dance performance, a play, or a concert. What is one object, idea, event, or emotion you saw or heard represented? What struck you about the way it was expressed?

▶ E. For a week, keep a log of all the representations you create and encounter in your daily life. At the end of the week, review your log, and write down some conclusions about your findings.

Understanding Creative Representation

Exercises A–J are based on the discussion of creative representation on *EYC* pp. 311–314. To construct your own knowledge, answer each question in your own words.

▶ A. What does Piaget mean when he refers to representation as "the symbolic evocation of absent realities" (*EYC* p. 311)?

B. What does Flavell mean by "internal imitation" in his statement about representation (*EYC* p. 311)?

C. How would you explain Golomb and Arnheim's ideas of representation as a creative problem-solving process (*EYC* p. 311)?

D. Why is personal investment part of the creative representation process?

E. What are symbols?

F. What are Ginsburg and Opper saying about "mental symbolism" (*EYC* pp. 312–313)?

G. What is Golomb saying about why children's early representations tend to be simple (*EYC* p. 313)?

H. How is creative representation "an exuberant, noisy activity of body and mind" (Golomb, *EYC* p. 314)?

I. What does Golomb mean when she says that in young children's creative representations, "producer and product are still inseparable" (*EYC* p. 314)? How does this idea relate to Golomb's statement that "representation does not aspire to copy the original" (*EYC* p. 314)?

J. What is creative representation? What are children doing when they create symbols?

Exercise 4

Starting With Direct Experiences

Creative representation begins as children interact with people and materials that engage their interest and spark their desire to savor and express some aspect of their experience.

A. Make a drawing or model of a cassowary. Next, draw or make a model of a cat. Which representation was easier for you to create? Why?

B. How do the actions of touching, seeing, smelling, tasting, and hearing help children create representations?

C. Review the *EYC* photo sequences in (1)–(3), and identify the direct experiences that serve as catalysts for the children's representations.

❶ Photos on p. 315

❷ Photo on p. 318

❸ Photos on p. 319

D. Exploring and using real materials provides children with meaningful experiences they may want to represent.

❶ Read "Realness" (*EYC* p. 129). How do Talbot's and Frost's ideas about the appeal of real objects support the idea that for young children, experience precedes creative representation?

❷ Return to Chapter 5, exercises 7C–E on pp. 53. How do the materials you listed in these exercises provide children with experiences they might want to represent?

E. Creative representation begins with actual experiences.

❶ How do the ingredients of active learning enable children to have real experiences?

❷ Why would visiting a fire station make a picture book about fire fighters and fire engines more meaningful to young children?

❸ In light of what you understand about experiencing and representing, would you prepare children for a trip to the fire station by first reading them a story about fire fighters and fire engines? Why or why not?

❹ As you talk with a fire fighter about plans for your preschool children's visit to the local fire station, which of the following activities would you suggest, based on your children's need for direct experiences?

- Hearing about how many gallons of water each hose delivers per minute
- Holding a fire hose
- Ringing a fire truck bell
- Seeing a map locating all the fire alarm boxes in town that are wired into the fire station
- Watching the fire fighters raise the bucket ladder
- Looking at a hose hanging up to dry
- Hearing about the medical qualifications of the emergency medical technicians
- Looking inside the rescue truck
- Visiting the living quarters of the fire fighters
- Hearing about how many gallons of coffee the fire fighters drink in a week
- Trying on fire boots, hats, and coats
- Hearing about chemicals used to put out fires
- Seeing photographs of fire fighters rescuing a kitten from a tree

F. Which one of the following sequences of experiences would be most likely to help children construct knowledge about the subject involved? Why do you think so?

Sequence 1

- First, feed, groom, walk, and play with a friendly dog.
- Second, pretend to be a dog.
- Third, draw a dog.

Sequence 2

- First, hear a story about how bread is made.
- Second, visit a local bakery, knead dough, see the bread go in and out of the ovens.
- Third, look at photos of bread baking.

Sequence 3

- First, march to a recording of marching band music.
- Second, hear a story about children watching a parade that includes a marching band.
- Third, stand on the sidelines while the local high school marching band practices on the football field.
- Fourth, touch and hold some of the instruments during a band's rehearsal break.

▶ G. Reorder the two sequences you did not select in exercise F in light of what you know about direct experience as the basis for understanding and creating representations, and explain the reason for your reordering.

▶ H. Why is the key experience *recognizing objects by sight, sound, touch, taste, and smell* an important part of children's symbol-making process?

▶ I. How do children who lack sight or hearing or speech create representations?

Exercise 5

The Role of Imitation in Creative Representation

▶ A. Look at the photographs on the *EYC* pages listed in (1)–(8). Explain **what** children are (or might be) imitating and **how** they are carrying out their imitations.

1. p. 179
2. p. 183
3. p. 199
4. p. 318
5. p. 319
6. p. 325
7. p. 489
8. p. 511

▶ B. What is each of these children from the opening anecdotes on *EYC* pp. 317–318 imitating?

1. Timmy
2. Joey
3. Tracy
4. Jonah
5. Nathan
6. Mikey
7. Kara
8. Alana
9. Andrew
10. Amanda
11. Jalessa

▶ C. Review your child-study notes and anecdotes from earlier chapters. What have you seen your study child(ren) imitating?

▶ D. In your own life, who and what have you imitated? Why? What role does imitation play in your life today?

▶ E. Look at the photograph on *EYC* p. 36, and read the statement by Forman and Kuschner on *EYC* p. 319. In an active learning environment, why is it important for adults to imitate children?

▶ F. Look at the photographs on *EYC* pp. 207 and 483 to answer exercises (1)–(3).

1. Who might these children be imitating?

2. Why do you think young children are inclined to imitate fantasy characters?

3. What is the role of choice and intrinsic motivation in imitation?

▶ G. How does imitation support the development of children's creative representation?

Exercise 6

Interpreting Representations Made by Others

▶ A. Read "How the Zebra Plant Got Its Name: Comparing a Plant and a Picture" (*EYC* p. 322). What strikes you about this conversation between Jeff and his teacher? What does this exchange tell you about Jeff's thinking and ability to represent?

▶ B. Read the anecdotes on *EYC* p. 320. Select one anecdote, and describe how the child is relating a model, photograph, or picture to a real place or thing.

▶ C. Why are young children interested in models, photographs, and pictures? Why is this interest in other people's representations important in their own development as symbol makers and readers?

Pretending and Role Playing

▶ **A.** What pretending and role-playing scenarios do you remember being involved in as a child? As an older person?

▶ **B.** What does Weininger mean when he describes pretending as *"what if" thinking leading to "as if" play (EYC* p. 323)?

▶ **C.** For exercises (1)–(3) read through the section on pretending and role playing (on *EYC* pp. 323–330), and look at the photographs.

❶ List all the pretend-play themes children are engaged in throughout the text and photographs of this reading selection. (For example, the pretend-play themes of the first three anecdotes are *rocket ship play, magic hunter,* and *going to the bank.* Then, list the pretend-play themes you have seen some of your study children from earlier chapters involved in.

❷ What categories might you use to classify the pretend-play themes you have identified? (After you have devised your own, see Garvey's categories on *EYC* p. 326, first column.)

❸ In an active learning setting, where do children's pretend-play and role-play themes come from?

▶ **D.** According to Smilansky (*EYC* p. 323), what is the role of imagination and make-believe/fantasy in pretending and role play? What is the role of imitation?

▶ **E.** Why do adults generally find it difficult to blend imitation of reality with imagination

and make-believe, whereas young children find this combination of ideas perfectly natural?

▶ **F.** What cautions do Fein and Schwartz (*EYC* p. 329) offer to adult supporters of role play, and why are these cautions important?

▶ **G.** For each element of pretend play listed in (1)–(5) (and described on *EYC* pp. 324–326), find an *EYC* **photograph,** an *EYC* **anecdote** (p. 323), and an **aspect of the barbershop** scenario (*EYC* pp. 325–326, 326) that illustrate that role-play element. Also find **anecdotes about some of your study children** to illustrate each element. Use a chart like the following to organize your answers.

Pretend Play Element	Illustration of Element			
	EYC Photo	EYC Anecdote	Barbershop Play	Study Children

❶ Pretending to be someone else
❷ Using one object to stand for another
❸ Using gestures, sounds, and words to define an object, situation, or setting
❹ Sharing pretend play and roles with others
❺ Talking with others within the context of the role-play situation

▶ **H.** For exercises (1)–(2), read "Details in Children's Barbershop Play Before and After the Trip to the Barbershop" (*EYC* p. 329) and Beth Marshall's week-by-week account of the barbershop play (*EYC* pp. 329–330).

❶ What does this account tell you about young children's need for time to carry out their pretend play?

❷ Adults often want to hurry children on to a new idea or play theme, but young children seem to need time for their play to evolve. Why?

▶ **I.** What does Garvey mean when she says that "as play develops, its forms become less determined by properties of the materials in the immediate situation and come increasingly under the control of plans or ideas" (*EYC* p. 325)? From your own observations, what are some examples of pretend play being determined by the properties of materials? Of pretend play being under the control of plans or ideas?

▶ **J.** How do Beth Marshall's observations about children's need for time to build detail into their play support Garvey's observations?

▶ **K.** Why are pretending and role playing significant cognitive, social, and emotional experiences for young children?

Making Models

▶ **A.** The photographs on the *EYC* pages listed in (1)–(14) show some models children have made or are making. For each photo, list the **materials the child used** and **what the model represents.**

❶ p. 51
❷ p. 179 (right-hand)
❸ p. 201 (right-hand)
❹ p. 226 (right-hand)

⑤ p. 315 (top right, bottom middle)

⑥ p. 330

⑦ p. 331

⑧ p. 333 (top photos)

⑨ p. 333 (bottom)

⑩ p. 401

⑪ p. 413

⑫ p. 433 (bottom)

⑬ p. 463

⑭ p. 519

▶ B. What kinds of models have you seen some of your study children making? Organize your answers in a chart like the following.

Child	Materials	What Model Represents

▶ C. Look at the clay models of people on *EYC* pp. 310 and 333. They were all made at the same time with the same materials by children working next to one another at small-group time. What does this suggest to you about the creative process of model-making in an active learning setting?

▶ D. Read about the development of model-making in "Anticipating a variety of approaches to model-making" (*EYC* pp. 332–333). Find and record *EYC* photographs, *EYC* anecdotes (p. 330), and anecdotes about your study child(ren) that illustrate approaches (1)–(4). Use a chart like the one at the top of the next column.

Approach	EYC Photo Page #	EYC Anecdotes	Study Child(ren) Anecdotes

❶ Exploration (sheer pleasure in action for action's sake)

❷ Romancing (embellishing forms with words)

❸ Simple models (economy and simplicity)

❹ Detailed models (distinct parts)

Exercise 9

Drawing and Painting

▶ A. Read the description of drawing and painting development "Anticipate a variety of approaches to drawing and painting" (*EYC* pp. 335–336). Then, look over the child anecdotes, drawings, or paintings on the *EYC* pages listed in the next column, and decide which approach(es) to painting and drawing is (or are) exemplified in each case. Use a chart like the one below to tally the approach(es) being used.

Abby, p. 334	p. 294
Jonah/Rachel, p. 334	p. 310
Alana, p. 334	p. 311 (top)
Brianna, p. 334	p. 313 (5 pictures)
Colin, p. 334	p. 336
Shannon, p. 334	p. 337
Hannah, p. 334	p. 338 (4 pictures)
Ben, p. 334	p. 351
p. 47	p. 363
p. 117 (left-hand)	p. 371
p. 122 (bottom)	p. 423
p. 173 (right-hand)	p. 470
p. 195	p. 473
p. 233	p. 480
p. 240	p. 488

▶ B. Young children "draw" with materials other than paints, markers, pencils, and crayons. What alternative drawing materials have children used in the photographs on the *EYC* pages listed in (1)–(4)?

❶ p. 256   **❸** p. 441

❷ p. 340   **❹** p. 452

Anecdote, Drawing, Painting Page #	Approaches			
	Marks & Scribbles	Shapes (Single Line Enclosing an Area)	Simple Figures ("Tadpole" People)	More Distinctive Figures

C. How might these and other three-dimensional materials (such as pebbles, yarn, wire, felt, and crepe paper) be useful to a blind or partially sighted child?

D. Look at drawings and paintings done by some of your study children from earlier chapters. What characterizes their work in terms of approach and materials?

Exercise 10

Supporting Children's Creative Representation Throughout the Day

(Exercise B involves a computer.)

A. If you are currently teaching or student teaching, think of your early childhood setting for these exercises about *providing materials;* if you are not teaching, consider your study child(ren)'s early childhood setting. Use a chart like the following to list the **materials currently in the setting** that support each of the creative representation key experiences listed in (1)–(6). Then list **materials you would like to add.** (You might refer to *EYC* materials suggestions on pp. 316, 320, 324, 331, and 335.)

Creative Representation Key Experience	Current Materials	Additional Materials

❶ Recognizing objects by sight, sound, touch, taste, and smell

❷ Imitating actions and sounds

❸ Relating models, pictures, and photographs to real places and things

❹ Pretending and role-playing

❺ Making models of clay, blocks, and other materials

❻ Drawing and painting

B. In *providing materials,* also consider appropriate computer software. If you have access to a computer and preschool software, try out some programs that encourage drawing and creative projects. (For ideas about appropriate software, consult the software reviews in the bimonthly magazine *Children's Software Revue,* www.childrenssoftware.com.) Which programs do you or would you like to provide for children in an early childhood setting?

C. Exercises (1)–(7) concern adults *participating respectfully in children's role play.*

❶ Recall and list the ways *you* have supported children's pretending and role play.

❷ What suggestions does Beth make within the barbershop play (*EYC* p. 326)? How does she make suggestions? How do the children respond?

❸ Why is it important to address a role-playing child as the person the child is pretending to be? How is this strategy related to taking cues from children?

❹ With a partner or a small group of friends, make up characters and improvise a scene around a situation of your own choosing.

How did you take cues and ideas from each other?

❺ In an active learning setting, why is it particularly important for adults to take cues and directions *from children* in role-play situations?

❻ How is children's pretending and role play similar to improvisational theater? To theatrical productions that follow a script?

❼ What social and communication skills does it take for a young child (or a person of any age) to be a member of a role-play ensemble?

D. Exercises (1)–(2) concern *listening to and conversing with children about models, drawings, and paintings.*

❶ In the adult-child dialogues on *EYC* pp. 333 and 337, what conversational moves is the adult making? Why? (Five conversational moves—*enforced repetition, closed question, open question, comment, acknowledgment*—are described on *EYC* p. 218.)

❷ How do the conversations in exercise (1) support what Thompson is saying (on *EYC* p. 337) about the need for adults to recognize and respectfully accept children's thoughts and ideas about their creations?

E. Read through the *creative representation support strategies* in the checklist on the facing page (which is from *EYC* p. 339). Under each of the six key experiences on the checklist, check the support strategies you are already using, write "E" in front of the strategies you have not used but would like to explore, and then read about each of these strategies in *EYC.*

Creative Representation Strategies: A Summary

Recognizing objects by sight, sound, touch, taste, and smell

___ Provide materials with distinctive sensory features:
   ___ Parts of things
   ___ Covers and things to cover up
   ___ Things with distinctive textures
   ___ Aromatic things
   ___ Things that make noise
   ___ Foods with a variety of tastes
___ Provide opportunities for children to notice sensory cues.
___ Notice and make imprints and rubbings with children.

Imitating actions and sounds

___ Watch for children's spontaneous imitations.
___ Imitate children's actions and sounds.
___ Build opportunities for imitation into the daily routine.

Relating models, photographs, and pictures to real places and things

___ Provide models for children to play with.
___ Provide photographs and pictures for children to look at:
   ___ Photograph the children in your program.
   ___ Provide children with a simple working camera.
   ___ Provide a variety of illustrated storybooks.
   ___ Include all sorts of catalogs and picture magazines in the art area.
   ___ Use photographs of children at small-group time.
___ Support and encourage children's comparisons of models and pictures to the things they represent.

Pretending and role playing

___ Provide materials and props for pretending and role play.
___ Support pretend play that moves from place to place.
___ Watch and listen for the elements of pretend play:
   ___ Pretending to be someone else.
   ___ Using one object to stand for another.
   ___ Using gestures, sounds, and words to define an object, situation, or setting.
   ___ Sharing pretend play and roles with others.
   ___ Talking with others within the context of the role-play situation.
___ Participate in pretend play respectfully, taking cues from players:
   ___ Follow the theme and content set by the players.
   ___ Offer suggestions from within the pretend situation.
   ___ Respect children's responses to your ideas.
   ___ Address the pretend person rather than the child.
___ Pretend at small- and large-group times.
___ Plan ways to support children's pretend play:
   ___ Add materials.
   ___ Take field trips.
   ___ Invite people and bring in animals to visit.
   ___ Discuss unsettling pretend-play themes as a teaching team.
___ Provide time for children's pretend play to unfold and develop.

Making models out of clay, blocks, and other materials

___ Provide a variety of model-making materials:
   ___ Clay   ___ Other materials
   ___ Blocks
___ Provide time and support for children to explore and gain skill with tools and materials.
___ Anticipate a variety of approaches to model-making:
   ___ Exploration   ___ Simple models
   ___ Romancing   ___ Detailed models
___ Find out from children what they are making:
   ___ Listen to children as they plan their models.
   ___ Listen to children as they work on their models.
   ___ Listen to children as they share their models.
___ At small-group time, ask children to make something out of clay, blocks, or other materials.

Drawing and painting

___ Provide materials for drawing and painting.
___ Provide time and support for children to explore and gain skill with drawing and painting materials and procedures.
___ Anticipate a variety of approaches to drawing and painting:
   ___ Marks and scribbles
   ___ Shapes
   ___ Simple figures
   ___ More distinctive figures
___ Watch and listen to children as they draw and paint.
___ Talk with children about their paintings and drawings.
___ Include drawing opportunities in planning, recall, small-group and large-group times.
___ Display and send home children's paintings and drawings.

F. For exercises (1)–(3), which involve *creative representation at recall time*, review *EYC* pp. 225–243.

❶ What is the relationship between creative representation and recall time?

❷ What creative representation key experiences have you seen (or might you see) children engaging in at recall time?

❸ From what you know about creative representation, why is recall an important element of the plan-work-recall sequence?

G. Exercises (1)–(3) concern *maintaining reasonable expectations about children's approaches to creative representation.*

❶ In an active learning approach to early childhood education, would it be reasonable to expect that all the children in your setting or group would be on the same level of role play, model-making, or drawing and painting at the same time? Why or why not?

❷ In an active learning setting, would you expect all the children to use role-play, model-making, or drawing and painting materials in the same way or to produce identical representations? Why or why not?

❸ What are the similarities and differences between encouraging children to create models of people out of clay and encouraging children to assemble puzzles depicting people? What kinds of knowledge are children constructing in each case?

Exercise 11

Child Study: Creating a Creative Representation Portfolio

As you teach, student teach, or observe your study child(ren), assemble a creative representation portfolio containing materials such as the following:

- Anecdotes related to each creative representation key experience
- Video clips or photographs of pretending and role-play scenarios
- Models (simple and detailed) that children create or photographs of their models
- Drawings and paintings children create using a range of approaches, including marks, scribbles, shapes, and simple and distinctive figures
- Representations children make at planning and recall times

When your creative representation portfolio is complete, find an opportunity to present it to teaching teams in your center, parents of preschoolers, or fellow early childhood students. Explaining your portfolio to others will sharpen your understanding of the process of creative representation that young children are involved in.

Exercise 12

Creative Representation Scenarios: What Would You Do?

Based on your understanding of the creative representation key experiences and the support strategies discussed on *EYC* pp. 311–341, decide how you might interact with and support the preschool children in the following scenarios.

A. *At work time in the house area, Yvonne and Tassini are dressing their "babies" for a walk to the "park" and gathering items they need to take along for a "picnic." Latanya stands nearby holding a dolly and watching Yvonne and Tassini closely.*

How might you support what appears to be Latanya's interest in this pretend-play situation?

B. *During large-group time, as the children are singing "Row, Row, Row Your Boat," a large flock of birds lands outside the window. The children stop singing and gather by the window, talking excitedly about the birds they see and hear outdoors.*

How might you, through creative representation, support the children's spontaneous interest in these birds?

C. *At small-group time, the children in your group are working with boxes, cardboard tubes, pipe cleaners, and tape. "Look at this," says Brendan, showing you something he has made, "it's a zord!" (You are not quite sure what a zord is.) Anna covers a box with layers of tape. Raoul flattens his box and on the "clean side" draws "army men."*

How might you support each of these children?

D. *At work time, Erica is dressing her baby and getting ready to "move." Maria asks, "Erica, can I play with you?" Erica says no. Frances brings Erica some doll clothes and asks Erica if she can play with her. Again, Erica says no. Later, Kacey joins Erica, saying "Mom, we need a bigger house, don't we?" "Yeah," replies Erica, "that's why we're moving today."*

What message is Erica sending you and any others who may want to join her pretend play?

E. *At planning time, Victor decides to make a tyrannosaur. "What will you use to make your tyrannosaur?" you ask. "I don't know," he says.*

How might you support Victor's plan to create a dinosaur?

F. *At small-group time, after a walk around the neighborhood, you encourage children to draw something they saw or brought back from the walk. One of the children in your group, Dorie, is blind.*

What drawing materials might you provide for Dorie?

G. *At small-group time, the children in your group are tracing around or drawing things they brought back from a walk around the neighborhood. Some are drawing things they saw on the walk. Niles is squealing as he covers a large sheet of paper with back-and-forth strokes of red crayon.*

How might you support Niles?

Exercise 13

Implementation Study: Trying Out Creative Representation Support Strategies

If you are currently teaching or student teaching or can work in an early childhood setting over a period of time, try out the creative representation support strategies on *EYC* p. 339 as opportunities arise during the child-initiated and adult-initiated times of the day. Support children's creative representation ideas at work time and outside time. Collect anecdotes, video clips, photos, models, drawings, and paintings for your creative representation portfolio. Plan and carry out a small-group time and a large-group time around children's interests in creative representation. At the end of each day of teaching, make a written record of your discoveries about creative representation and how to support young symbol makers.

This implementation exercise is crucial for your understanding of the creative representation key experiences and ways to support them. Do not be discouraged if things do not go the way you expect them to. It is only with practice that adults learn from children how they create representations and how to encourage their representational initiatives.

Exercise 14

Child Assessment: COR Items Related to Creative Representation

One way to assess preschool children's understanding and use of creative representation is to match the children's anecdotes (collected each day and discussed at daily team planning time) with the most relevant level-descriptors for items J–L from the High/Scope Child Observation Record (COR) for Ages 2½–6. These items are presented on the next page. Based on the following anecdotes, at what level (1–5) would you place Daniel on COR item J?[24] (After making your own assessment, you may wish to look at the item J level suggested for Daniel on page 143 of this chapter.)

> 6/2 At work time in the toy area with Jack, Daniel fit together the Lasy builders to make "robots" with "legs, arms, head, body, and gripper hands."

[24]*Anecdotes used in this COR item and in the COR items in subsequent key experience chapters were collected and recorded by High/Scope Demonstration Preschool teachers Carol Markley and Beth Marshall.*

6/5 At work time in the toy area, working with the Lasy builders, Daniel made a "helicopter man" with two propellers, a head, and a body.

6/12 At work time in the toy area, with the Lasy builders, Daniel made a "transformer" with head, arms, legs, feet, and a body. "To make it fly, you put the arms up and the feet down, and then it's a jet," he told Carol.

6/13 At small-group time, Daniel rolled some Play-Doh with his palm into a "worm or snake." He made a "baby" and a "bigger brother." (The baby *was* smaller than the bigger brother.)

6/15 At work time in the block area, Alex and Daniel built a house for Beth's dog, who was visiting for the day. The house included "walls, a door, and a blanket bed."

Exercise 15

Further Understanding of the Creative Representation Process

Go to the library and examine one or more of the following four books. Record your observations and discoveries.

- *The Child's Creation of a Pictorial World* by Claire Golomb (1992)

- *Young Children's Sculpture and Drawing* by Claire Golomb (1974)

- *Facilitating Play: A Medium for Promoting Cognitive, Socio-Emotional, and Academic Development in Young Children* by Sara Smilansky and Leah Shefatya (1990)

- *Imagination and Education*, Keiran Egan and Dan Nadaner, editors (1988)

COR Item J. Making and building

Level 1   Child does not yet explore or use making-and-building materials such as clay, sand, or blocks.

Level 2   Child explores making-and-building materials.

Level 3   Child uses materials to make something (a stack of blocks, a sand pile) but does not say whether it is meant to represent something else (a tower, a beach).

Level 4   Child uses materials to make a simple representation and says or demonstrates what it is (says a stack of blocks is a tower; says a stack of balls is a snowman).

Level 5   Child uses materials to make or build things with at least three details represented (a house with a door, windows, and a chimney).

Supporting Anecdotes:

COR Item K. Drawing and painting

Level 1   Child does not yet draw or paint.

Level 2   Child explores drawing and painting materials.

Level 3   Child draws or paints simple representations (a ball, a house).

Level 4   Child draws or paints representations with a few details.

Level 5   Child draws or paints representations with many details.

Supporting Anecdotes:

COR Item L. Pretending

Level 1   Child does not yet pretend.

Level 2   Child uses one object to stand for another or uses actions or sounds to pretend.

Level 3   Child assumes the role of someone or something else, or talks in language appropriate to the assumed role.

Level 4   Child engages in cooperative pretend play with another child.

Level 5   Child steps out of pretend play to give directions to another ("When you are the baby bear, speak in a voice like this").

Supporting Anecdotes:

Creative Representation Issues to Ponder and Write About

▶ A. How does understanding creative representation help adults support active learners?

▶ B. How is role play related to children's social development?

▶ C. What is the relationship between *pretending and role playing* in the early years and *drama* in the later years?

▶ D. What is the difference, if any, between representation and artistic expression?

▶ E. How does active learning help children construct knowledge about representation?

▶ F. What compels human beings to create representations?

▶ G. What enables children to create representations of creatures they have never seen, such as monsters and elves?

▶ H. What is the role of imagination in creative representation?

▶ I. How do children's family cultures influence their approach to creative representation?

Related Publications

Ansbach, Ursula. 2000. "Master Pretenders: Dramatic Arts in the Preschool Classroom." *High/Scope Extensions* (January/February): 1–3.

Epstein, Ann S. 1999a. "Supporting Young Artists." *High/Scope ReSource* (Winter):10–12.

Epstein, Ann. S. 1999b. "Thinking About Art With Young Children." *High/Scope Extensions* (May/June):1–3.

Epstein, Ann S., and Eli Trimis. In press. *Supporting Young Artists: The Development of the Visual Arts in Young Children.* Ypsilanti, MI: High/Scope Press.

Graves, Michelle. 1989. *The Teacher's Idea Book: Daily Planning Around the Key Experiences*, 27–35. Ypsilanti, MI: High/Scope Press.

Graves, Michelle. 1996. "Field Trips: A New Definition." In *Supporting Young Learners 2: Ideas for Child Care Providers and Teachers*, Nancy A. Brickman, ed., 257–64. Ypsilanti, MI: High/Scope Press.

Graves, Michelle. 1996. The *Teacher's Idea Book 2: Planning Around Children's Interests*. Ypsilanti, MI: High/Scope Press.

High/Scope Child Observation Record (COR) for Ages 2½–6. 1992. Ypsilanti, MI: High/Scope Press.

Hohmann, Mary. 1996. "Supporting Children's Development in Drawing and Painting." *High/Scope Extensions* (November/December): 1–3

Johnston, Diana Jo. 1996. "Primary-Grade Field Trips That Work." In *Supporting Young Learners 2: Ideas for Child Care Providers and Teachers*, Nancy A. Brickman, ed., 265–66. Ypsilanti, MI: High/Scope Press.

Marshall, Beth. 1996. "Lights, Camera, Action! Spotlight on Pretend Play." In *Supporting Young Learners 2: Ideas for Child Care Providers and Teachers*, Nancy A. Brickman, ed., 179–86. Ypsilanti, MI: High/Scope Press.

Marshall, Beth. 1997. "Ban It, Ignore It, or Join It? What to Do About Superhero Play." *High/Scope Extensions* (November/December): 1–3.

Tompkins, Mark. 1996. "A Partnership With Young Artists." In *Supporting Young Learners 2: Ideas for Child Care Providers and Teachers*, Nancy A. Brickman, ed., 187–92. Ypsilanti, MI: High/Scope Press.

Related Videos

Adult-Child Interactions: Forming Partnerships With Children. 1996. Color videotape, 60 min. Ypsilanti, MI: High/Scope Press.

Creative Representation. 2000. Color videotape, 40 min. Ypsilanti, MI: High/Scope Press.

Experiencing and Representing. 1975. Four color videos of slides transferred to film, then to video, 48 min. total. Ypsilanti, MI: High/Scope Press:
Part 1. *A Way Children Learn* (12 min.)
Part 2. *Starting With Direct Experience* (12 min.)
Part 3. *From Direct Experience to Representation* (8 min.)
Part 4. *Strategies for Supporting Representational Activity* (16 min.)

Supporting Young Artists: Exploring and Creating With Clay. 2000. Color video, 53 min. Ypsilanti, MI: High/Scope Press.

Supporting Young Artists: Exploring and Creating With Dough. 2000. Color video, 59 min. Ypsilanti, MI: High/Scope Press.

Supporting Young Artists: Exploring and Creating With Drawing and Painting. 2000. Color video, 59 min. Ypsilanti, MI: High/Scope Press.

Supporting Young Artists: Exploring and Creating With Paper. 2000. Color video, 55 min. Ypsilanti, MI: High/Scope Press.

Answer to Exercise 14

Daniel's level on COR item J:

Level 4 on the basis of anecdote from 6/13

Level 5 on the basis of anecdotes from 6/2, 6/5, 6/12, 6/15

Level 5 overall

T hree- and four-year-olds have progressed to the stage of using language to convey their feelings and desires, interact with others, ask questions and think about things, represent what they know, and talk about imaginary situations. At the same time, they are mastering grammar, constructing the meaning of specific words, and "writing" and "reading" in their own particular, though unconventional, ways.

—*Educating Young Children, p. 343*

Language and Literacy

11

Speaking, Listening, Writing, and Reading

▶ A. For the following activity in talking, listening, and writing, you will need a partner:

- Tell your partner a story about a favorite chair. Then, listen to your partner's story about his or her favorite chair.

- Take turns describing and listening to your partner describe an experience with an uncomfortable chair.

- Together, write a story, a poem, or song lyrics about chairs. Then present what you have written to another pair doing this exercise. What struck you about your collective experiences?

▶ B. With a partner, have a conversation about a topic of personal interest to you both. After you have completed your dialogue, write a statement that in some way reflects the thoughts, feelings, or ideas that arose from this exchange.

▶ C. To experience enjoying books, go to a library or bookstore, and browse through any books, magazines, journals, catalogs, or newspapers of interest to you. What made this an enjoyable experience?

▶ D. To experience emergent reading, find and "read" a children's storybook or a comic book written in a foreign language that you do not read or speak.[25] Describe the experience.

[25]*This exercise originated with High/Scope editor Nancy Brickman and High/Scope consultant Michelle Graves.*

▶ E. Based on what you just did in exercises A–D, what is *language and literacy*? How is it related to creative representation?

Recalling Your Own Experiences With Language and Literacy

Discuss the following memories with a partner or several friends, and record your answers.

▶ A. What are your earliest memories of talking, of trying to make yourself understood by others?

▶ B. When you were a young child, what did you like to talk about (or what do you remember talking about)? With whom did you talk? Who really listened to you?

▶ C. What stories or poems do you remember people telling you (rather than reading to you)? Who told you these stories or poems? Under what circumstances?

▶ D. What stories or poems do you remember telling or making up? To whom did you tell them? Why?

▶ E. As a child, were there people you really liked to talk with and listen to (or eavesdrop on) even though you may not have understood everything they said? Who? Why?

▶ F. What, if any, recollections do you have of hearing languages, dialects, or accents other than your own? Did you have the opportunity to communicate with these people? If so, how?

G. What, if any, recollections do you have of learning to comprehend and speak a second language as a young child? As an older person?

H. What experiences have you had "reading" signs, maps, and menus written in languages you did not understand?

I. In your experience, what makes a person easy to converse with?

J. Describe your earliest memories of learning to write and read. (These memories may or may not have to do with school.)

K. What, if anything, do you remember about being read to as a young child? What picture books or storybooks do you recall from your childhood?

L. What childhood memories do you have about print matter—books, magazines, newspapers, comics, instruction manuals, billboards, cards, recipes, menus? What childhood memories do you have about libraries, bookmobiles, or bookstores?

M. What do you like to read about?

N. What kind of writing do you like to do?

O. For a week, keep a log of language and literacy experiences you engage in and observe in your daily life. At the end of the week, review and reflect on your findings.

Understanding Whole Language and Emergent Literacy

These exercises are based on the discussion "Basic Beliefs About Language and Literacy" on *EYC* pp. 343–345.

A. What is meant by the *whole language* approach?

B. What is *literacy*?

C. What does the term *emergent literacy* mean?

D. What does Wells mean when he says "We are all meaning makers" (*EYC* p. 343)? How is being a "meaning maker" related to being a symbol maker (as discussed in *EYC* Chapter 10, "Creative Representation")?

E. Why do people want to communicate? Why do people use spoken and written language as a means to communicate?

F. According to Temple, what role does error play in learning to speak and write (*EYC* p. 344)?

G. What role does social interaction play in language and literacy development?

H. How does active learning support the development of language and literacy?

I. For further understanding of the theories behind emergent literacy and the whole language approach, go to the Internet or library and find one or more of the books or articles listed on *EYC* pp. 371–373. Record your findings and reflections.

Language Begins With the Desire to Communicate

Children learn to talk by talking, by attempting to verbally communicate experiences they want to share with the important people in their lives.

A. What is Tough saying about how children learn to use language (*EYC* p. 346)?

B. Read the anecdotes on *EYC* pp. 346 and 349. What subjects are the children listed in (1)–(11) eager to talk about?

❶ Jason   ❼ Jonah

❷ Alma   ❽ Abby/Rachel

❸ Douglas   ❾ Jason

❹ Hannah   ❿ Jason/Jonah

❺ Colin/Nicholas   ⓫ Abby

❻ Corrin

C. What do some of your study children (from earlier exercises) like to talk about?

D. From your answers to exercises B and C, what strikes you about the conversational topics young children find personally meaningful? What, if any, is the relationship between child-initiated conversation topics and the pretend-play themes you identified in Chapter 10, for exercise 7C(1) on p. 136?

Describing the World of Experience

As children talk about topics and experiences of particular interest to themselves, they are often moved to describe significant objects, events, and relationships.

▶ A. What is each of the following children describing in the anecdotes on *EYC* p. 353?

❶ Brianna	❼ Hannah
❷ Brian	❽ Douglas
❸ Kacey	❾ Alana
❹ Trey	❿ Jonah
❺ Amanda	⓫ Sarah
❻ Douglas	

▶ B. What descriptions have you heard from some of your study children from earlier exercises?

▶ C. On *EYC* p. 355, first column, what characterizes Troy's and Brian's descriptions?

▶ D. If you were in a country whose language you did not speak or read, among people who did not speak your language, how might you communicate your desire for a place to wash or eat or sleep?

▶ E. Why do young children often fill in with gestures or pause to search for words as they strive to describe something they have seen or experienced?

▶ F. Turn to the recall time anecdotes on *EYC* p. 225. What is the relationship between what these children are saying and the language and literacy key experience *describing objects, events, and relations?*

Exercise 6

Enjoying Language

▶ A. The following children appear in the anecdotes on *EYC* pp. 356–357. How is each of them enjoying language by playing with the structures, sounds, and meanings of language?

❶ Kenneth	❼ Jonah
❷ Jessa	❽ Colin
❸ Andrew	❾ Tomo
❹ Jessa	❿ Penny
❺ Colin	⓫ Jason
❻ Douglas	

▶ B. How do some of your study children from earlier exercises have fun with language?

▶ C. Why do young children play with language? Why is this "silly" activity important?

▶ D. Thorndike, Wells, and Caplan (*EYC* p. 358) have found that young children who are read to from picture books and storybooks become better readers than children who are not read to. Why do you think this is the case? How does reading to children add to their enjoyment of language and help them untangle the code of written language?

▶ E. To the child, what is the difference between hearing a story *read* and having a story *told?* Why are both experiences important in developing a child's language and literacy?

▶ F. Why is it important for young children to make up their own stories, rhymes, and jokes?

▶ G. What emotions are Colin, Tomo, and Jason expressing in their stories (*EYC* p. 357)?

▶ H. There are children who talk a lot, children who talk a moderate amount, and children who talk very little. What assumptions do adults often make about each of these three types of children? In an active learning setting, why would it be important to avoid making assumptions about children's ability to verbally communicate and to instead focus on listening to and interacting with them?

Exercise 7

Early Writing

▶ A. How does Temple explain why young children do not begin to write by reproducing alphabet letters (*EYC* pp. 361–362)?

▶ B. Read the description of emergent forms of writing entitled "Anticipate various emergent forms of writing" (*EYC* pp. 361–363). Then look at the *EYC* photographs on the pages listed in (1)–(13), and decide which form or combination of forms of early writing is evident in each photo. Use a chart like the one at the top of the next page to tally the form(s) being used.

Photo Page #	Forms of Emergent Writing				
	Drawing	*Scribbling*	*Letterlike Forms*	*Invented Spelling*	*Conventional*

❶ p. 122 (bottom photo)

❷ p. 188

❸ p. 195

❹ p. 240

❺ p. 315 (bottom left photo)

❻ p. 338 (all photos)

❼ p. 345

❽ p. 351 (top left of photo)

❾ p. 361

❿ p. 362

⓫ p. 363

⓬ p. 364

⓭ p. 442 (right-hand photo)

❹ Corrin

❺ Alana

❻ Abby

❼ Andrew

❽ Alana

❾ Bryant

❿ Deola

⓫ Andrew

⓬ Douglas

⓭ Chrysten

⓮ Corrin

⓯ Jalessa

▶ C. What strikes you about the range of children's early writing skills shown in the group of photos in exercise B? How does this variety of early writing samples support the idea that each child develops at his or her own pace?

▶ D. Why might each of the following children (from the anecdotes on *EYC* p. 360) be motivated to write?

❶ Douglas

❷ Brianna

❸ Bryant

▶ E. What is the role of choice (intrinsic motivation, active learning) in learning to write?

▶ F. How are Ben, Kenneth, and Andrew *having fun with language* while *writing in various ways* (*EYC* p. 361, second column)?

Early Reading

▶ A. The children listed in (1)–(15) are from anecdotes on *EYC* pp. 365–366. Use a chart like the one at the bottom of this page to tally the forms of emergent reading they are engaging in.

❶ Douglas

❷ Julia

❸ Trey

❹ Abby

❺ Kenneth

❻ Chrysten

❼ Collin

❽ Aimee

❾ Kenneth/Chelsea

❿ Amanda

⓫ Audie

⓬ Aimee

⓭ Petey

⓮ Alana

⓯ Issac

▶ B. How does the use of children's personal symbols (see photograph on *EYC* p. 369) support children's emergent reading?

▶ C. The first writing young children are apt to read is composed of their own drawings, scribbles, and letterlike forms. Why is this the case?

▶ D. What kinds of knowledge are children constructing when they read their own writing?

▶ E. How is emergent reading related to the creative representation process—imitation, relating pictures to real things, pretending, drawing and painting?

Child's Name	Forms of Emergent Reading				
	Picture Reading	*Memorizing*	*Symbol/Sign Reading*	*Reading Own Writing*	*Identifying Letters/Words*

► F. Why is it important for young children to have time and many opportunities to read their own writing?

Exercise 9

Requesting "Real" Writing

► A. Sometimes children in active learning settings request adults to write for them. Why might they occasionally do this rather than write for themselves in their own way?

► B. Why might each of these children (from the anecdotes on *EYC* p. 370) have requested adults to write for them?

❶ Jonah

❷ Aimee

❸ Chrysten

❹ Colin

Exercise 10

Supporting Children's Language and Literacy Throughout the Day

(Exercise B involves a computer.)

► A. For this exercise about *providing materials*, if you are currently teaching or student teaching, think about your early childhood setting. If you are not teaching, think about the early childhood setting of one of your study children from earlier chapters. For each type of supporting material listed in (1)–(3), list **materials currently in the setting** and **materials you would like to add.** (You may wish to

refer to the materials suggestions on *EYC* pp. 350, 361, and 366.)

❶ Materials that support conversation

❷ Materials that support emergent writing

❸ Materials that support emergent reading

► B. In *providing materials*, if you have access to a computer and preschool software, try out the programs that support language and literacy. (For software titles, see the software reviews in the bimonthly magazine *Children's Software Revue:* www.childrenssoftware.com.) Which programs do you or would you like to provide in an early childhood setting?

► C. Exercises (1)–(6) deal with *providing a supportive atmosphere.*

❶ How do the elements of support discussed in *EYC* Chapter 2—*sharing of control between children and adults, focusing on children's strengths, forming authentic relationships with children, making a commitment to support children's play, adopting a problem-solving approach to social conflict*—help create a setting in which children feel free to talk?

❷ Why is the opportunity to speak freely important to children's language and literacy development?

❸ What effect does correcting a child's speech or grammar have on the child? How is correcting a child's speech related to the conversational move *enforced repetition* (*EYC* p. 218)? Why is it important for adults to focus on *what* the child is saying rather than on *how* the child is saying it?

❹ What are adults' worst fears about allowing children to speak freely?

❺ Review the subjects of children's spontaneous conversations that you listed in exercise 4B on p. 146. Which of these subjects might make some adults uncomfortable? Why?

❻ What subjects might you feel uncomfortable discussing with children? How might you support a child's interest in a subject that you are uncomfortable with?

► D. Exercises (1)–(6) deal with *taking cues from children.*

❶ What conversational moves are made by Ms. Flores (*EYC* p. 347), Mr. Yanez (*EYC* p. 351), and the adult talking with Troy and Erin (*EYC* pp. 352–353)? (See *EYC* p. 218 for explanation of the five types of conversational moves.)

❷ Why is listening to children essential to their development of language?

❸ How does listening to children support their development as listeners?

❹ What does Hiebert mean about substantive talk (*EYC* p. 353)?

❺ What is the role of reciprocity in substantive talk?

❻ In an active learning setting, who generally selects the topic of conversation?

► E. What cues are the children giving about their interest in writing and reading in the photographs on the *EYC* pages listed in (1)–(6) below?

❶ p. 355   ❹ p. 364

❷ p. 356   ❺ p. 365

❸ p. 358   ❻ p. 367

F. As a group, what do the following *EYC* photographs say about the adult's role in *reading aloud* to children: p. 20 (bottom photo), p. 21 (top left photo), p. 72, p. 77 (bottom left photo), p. 113, p. 138, p. 162, p. 209, p. 264, p. 358?

G. Read through the *language and literacy support strategies* in the checklist at the right (which is from *EYC* p. 373). Under each of the six key experiences on the checklist, check off the support strategies you are already using, write "E" in front of the strategies you have not used but would like to explore, and then read about each of these strategies in *EYC*.

H. Exercises (1)–(4) concern *taking cues from children about when they are interested in learning to identify and write conventional alphabet letters.*

❶ Why would or wouldn't it be important to provide wooden, plastic, and magnetic letters as well as letter stamps and ink pads (along with markers, crayons, pencils, paints, brushes, and paper) in appropriate interest areas in an active learning early childhood setting?

❷ If you provided these materials for children in an active learning setting, would you expect all children to use them at the same time? In the same way? Why or why not?

❸ From your own observations, is there any difference between the satisfaction children derive from tracing letters and the satisfaction children derive from making letters freehand? Explain.

❹ Based on an understanding of how children's writing develops, why is it important to refrain from writing on children's paintings and drawings unless children ask you to do so?

Language and Literacy Strategies: A Summary

Talking with others about personally meaningful experiences
___ Establish a climate in which children feel free to talk.
___ Be available for conversation throughout the day:
   ___ Place yourself at the children's physical level.
   ___ Listen carefully to what children are saying.
   ___ Give children control of conversations.
   ___ Accept children's hesitations and nonverbal utterances.
   ___ Learn and remember each child's particular interests.
___ Encourage children to talk with one another throughout the day:
   ___ Provide opportunities for cooperative projects and play.
   ___ Support children who wish to plan and recall together.
   ___ Refer one child's questions and problems to another child.
   ___ Interpret and deliver messages.
   ___ Explain the context of children's statements.
   ___ Acknowledge conflicting viewpoints.
___ Converse with *all* children:
   ___ Make time to talk with children.
   ___ Look for comfortable opportunities for dialogue.
   ___ Be aware of your personal preferences.

Describing objects, events, and relations
___ Provide children with interesting materials and experiences.
___ Listen as children describe things in their own way.
___ Encourage children to talk about their plans.
___ Let children be the leaders in "describing" games.

Having fun with language: Listening to stories and poems, making up stories and rhymes
___ Listen to children throughout the day.
___ Read to children individually and in small, intimate groups.
___ Tell stories, recite poems and rhymes.
___ Make up stories, chants, and rhymes.

Writing in various ways: Drawing, scribbling, letter-like forms, invented spelling, conventional forms
___ Provide a variety of writing and drawing materials.
___ Anticipate various emergent forms of writing:
   ___ Drawing
   ___ Scribbling
   ___ Letterlike forms
   ___ Invented spelling
   ___ Conventional forms
___ Encourage children to write in their own way:
   ___ Ask children to write stories.
   ___ Encourage children to write to one another.
   ___ Accept children's additions to your writing.
___ Display and send home samples of children's writing.

Reading in various ways: Reading storybooks, signs and symbols, one's own writing
___ Provide a print-rich environment:
   ___ Stock the interest areas with reading materials.
   ___ Look for things to read outside.
___ Provide each child with a personal symbol.
___ Provide storybooks for children to read.
___ Encourage children to read to one another.

Dictating stories
___ Write down children's personal dictations.
___ Write down group dictations.
___ Save dictations and encourage children to act out their experiences.

Child Study: Creating a Language and Literacy Portfolio

As you teach, student teach, or observe your study child(ren), create a language and literacy portfolio by collecting materials such as the following:

- Anecdotes related to each language and literacy key experience

- Recordings or transcripts of conversations children have with you and with other children

- Samples of children's emergent writing, including drawing, scribbling, letterlike forms, invented spelling, conventional forms

- Tapes or transcripts of children's stories, rhymes, jokes

- Videotape clips or photographs of children reading in various ways—reading pictures, symbols, signs, their own writing

When your language and literacy portfolio is complete, find an opportunity to present it to teaching teams in your center, parents of preschoolers, or fellow early childhood students. Assembling and explaining your portfolio to others will add to your own understanding of preschool language and literacy.

Language and Literacy Scenarios: What Would You Do?

Based on your understanding of the language and literacy key experiences and the support strategies discussed on *EYC* pp. 346–373, decide **how you might interact with and support the way preschool children are communicating** in each of the following scenarios.

▶ A. *At work time, **Alex, Kevin, Rachel,** and **Raina** are having a conversation as they use sand and water to make "salt." Alex says, "Everybody, us needs some more water." "I'll get it," Kevin replies. "Her will get it," Alex tells him, nodding toward Raina, "all right?" Raina looks at Alex.*[26]

▶ B. *At recall time, **Zach** describes the "wormer" he made. "Well, it was . . ." He pauses and gestures with his hands. "It had this part that went like . . ." He twists and thrusts his arm forward. "And then it, well it . . . it ate a hole!"*

▶ C. *At outside time, **Rachel** shows you how to make a " 'pecial cake," giving you these instructions: "You this," she says, using her hand to flatten a mound of damp sand. "And all this," she says, poking all her fingers into the damp, flattened sand.*

---

[26]*To see how High/Scope Demonstration Preschool teacher Carol Markley supported Alex, Kevin, Rachel, and Raina in this work time situation, see the High/Scope video **Adult-Child Interactions: Forming Partnerships With Children,** Part I, Scene 1, "Making Pretend Salt."*

▶ D. *At work time, **Evan** is pushing a toy bulldozer through a pile of blocks and making a motor-like sound. When he sees you, he communicates by smiling, patting the floor next to him, and then offering you a toy dump truck.*

▶ E. *"You know what I got from my grandma?" **Teresa** asks you as she comes through the door in the morning. "A [here she says a word you can't understand]—you can put stuff in, and the handles have these streamer things—green and purple—and my dad says maybe I can bring it when he's off work. I think that's going to be soon!"*

▶ F. *"Boo-hoo, you look like goo!" **Ryan** says, having fun with language at snack time.*

▶ G. *"I can write my cat's name. Watch," **Liza** tells you as she prints B R N D. "Brandy," she reads.*

▶ H. *Here's the list I wrote," **Jezra** says, handing you a sheet of scribbles. "Now you go to the store and get all those things for the camping trip."*

▶ I. ***Geena** is "reading" to her stuffed monkey from a picture-book version of **Hansel and Gretel**. "Stay away from that house!" she reads, pointing to the illustration of a gingerbread house. "There might be bad poison candy that makes you sick—and knives and stuff."*

▶ J. *"This is for my mom so she'll feel better," **PJ** tells you, showing you his drawing. "This says 'Love,'" he explains, pointing to a printed L followed by shapes and scribbles. "My dad can take it to the hospital."*

▶ K. *At planning time, when you ask **Sasha** what he plans to do at work time, he indicates* *his plan by throwing his arm around the shoulders of his friend Mike, gesturing broadly toward the block area with the other arm, and making a noise that sounds something like the word "big."*

▶ L. *Laramie and Forest laugh and talk together throughout work time. At recall time, however, they look down at their hands and remain silent when you ask them what they did at work time.*

▶ M. *Troy rarely talks indoors. Outdoors, however, he talks freely as he runs, jumps, climbs, throws, and catches.*

Exercise 13

Implementation Study: Trying Out Language and Literacy Support Strategies

If you are currently teaching or student teaching or can work in an early childhood setting over a period of time, try out the language and literacy support strategies on *EYC* p. 373 as opportunities arise during the child-initiated and adult-initiated times of the day. Support children's communication, conversation, emergent writing, and emergent reading at work time and outside time. Plan and carry out a small-group time and a large-group time around children's interests in language and literacy. Collect anecdotes, recordings, emergent writing samples, video clips, and photographs for your language and literacy portfolio. At the end of each day of teaching, write down your reflections about the ways young children speak, listen, write, and read.

This implementation exercise is crucial for your understanding of the language and literacy key experiences and ways to support them. Do not be discouraged if things do not go the way you expect them to. It is only with practice that adults learn from children how they construct knowledge about language and literacy and how their communication initiatives can be supported.

Exercise 14

Child Assessment: COR Items Related to Language and Literacy

One way to assess preschool children's understanding and use of language and literacy is to match their anecdotes (collected each day and discussed at daily team planning) with the most relevant level descriptors for items Q–V from the High/Scope Child Observation Record (COR) for Ages 2½–6. These COR items are presented on the facing page. Based on the following anecdotes about Andy, at what level (1–5) would you place him on COR item R? (After making your own assessment, you may wish to look at the item R level suggested for Andy on p. 154 of this chapter.)

> 2/12 At work time at the sand table, Andy said, "You know, sand is made from ground-up rocks, so this sand must be made from white rocks."

> 2/28 At work time, when the power went out in the classroom, Andy said, "The sun doesn't go out because the electricity doesn't go to it."

> 3/11 At work time, when Andy flipped the sand timer over to signal cleanup time, he said, "If this was electric, it couldn't work."

> 3/16 At work time, while playing with the doll house, Andy rearranged the furniture by putting the nightstand and the lamp between the two beds, saying "They can both get some light if I move the lamp to the middle."

> 3/25 At work time in the block area, Andy made several Power Rangers out of Bristle Blocks and said, "These two small guys need one battery, but these two big guys need two batteries."

Exercise 15

Language and Literacy Issues to Ponder and Write About

▶ A. Why do many early childhood educators wish to teach young children to recite, recognize, and write alphabet letters?

▶ B. In an active learning setting, how do children learn about alphabet letters and letter sounds?

▶ C. Children who lack hearing, sight, or speech nevertheless retain the desire to communicate. Why is it important for adults to focus on their communication initiatives rather than on their deficits?

▶ D. What is the relationship between *language and literacy* and *creative representation*?

COR Item Q. Understanding speech

Level 1   Child seldom responds when spoken to by others.
Level 2   Child follows simple directions ("Come to the circle").
Level 3   Child responds to simple, direct, conversational sentences.
Level 4   Child participates in ordinary classroom conversation.
Level 5   Child follows multistep or complex directions.

Supporting Anecdotes:

COR Item R. Speaking

Level 1   Child does not yet speak or uses only a few one- or two-word phrases.
Level 2   Child uses simple sentences of more than two words.
Level 3   Child uses sentences that include two or more separate ideas.
Level 4   Child uses sentences that include two or more ideas with descriptive details ("I stacked up the red blocks too high and they fell down").
Level 5   Child makes up and tells well-developed, detailed stories, rhymes, or songs.

Supporting Anecdotes:

COR Item S. Showing interest in reading activities

Level 1   Child does not yet show interest in reading activities.
Level 2   Child shows interest when stories are read.
Level 3   Child asks people to read stories or signs or notes.
Level 4   Child answers questions about a story that has been read or repeats part of the story.
Level 5   Child often reads a book or tells the story while turning the pages.

Supporting Anecdotes:

COR Item T. Demonstrating knowledge about books

Level 1   Child does not yet pick up books and hold them conventionally.
Level 2   Child picks up books and holds them conventionally, looking at the pages and turning them.
Level 3   Child picture-reads, telling the story from the pictures on the cover or in the book.
Level 4   Child follows the print on a page, moving his or her eyes in the correct direction (usually left to right and top to bottom).
Level 5   Child appears to read or actually reads a book, pointing to the words and telling the story.

Supporting Anecdotes

COR Item U. Beginning reading

Level 1   Child does not yet identify letters or numbers.
Level 2   Child identifies some letters and numbers.
Level 3   Child reads several words, or a few simple phrases or sentences ("I love Mom").
Level 4   Child reads a variety of sentences.
Level 5   Child reads simple stories or books.

Supporting Anecdotes:

COR Item V. Beginning writing

Level 1   Child does not yet attempt to write.
Level 2   Child writes using squiggles and marks as letters.
Level 3   Child copies or writes identifiable letters, perhaps including own name.
Level 4   Child writes some words or short phrases besides own name.
Level 5   Child writes a variety of phrases or sentences.

Supporting Anecdotes:

E. Some children are very quiet. How do they have fun with language?

F. How do emergent reading and emergent writing serve a non-English-speaking child in an active learning early childhood setting where English is the language spoken?

G. How does young children's understanding of grammar emerge?

H. To support children's language and literacy development, why is it important for adults to curb their own need to talk and to instead spend a lot of time listening to children?

I. How is children's talking related to later reading comprehension?

Related Publications

Evans, Betsy. 1996. "All the Ways Preschoolers Read." *High/Scope Extensions* (September): 1–3.

Frede, Ellen. 1984. *Getting Involved: Workshops for Parents*, 77–181. Ypsilanti, MI: High/Scope Press.

Gainsley, Suzanne. 1999. "Message Board: A Preschool Communication Center." *High/Scope Extensions* (October): 1–3.

Graves, Michelle. 1989. *The Teacher's Idea Book: Daily Planning Around the Key Experiences*, 19–25. Ypsilanti, MI: High/Scope Press.

High/Scope Child Observation Record (COR) for Ages 2½–6. 1992. Ypsilanti, MI: High/Scope Press.

Hohmann, Charles. 1998. "Reading Research: New Findings." *High/Scope Extensions* (March/April): 5.

How Young Children Learn to Read in High/Scope Programs: A Series of Position Papers. 2001. Ypsilanti, MI: High/Scope Press.

Maehr, Jane. 1991. "Right! Young Children Can Write!" In *Supporting Young Learners: Ideas for Preschool and Day Care Providers*, Nancy A. Brickman and Lynn S. Taylor, eds., 77–86. Ypsilanti, MI: High/Scope Press.

Maehr, Jane M. 1991. *High/Scope K–3 Curriculum Series: Language and Literacy.* Ypsilanti, MI: High/Scope Press.

McDonald, Bettye. 1991. "Communication: Why It's So Important in the High/Scope Curriculum." In *Supporting Young Learners: Ideas for Preschool and Day Care Providers*, Nancy A. Brickman and Lynn S. Taylor, eds., 71–76. Ypsilanti, MI: High/Scope Press.

Morrison, Kathy, and Tina Dittrich. 2000. *Literature-Based Workshops for Language Arts—Ideas for Active Learning, Grades K–2.* Ypsilanti, MI: High/Scope Press.

Storer, Eileen, Marilyn Barnwell, Chantal LaFortune, et. al. 1998. "Supporting Children's Language Choices." *High/Scope Extensions* (November/December): 1–3.

Related Videos

Adult-Child Interactions: Forming Partnerships With Children. 1996. Color video, 60 min. Ypsilanti, MI: High/Scope Press.

High/Scope K–3 Curriculum Series: Language & Literacy. 1990. Color video, 17 min. Ypsilanti, MI: High/Scope Press.

Language and Literacy (Preschool Key Experience Series). 2000. Color videotape, 60 min. Ypsilanti, MI: High/Scope Press.

Answer to Exercise 14

Andy's level on COR item R:

Level 3 on the basis of anecdotes from 2/28, 3/16

Level 4 on the basis of anecdotes from 2/12, 3/11, and 3/25

Level 4 overall

> **P**reschoolers are beginning to appreciate, understand, and make decisions about themselves and the people in their world. . . . The social relations young children form with peers and adults are profoundly important because it is from these relationships that preschoolers generate their understanding of the social world."
>
> —*Educating Young Children*, pp. 375, 376

12

Initiative and Social Relations

Initiating and Carrying Out Individual and Group Work

Carry out the individual and group work described below.

- *Individual work:* Think of something you would particularly like to do for the next hour or so. Then, tell your plan to a friend, and get started. After you have completed your idea or come to a stopping point, share something about what you did with the friend to whom you told your plan.

- *Group work:* With a group of friends, make a plan to do something cooperatively, and then do it. For example, you might make up a cooperative game; choose a poem and together present it through dance, mime, painting, or music; plan an overnight camping, hiking, or canoe trip; create a group sculpture using scrap materials; or act out a scientific or mathematical concept.

Based on your individual and group work, in your own words, define *initiative* and *social relations*.

Recalling Your Own Initiatives and Relationships

With a partner or several friends, discuss and record your answers to the following questions.

▶ A. What do you remember about making choices, solving problems, taking care of your own needs, and expressing feelings as a young child? As an older child?

▶ B. How did your family and friends respond to your initiatives, choices, and ideas?

▶ C. In what ways do you currently express initiative?

▶ D. To what extent did your parents/ guardians/relatives believe that young children should be encouraged to make choices, solve problems, take care of their own needs, and express their feelings in words?

▶ E. What do you remember about relationships you formed with adults and peers as a young child? As an older child?

▶ F. What collaborative play do you remember participating in as a child?

▶ G. Within your family, how did people deal with social conflict? In school, how did adults deal with social conflict?

▶ H. How did you and your peers deal with social conflict among yourselves?

▶ I. List words you associate with each of the terms *conflict, power,* and *problem solving.*[27]

❶ With which of the three terms do you have the most negative associations? The fewest negative associations?

❷ What is the relationship between these three terms? What opportunities for a balance of power (sharing control) and problem solving do conflicts provide?

---

[27]*This exercise was created by High/Scope certified trainer Betsy Evans as part of a workshop series on a problem-solving approach to conflict.*

❸ How might your attitudes toward conflict and power influence your willingness to deal with them?

▶ J. For a week, keep a log of the initiatives and social relations you engage in or observe in your daily life. At the end of the week, write down your reflections on your findings.

Exercise 3

Understanding Initiative and Social Relations

This exercise is based on the discussion of "Characteristics of Preschoolers' Initiative and Social Relations" and "The Construction of Social Understanding" on *EYC* pp. 375–377.

▶ A. What is *intentionality*? How is it related to choice? To intrinsic motivation? To active learning?

▶ B. What is Moore saying about the role of conflict and encouragement in young children's *desire for friendships* (*EYC* p. 376)?

▶ C. What is Asher saying about the conflict young children often face between their initiatives and their social relationships?

▶ D. What examples can you give of the kinds of *social competence* Radke-Yarrow describes (*EYC* p. 376)?

▶ E. According to Kohlberg and Likona, what is the relationship between children's social interactions and the knowledge they construct about interpersonal relations (*EYC* p. 376)?

▶ F. What is Hartup saying about the role friendships play in children's overall development (*EYC* p. 377)?

▶ G. How do social relationships and initiative influence and temper each other?

Exercise 4

Expressing Intentions

▶ A. What **intentions** (choices, plans, decisions) are expressed by the following children from the anecdotes on *EYC* pp. 378–379? During what **time of day** are they expressing them? Use a chart like the following to organize your answers.

Child(ren)	Intention Expressed	Time of Day

❶ Andrew/Alana ❻ Colin/Nicholas

❷ Amanda ❼ Aimee

❸ Petey ❽ Megan

❹ Jonah ❾ Julia

❺ Alana ❿ Mark/Daniel

▶ B. Children express many of their choices and decisions through gestures and actions. What choices and decisions are implied by the actions and gestures of the children in the photographs on the following *EYC* pages?

❶ p. 10   ❺ p. 48
❷ pp. 14–15 ❻ p. 379
❸ p. 17   ❼ p. 381
❹ p. 23

▶ C. What choices, plans, and decisions have you seen and heard some of your study children from earlier chapters make throughout the day?

▶ D. Why is choice an essential ingredient of active learning?

▶ E. In an active learning setting, why do children make choices and decisions throughout the day rather than just at planning time?

▶ F. What is Elkind saying about initiative and interference with initiative on *EYC* p. 169?

Exercise 5

Problem Solving

▶ A. Read the anecdotes on *EYC* p. 381. What strikes you about the problems Isaac, Hannah, Jonah, and Alana are solving?

▶ B. What kind of knowledge are the children in these problem-solving situations constructing about the physical world, other people, and themselves?

▶ C. What problems have some of your study children encountered in play? How have they solved or tried to solve them?

▶ D. What does the knot-tying photo sequence on *EYC* p. 382 tell you about this child's approach to problem solving?

Taking Care of One's Own Needs

▶ A. What physical, social, and emotional needs are the following children taking care of in the anecdotes and photographs on *EYC* pp. 383–385?

① Alex   **⑥** Isaac

② Wendy   **⑦** Erin

③ Andrew   **⑧** Jason

④ Isaac   **⑨** Photo on p. 384

⑤ Abby   **⑩** Photo on p. 385

▶ B. Read "In the Eye of the Beholder: Dressing in Two Different Social Climates" (*EYC* p. 50). What strikes you about this scenario in terms of the key experience *taking care of one's own needs?*

▶ C. What physical, social, and emotional needs have you seen some of your study children taking care of?

▶ D. Young children *want* to do things for themselves. Why is it important for them to be able to follow through on their self-help initiatives?

Expressing Feelings in Words

▶ A. What feelings are the following children describing in the anecdotes presented on *EYC* pp. 385–386?

① Andrew   **⑦** Corrin

② Aimee   **⑧** Jonah

③ Kacey   **⑨** Abby

④ Brian   **⑩** Anya/Isaac

⑤ Bryant   **⑪** Abby/Hannah

⑥ Chelsea   **⑫** Jason

▶ B. In "'I Want My Mommy!' A Cry for All Ages" (*EYC* p. 387), what feelings do Chris and Christina express and how do they express them?

▶ C. At the fire station (*EYC* pp. 387–388), what are Timmy's feelings and how does he indicate them?

▶ D. What feelings are children expressing in the three stories they tell on *EYC* p. 389, first column?

▶ E. What feelings do some of your study children express? How?

▶ F. On what occasions do you remember expressing feelings as a young child? How did you express them?

▶ G. Although preschool-aged children are developing the capacity to name and talk about their feelings, they often express feelings through gestures and actions. Why might this be the case?

Participating in Group Routines

▶ A. In the anecdotes on *EYC* p. 389, what group routines are the following children participating in?

① Isaac   **④** Deanne/Kalynn

② Megan   **⑤** Brian

③ James   **⑥** Jason

▶ B. What group routines have you seen some of your study children participating in?

▶ C. In an active learning setting, what role does choice play insofar as children's participation in group routines is concerned?

▶ D. In the story of Ricky at small-group time (*EYC* p. 391, third column), how is Ricky expressing his feelings and making choices about the way he participates in small-group time?

Being Aware of the Needs of Others

▶ A. In the anecdotes on *EYC* pp. 391–392, what strikes you about the children's sensitivity to the needs and feelings of their peers?

▶ B. Which anecdote is your favorite? Why?

▶ C. How are children responding to the needs and feelings of their peers in the photographs on *EYC* pp. 392 and 394?

▶ D. How have you seen some of your study children responding to the feelings, interests, and needs of others?

▶ E. On *EYC* p. 392, what is Harris saying about the relationship between children's capacity to represent and their capacity to notice and respond to the feelings and needs of others?

▶ F. Read "Preschoolers Care for One Another" on *EYC* p. 393. How does William Ayers's story about Cameron support McCoy's and Master's observations about young children on *EYC* p. 392?

Exercise 10

Building Relationships

▶ A. In the anecdotes on *EYC* pp. 394–395, how are the following children building relationships with peers and adults?

❶ Brian
❷ Kacey
❸ Mikey
❹ Aimee
❺ Petey
❻ Alana
❼ Callie
❽ Corrin (about Ben)
❾ Kenneth
❿ Corrin (about Sam)
⓫ Bryant
⓬ Douglas
⓭ Jonah
⓮ Isaac
⓯ Colin

▶ B. How have some of your study children built relationships with peers and adults?

▶ C. According to Hartup and Moore, why are peer relationships among young children important (*EYC* p. 395)?

▶ D. What do Sroufe and Fleeson mean when they say (on *EYC* pp. 395–396) that "early relations forge one's expectations concerning relationships. Expectations are carriers of relationships"?

Exercise 11

Playing Together

▶ A. In the anecdotes on *EYC* pp. 399 and 400–401, **what play ideas** draw the following children together? In **what type of play**— *exploratory play, constructive play, pretend play, games*—are the children engaged? Organize your answers in a chart like this.

Children	Collaborative Play Ideas	Play Type

❶ Brian/Kenneth/Bryant (p. 399)
❷ Anna/Jessa
❸ Matthew/Emily
❹ Peter/Jason
❺ Amanda/Colin/Ashley/Nicholas
❻ Emma/Maria
❼ Ashley/Isaac
❽ Eli/Evan/Jason/Peter/Isaac
❾ Anna/Jessa (p. 400)
❿ Tommy, Randy
⓫ Hillary/Hannah (p. 401)
⓬ Max/Athi
⓭ Caroline/Ilana
⓮ Callie/Aimee/Corrin/Chelsea
⓯ Corey/Jeff

▶ B. With whom do some of your study children play collaboratively? What collaborative play situations have you observed?

▶ C. What is the relationship between the initiative and social relations key experience *creating and experiencing collaborative play* and the creative representation key experience *pretending and role playing*?

▶ D. On *EYC* p. 399, Das and Berndt describe criteria children use for selecting playmates. Explain how each of these criteria, listed in (1)–(5), might apply to Bryant's decision to join Anna and Douglas (*EYC* pp. 401–402).

❶ Lack of aggressive behavior
❷ Similarity
❸ Sociability
❹ Perceptions of being liked by peer
❺ Prior association

▶ E. On *EYC* p. 399, what do Rubin and Everett have to say about the opportunity for growth that is provided by collaborative play?

▶ F. Why do you think collaboration increases the complexity of children's play?

▶ G. What role does choice play in collaborative play?

▶ H. Are all young children ready to engage in collaborative play at the same age? Why or why not?

▶ I. What do the photographs on *EYC* pp. 396, 398, 400, 401, and 402 suggest to you about the spirit and nature of children's collaborative play?

Exercise 12

Solving Social Conflicts

▶ A. In the anecdotes on *EYC* p. 403, what needs lead to the social conflicts experienced by the following children? What, if any, objects are involved in each dispute?

❶ Jonah/Owen ❸ Alice/Sam

❷ Colin/Nicholas ❹ Emma/Joe

▶ B. What social conflicts have you seen some of your study children involved in, and what, if any, objects have been involved?

▶ C. Why does conflict arise between young children in the course of their play? How does social conflict within what Rubin and Everett (*EYC* p. 399) call "egalitarian relationships" promote children's social, emotional, and intellectual understanding?

Exercise 13

Supporting Children's Initiative and Social Relations Throughout the Day

▶ A. Exercises (1)–(5) concern *providing a psychologically safe and supportive climate* for children.

❶ Read Holloway and Reichhart-Erickson's statement about the adult's role in children's development of social competence (*EYC* p. 396). How is their statement related to the elements of support discussed in *EYC* Chapter 2—*sharing of control between children and adults, focusing on* *children's strengths, forming authentic relationships with children, making a commitment to support children's play, and adopting a problem-solving approach to social conflict?*

❷ How would you interpret what Katz and McClellan are saying about the need for firmness (*EYC* p. 396) in terms of *forming authentic relationships with children?*

❸ Which of the following two adult statements would be more supportive to a child? Why?

• "You're being too loud, Brin. You're driving me crazy!"

• "I feel frustrated by such a loud voice, Brin. I can't hear what other people are saying."

❹ According to Howes (*EYC* p. 397), having stable relationships with adults and peers has positive effects on young children. Conversely, what adverse effects does a constantly changing cast of adults and peers have on young children's sense of safety and support?

❺ Review the examples of reasonable, routine expectations for preschool-aged children listed on *EYC* p. 391. List the expectations you have for the young children in your care, and identify which ones are consistent, agreed upon, suited to children's development and understanding. Which ones might you want to modify in light of what you know about active learning?

▶ B. How are the adults listed in (1)–(4) *patient with the children?*

❶ Becki, scenario on *EYC* p. 383

❷ Neenah, scenario on *EYC* p. 383

❸ Jackie, scenario on *EYC* p. 384

❹ Adult, conversation on *EYC* p. 393

▶ C. How are adults responding to children's needs and feelings by *looking at situations from the child's point of view* in the *EYC* scenarios listed in (1)–(5)?

❶ Jason and the sand, p. 382

❷ Jonah and his blanket, p. 384

❸ Kenneth digging a hole, p. 385

❹ Timmy and the fire station, pp. 387–388

❺ Mikey joining role play, pp. 402–403

▶ D. Exercises (1)–(4) concern *listening to children.*

❶ According to Dimidjian, what is the role of the adult who listens to children's concerns (*EYC* p. 388)?

❷ What role did Beth play for Kacey (*EYC* p. 389)? How?

❸ What strikes you about the adult's role as listener in the three scenarios on *EYC* pp. 393–394?

❹ Read "Genuine Conversations" (*EYC* p. 397). What is "a sense of shared quest" and why is it important in conversations between children and adults?

▶ E. Exercises (1)–(4) concern using the six *problem-solving steps for resolving conflicts:* (1) approach calmly; (2) acknowledge feelings; (3) gather information; (4) restate the problem; (5) ask for ideas for solutions, and choose one together; (6) be prepared to give follow-up support.

❶ What strikes you about the problem-solving process Emma, Joe, and Betsy participate in (*EYC* pp. 403, 405)?

❷ In the dispute over the spoon in "Effective Mediation" (*EYC* p. 406), how did the solution evolve? How did Betsy, the teacher, support the process?

❸ In Sara's and Mei Mei's dispute in "Effective Mediation" (*EYC* p. 406), how does Betsy, the teacher, turn a tattling situation back to the children for problem solving?

❹ What strikes you about Luke and Lawrence's problem-solving process as it unfolds in the scenario on the facing page?[28] In the margins beside the scenario, note (by number) which of the six problem-solving steps is occurring.

▶ F. Read through the *initiative and social relations support strategies* in the checklist on pp. 164 of this study guide (which also appears on *EYC* p. 407). Under each of the key experiences on this checklist, check off the support strategies you are already using, write an "E" in front of the strategies you have not used but would like to explore, and then read about each of these strategies in *EYC*.

Exercise 14

Child Study: Creating an Initiative and Social Relations Portfolio

As you teach, student teach, or observe your study children from earlier chapters, create an initiative and social relations portfolio by collecting materials such as the following:

- Anecdotes related to each initiative and social relations key experience
- Samples of children's plans
- Tapes or transcripts of children's problem-solving conversations

[28]*This real-life scenario was provided by preschool teacher and High/Scope certified trainer Rachel Underwood as part of a High/Scope workshop series on a problem-solving approach to conflict.*

- Videotape clips or photographs of children's initiatives and collaborative play

When your initiative and social relations portfolio is complete, find an opportunity to present it to teaching teams in your center, parents of preschoolers, or fellow early childhood students. Assembling and explaining your portfolio to others will add to your own understanding of the way children initiate ideas and relate to peers and adults.

Exercise 15

Initiative and Social Relations Scenarios: What Would You Do?

Based on your understanding of the initiative and social relations key experiences and the support strategies discussed on *EYC* pp. 378–407, describe how you might interact with and support the preschool children in the following scenarios.

▶ A. *At large-group time, the children decide which roles they want as they prepare to re-enact a favorite story,* **The Three Billy Goats Gruff.** *"Sheila and me will be the trolls," says Derrick. "Me, too!" adds Victor. Other children decide to be goats of various sizes. Several children make themselves into a "bridge for the trolls to hide under." "I'm 'na be the monkey!" says Josef. "There is no monkey is this story," Les tells Josef. "Well, yes 'cause I tell the baby goats to watch out, okay?" "You mean in a tree?" Les asks. "Yeah!" says Josef.*

How might you support Josef's choice?

▶ B. *At work time, Brendan tries three different ways of connecting the Lasy builders to carry out an idea he has in mind. "I just don't get it!" he*

says and tries again.

How might you support Brendan's problem solving?

▶ C. *Rachel can't get any glue to come out of her squeeze bottle. First, she looks for another bottle to use, but the other glue bottles are either in use or do not work any better than the one she already has. Then she tries to unscrew the top, and Douglas helps her. Once the top is off, she looks inside and says, "All gone!" Finding the gallon container of glue under the sink, she and Douglas unscrew the top, and Rachel pours glue from the gallon container into her bottle. Glue runs into the small bottle and also down the sides onto the table.*

How might you support Rachel as she takes care of her own needs?

▶ D. *Lanie's friends call her over to the big slide they are sliding down in the park. Lanie runs to you and clings to your leg, saying "I scared! I scared!"*

How might you support Lanie?

▶ E. *One morning at greeting circle, 2-year-old Leroy sits in his mom's lap, watching children come to the book area and "read" to one another. Kenneth notices Leroy and says, "He needs a book!" Kenneth goes to the bookshelf, picks out* **The Big Book of Cars and Trucks,** *and gives it to Leroy. Leroy hides his face against his mom.*

How might you support Kenneth and Leroy?

▶ F. *At work time in the house area, Leah and Kelly put on long gloves and try to decide who will be "Beauty." Leah wants Kelly's bracelet, so*

A Conflict Between Luke and Lawrence

Problem-Solving Process	Step Number	Problem-Solving Process	Step Number
Luke and Lawrence are 3 years old. They attend a child care center in a hospital where their parents work. It is the middle of work time. Luke and Lawrence are both tugging on the new baby stroller and hitting each other. "I want it!" Luke shouts. "I want it!" Lawrence shouts. Both children start to cry. Rachel, the teacher, moves quickly and calmly toward the two boys. She gets down on their physical level and gently puts her hands on each of them. "Luke, you look angry," she says. "Lawrence, you look angry, too. It's not okay to hit when you are angry, but we can talk about what is making you feel upset." Both children stop crying and look at the teacher, who keeps her voice soft and her body language gentle as she says, "What is happening here? What seems to be the problem?" "I had the stroller, and I want it!" says Luke. "I want it!" says Lawrence. Rachel, noticing that both children's emotions are escalating, intervenes by saying "So, Luke, you want the stroller, and Lawrence, you want the stroller too. So the problem is that you both want the stroller." Everyone appears to consider this statement. "Hmmm," Rachel continues, "I wonder what you could do about that? How can you solve this problem?" Everyone is silent. Rachel feels somewhat uncomfortable in the silence, but she waits for the children to respond. Suddenly, Luke's face lights up. "We could buy a new one!" he says excitedly. Rachel wants to support Luke's solution and says, "I wonder how that could happen." Luke curls up his nose and says, "Nah," and returns to deep thought. Then he says, "We could *make* another one!" "Is there a way we could do that?" Rachel asks. "Yes, in the block area," Luke says, "and Lawrence could play with it!" Rachel checks this idea with Lawrence. "If we build another stroller, would you like to play with it, Lawrence?" she asks. "No," replies Lawrence. "It doesn't sound like that solution will work," says Rachel. "Do you have any other ideas?"		Rachel asks a group of children playing nearby for ideas about ways to solve Luke and Lawrence's problem. Sara looks up from the car she is pushing and says, "Share," then returns to her play. "Sara says you could share," Rachel says to Luke and Lawrence. "What does that mean?" "We could *both* push the stroller *together!*" Luke says. Again, Rachel checks this idea with Lawrence: "Lawrence, Luke says you could both push the stroller together. What do you think of that idea?" "But I want to push it all by myself!" Lawrence says. "Um," says Rachel, "does anyone else have any suggestions?" David looks up from his puzzle. "They could take turns," he says. "Yes!" says Luke. "I could push the stroller all the way down there [points to the wall at the far end of the center] and back here, and then I could give it to Lawrence, and he could push it all the way down there and back and give it to me!" "What do you think of that idea?" Rachel asks Lawrence. "How about if Luke pushed the stroller all the way down to the wall and back to you, and you pushed it all the way down to the wall and gave it back to Lawrence?" "Yes," Lawrence replies. "So, you decided to take turns," Rachel says. "Luke, you are going to push the stroller first, and when you have pushed it to the wall and back, you are going to give it to Lawrence." "Yes," Luke says. "Well, it looks like you have solved the problem of both wanting to play with the stroller. Lawrence, what will you do while you are waiting for Luke to give the stroller to you?" "I want you to wait with me and watch Luke," Lawrence replies. "Sure, I can do that," says Rachel. "Usually when I'm waiting I like to read a book. Could I do that?" "No," says Lawrence. "I just want you to wait with me." "Sure," says Rachel. Luke and Lawrence continue playing with the stroller, taking turns for the next 35 minutes until the end of work time.	

Initiative and Social Relations Strategies: A Summary

Making and expressing choices, plans, and decisions
___Establish an option-rich environment and consistent daily routine.
___Express and maintain interest in the choices children make.
___Give children time to make choices, plans, and decisions.
___Encourage children to make choices and decisions throughout the day.

Solving problems encountered in play
___Encourage children to describe the problems they encounter.
___Give children time to generate their own solutions.
___Assist frustrated children.

Taking care of one's own needs
___Provide children with time to do things for themselves.
___Encourage children to use common tools.
___Support children's attempts to take care of their emotional needs.

Expressing feelings in words
___Establish and maintain a supportive environment.
___Acknowledge and accept children's feelings.
___Listen for the names children give to their feelings.
___Talk with children about their concerns.
___Encourage children to tell stories.

Participating in group routines
___Establish consistent group routines:
___High/Scope daily routine elements
___Group maintenance routines
___Reasonable expectations
___Make active learning a part of group routines.
___Focus on children's interests, intentions, and strengths.

Being sensitive to the feelings, interests, and needs of others
___Respond to children's feelings, interests, and needs.
___Recognize and comment on children's sensitivities.
___Support children's concerns for absent group members.

Building relationships with children and adults
___Establish supportive relations with children:
___Treat children with kindness.
___Have genuine conversations with children.
___Maintain a stable group of children and adults.
___Look for relationships between children.
___Refer one child to another.

Creating and experiencing collaborative play
___Provide materials that encourage collaborative play.
___Provide space for collaborative play.
___Watch for children playing together.
___Encourage children who play together to plan and recall together.
___Allow time for collaborative play to evolve.
___Form partnerships with emerging players.
___Provide opportunities for collaborative play at small-group time.

Dealing with social conflict
___Keep children's developmental characteristics in mind:
___Acknowledge and talk about what each child is feeling.
___Engage children as active participants in the problem-solving process (rather than solve problems for them).
___Give children specific information.
___Maintain a supportive environment to keep conflicts at a minimum:
___Maintain limits and expectations for behavior that are *developmentally appropriate.*
___Provide many choices for play.
___Establish and follow a consistent daily routine.
___Model respectful ways of interacting with others and using materials.
___Plan for transitions.
___Help children resolve conflicts when they arise:
___*Step 1:* Approach the situation calmly.
___*Step 2:* Acknowledge children's feelings.
___*Step 3:* Gather information.
___*Step 4:* Restate the problem.
___*Step 5:* Ask for ideas for solutions, and choose one together.
___*Step 6:* Be prepared to give follow-up support.

she can be "Beauty," but Kelly says, "No. It's mine, and I'm not giving it to you." They finally decide that Leah can be "Beauty" and Kelly can be "Beauty Jasmine" and wear her bracelet. When Megan comes over and puts on another pair of long gloves, Leah tells her, "You can't be a Beauty 'cause we already have enough." Megan sits with her gloves on and watches.

How might you support what appears to be Megan's desire to join this play?

▶ G. *Callie, Corrin, Chelsea, and Aimee are cutting and tearing construction paper into tiny bits. "We're making that throwing stuff like they have at weddings," they tell you.*

How might you support the children's collaborative play?

▶ H. *Jack and Dan are tugging on one pair of blue sunglasses that they both want to wear. Leah, another child, offers the boys a pair of red sunglasses, which they reject. Still holding onto the blue sunglasses, they begin to hit each other with their free hands.*

How might you use the six problem-solving steps to help Jack and Dan resolve this dispute?

Exercise 16

Implementation Study: Trying Out Initiative and Social Relations Support Strategies

If you are currently teaching or student teaching or can work in an early childhood setting over a period of time, try out the initiative and social relations support strategies on *EYC* p. 407 during the child-initiated and adult-initiated times of the day. Support children's initiative, social relations, and problem solving at work time and outside time. Plan and carry out a small-group time and a large-group time around children's initiatives and social relations. Collect anecdotes, recordings, photographs, and samples of children's plans for your portfolio. At the end of each day of teaching, write down your discoveries about the ways young children initiate ideas and relate to peers and adults.

This implementation exercise is crucial for your understanding of the initiative and social relations key experiences and ways to support them. Do not be discouraged if things do not go the way you expect them to. It is only with practice that adults learn from children how they construct knowledge about themselves and others and how to encourage their initiatives and attempts at problem solving.

Exercise 17

Child Assessment: COR Items Related to Initiative and Social Relations

One way to assess preschool children's initiative and social relations is to match their anecdotes (collected each day and discussed at daily team planning time) with the most relevant level descriptors for items A–I from the High/Scope Child Observation Record (COR) for Ages 2½–6. These COR items are presented on the following two pages. Based on the following anecdotes about Leah, at what level (1–5) would you place her on COR item I? (After making your own assessment, you may wish to look at the item I level suggested for Leah on p. 168 of this chapter.)

7/7 At work time, Leah and Kelly put their arms around each other and hugged.

7/15 At work time in the art area, Leah and Madison were picking out stamps to use. Leah said, "I'll get the ones I like, and you get the ones you like, okay?"

7/30 At work time in the toy area, when Kelly was crying, Leah said, "Do you want me to play with you?" Kelly looked up. "I'm trying to make her feel better," Leah said to Carol, a teacher, and then turned again to Kelly. "Do you want me to make a silly face?" Kelly nodded yes and stopped crying.

7/31 At work time playing beauty shop, Leah said to Kelly, "I asked Santa for a dolly, but he brought me a doggie instead." "I got a doctor kit!" Kelly said. "Hey, that's no fair! I would like a doctor kit!" Leah replied.

8/9 At small-group time, Leah and Madison put their chairs and paints together and began to paint on the same sheet of paper. "This is fun!" Leah said to Madison.

Exercise 18

Initiative and Social Relations Issues to Ponder and Write About

▶ A. How is encouraging children to make choices, plans, and decisions related to the role of citizens in a democracy?

▶ B. What choices do people have about their interactions with adults and children?

COR Item A. Expressing choices

Level 1   Child does not yet express choices to others.
Level 2   Child indicates a desired activity or place of activity by saying a word, pointing, or some other actions.
Level 3   Child indicates desired activity, place of activity, materials, or play-mates with a short sentence.
Level 4   Child indicates with a short sentence how plans will be carried out ("I want to drive the truck on the road").
Level 5   Child gives detailed description of intended actions ("I want to make a road out of blocks with Sara and drive the truck on it").

Supporting Anecdotes:

COR Item B. Solving problems

Level 1   Child does not yet identify problems.
Level 2   Child identifies problems, but does not try to solve them, turning instead to another activity.
Level 3   Child uses one method to try to solve a problem, but if unsuccessful, gives up after one or two tries.
Level 4   Child shows some persistence, trying several alternative methods to solve a problem.
Level 5   Child tries alternative methods to solve a problem and is highly involved and persistent.

Supporting Anecdotes:

COR Item C. Engaging in complex play

Level 1   Child does not yet take initiative in choosing materials or activities.
Level 2   Child shows interest in simple use of materials or simple participation in activities.
Level 3   Child, acting alone, uses materials or organizes active play involving two or more steps.
Level 4   Child, acting alone, carries out complex and varied sequences of activities.
Level 5   Child joins with others in carrying out complex and varied sequences of activities.

Supporting Anecdotes:

COR Item D. Cooperating in program routines

Level 1   Child does not yet follow program routines.
Level 2   Child sometimes follows program routines.
Level 3   Child participates in program routines when directed to do so.
Level 4   Child participates in program routines without being asked.
Level 5   Child continues program routines even when an adult is not nearby.

Supporting Anecdotes:

COR Item E. Relating to adults

Level 1   Child does not yet interact with adults in the program.
Level 2   Child responds when familiar adults initiate interactions.
Level 3   Child initiates interactions with familiar adults.
Level 4   Child sustains interactions with familiar adults.
Level 5   Child works on complex projects with familiar adults (shares labor, follows rules).

Supporting Anecdotes:

COR Item F. Relating to other children

Level 1   Child does not yet play with other children.
Level 2   Child responds when other children initiate interactions.
Level 3   Child initiates interactions with other children.
Level 4   Child sustains interactions with other children.
Level 5   Child works on complex projects with other children (shares labor, follows rules).

Supporting Anecdotes:

COR Item G. Making friends with other children

Level 1   Child does not yet identify classmates by name.
Level 2   Child identifies some of the children by name and occasionally talks about them.
Level 3   Child identifies a classmate as a friend.
Level 4   Child is identified by a classmate as a friend.
Level 5   Child appears to receive social support from a friend and shows loyalty to the friend.

Supporting Anecdotes:

COR Item H. Engaging in social problem solving

Level 1   Child does not yet work with others to solve a conflict, but instead runs away or uses force.
Level 2   Child finds acceptable ways to get others to pay attention to problems (does not hit or kick to get attention).
Level 3   Child requests adult help in solving problems with other children.
Level 4   Child sometimes attempts to solve problems with other children independently, by negotiation or other socially acceptable means.
Level 5   Child usually solves problems with other children independently (shares materials, takes turns).

Supporting Anecdotes:

COR Item I. Understanding and expressing feelings

Level 1   Child does not yet express or verbalize feelings.
Level 2   Child expresses or verbalizes feelings, but sometimes in unacceptable ways.
Level 3   Child shows awareness of the feelings of others.
Level 4   Child usually expresses feelings in acceptable ways.
Level 5   Child responds appropriately to the feelings of others.

Supporting Anecdotes:

► C. Why might adults sometimes be uneasy with the choices children make?

► D. What are some of the choices you have made that are different from the choices your parents and grandparents made?

► E. Why do some adults feel uncomfortable when young children do things for themselves?

► F. Are the feelings of young children any more or less complex than the feelings of older people? Why or why not?

► G. Who usually expresses feelings more openly, young children or adults? Why?

► H. What are the pros and cons of avoiding social conflict?

Related Publications

Evans, Betsy. 1996. "Helping Children Resolve Disputes and Conflicts." "Watch Your Language!" "Punishment: What Does It Teach?" "Language That Sets Limits." "From Superheroes to Problem Solving." "'Super Strategies' for Superheroes." In *Supporting Young Learners 2: Ideas for Child Care Providers and Teachers*, Nancy A. Brickman, ed., 27–56. Ypsilanti, MI: High/Scope Press.

Evans, Betsy. 2002. *You Can't Come to My Birthday Party! Conflict Resolution With Young Children.* Ypsilanti, MI: High/Scope Press.

Frede, Ellen. 1984. *Getting Involved: Workshops for Parents*, 271–97. Ypsilanti, MI: High/Scope Press.

Graves, Michelle. 1996. *The Teacher's Idea Book 2: Daily Planning Around Children's Interests*, 69–87. Ypsilanti, MI: High/Scope Press.

Graves, Michelle. 1998. "Children's Problem-Solving: When to Step In, When to Stand Back." *High/Scope Extensions* (September): 1–3.

Graves, Michelle. 1999. "A Child Development Approach to Rules and Limits." *High/Scope Extensions* (November/December): 1–3.

High/Scope Child Observation Record (COR) for Ages 2½–6. 1992. Ypsilanti, MI: High/Scope Press.

Related Videos

Adult-Child Interactions: Forming Partnerships With Children. 1996. Color video, 60 min. Ypsilanti, MI: High/Scope Press.

Initiative and Social Relations. 2001. Color videotape, 60 min. Ypsilanti, MI: High/Scope Press.

Supporting Children in Resolving Conflicts. 1998. Color videotape, 24 min. Ypsilanti, MI: High/Scope Press.

Supporting Children's Active Learning: Teaching Strategies for Diverse Settings. 1989. Color video, 13 min. Ypsilanti, MI: High/Scope Press.

Answer to Exercise 17

Leah's level on COR item I:

Level 4 on the basis of anecdotes from 7/7, 7/15, 7/31, 8/9

Level 5 on the basis of anecdote from 7/30

Level 4 overall

*B*y the time they reach preschool age, children move with increasing skill, and they exhibit a newfound ability to tailor the way they move to suit their play and intentions.

—*Educating Young Children*, p. 411

13

Movement

Moving in a Variety of Ways

Experiencing Movement

To carry out this activity, you will need a group of friends and a ball or balloon for each person:

- Sit in a circle, and choose a person to begin. That person moves one part of his or her body, and then everyone else tries out the same movement. Then a person on either side of the first person selects a movement to try, for everyone else to imitate. Repeat this process as you take turns around the circle. Move various body parts in as many ways as you can without leaving your spot.

- Stand up. As a group, pick two points in the room or outside to move between. Then move between these points in as many ways as you can think of—running, crawling, rolling, hopping, and so forth.

- Still standing, blow up a balloon for each person, or pass out the balls. Then, try all the ways you can think of to move with balloons or balls.

- Form a circle. Take turns expressing a common action, feeling, object, or animal *through movement alone*. As a group, guess what each person is expressing through his or her motions.

- Remain in a circle. As a group, take turns doing the following: In words alone (no motions), describe a common movement or movement sequence, for example, tooth brushing or pushing a grocery cart. Listeners act out the movement you are describing.

- As a group, decide on a song or nursery rhyme you all know. As you sing or say it together the first time, rock back and forth or sway from side to side to the steady beat of the song or rhyme. As you sing it or say it the second time, with both hands, pat the steady beat on some part of your body. As you sing it or say it the third time, walk to the steady beat.

Observing Movement

Find a comfortable location in a public place, and spend 15–20 minutes watching people move. For example, you might watch people in a park, people along a busy street, workers at a construction sight, soccer players, toddlers in a child care center.

Based on your activities *experiencing movement* and *observing movement*, what is movement? How and why do people move?

Recalling Movement Experiences

With a partner or several friends, discuss and record your answers to the following questions.

► A. What do you remember about early movement experiences, such as learning to walk, riding a tricycle, pulling a wagon, dancing, digging, climbing stairs?

► B. What do you remember about later play-related movement, such as skating, skipping, swimming, playing tag or hide-and-seek, surfing, skateboarding, playing hopscotch, jumping rope, playing kick ball or toss-and-catch, sledding, tumbling, swinging, climbing trees, building forts?

C. What do you recall about organized movement experiences, such as gym class, sports leagues and teams, dance class, marching band, martial arts?

D. What kinds of movement experiences do you currently enjoy?

E. What kinds of physical-labor movement have you experienced, such as moving boxes, painting, washing windows, digging, picking fruits or vegetables?

F. For a week, keep a movement log. Record the kinds of movement you observe and engage in each day. At the end of the week, when you review your entries, write down your reflections on your findings.

Exercise 3

Moving in Place

A. What is *nonlocomotor* movement? Give some examples.

B. In the three anecdotes on *EYC* p. 412, what nonlocomotor movements are children engaged in?

C. What nonlocomotor movements do you see in the photos on the following *EYC* pages?

1 p. 105   6 p. 381
2 p. 149   7 p. 414
3 p. 156   8 p. 441
4 p. 267   9 p. 448
5 p. 270

D. What nonlocomotor movements have you seen some of your study children from other chapters engaging in?

E. Recall or watch an infant who does not yet crawl or walk. What nonlocomotor movements do you see?

F. Perform some nonlocomotor movement. Then try varying the quality of the movement by changing its direction, size, level, intensity, shape, and timing. (For explanations of these movement qualities, see *EYC* p. 414.) Give examples of when, in young children's play, you might see variations in these qualities of nonlocomotor movement.

Exercise 4

Moving From Place to Place

A. What is *locomotor* movement? Give examples.

B. In the five anecdotes on *EYC* p. 415, what locomotor movements are the following children performing?

1 Kenneth and group
2 Mikey
3 Corrin
4 Playground group
5 Anna/Jessa

C. What locomotor movements do you see in the photos on the following *EYC* pages?

1 p. 14   11 p. 318
2 p. 29   12 p. 415
3 p. 52   13 p. 416
4 p. 65   14 p. 417
5 p. 70 (top photo)   15 p. 435
6 p. 157   16 pp. 483 and 207
7 p. 159   17 p. 489
8 p. 255
9 p. 278
10 p. 311 (bottom photo)

D. What locomotor movements have you seen some of your study children engaging in?

E. Perform a locomotor movement. Then try varying the direction, size, level, pathway, intensity, and timing of the movement. (For explanations of these movement qualities, see *EYC* pp. 417–418.) Give examples of when, in young children's play, you might see variations in these qualities of locomotor movement.

Exercise 5

Moving With Objects

A. In each of the five anecdotes on *EYC* p. 418, describe the movement with objects.

B. Describe the **movement** and the **objects being used** in the photos on the following *EYC* pages.

① p. 10
② p. 17
③ p. 36
④ p. 83
   (left-hand photo)
⑤ p. 118
⑥ p. 124
⑦ p. 163
⑧ p. 219
⑨ p. 239
⑩ p. 261
⑪ p. 272
⑫ p. 286
⑬ p. 287

⑭ p. 300
⑮ p. 325
⑯ p. 389
⑰ p. 402
⑱ p. 410
   (bottom left photo)
⑲ p. 410
   (top right photo)
⑳ p. 411
㉑ p. 418
㉒ p. 419
㉓ p. 443
㉔ p. 490
㉕ p. 514

▶ C. With what objects do some of your study children enjoy moving?

Exercise 6

Moving Creatively

▶ A. In each of the four anecdotes on *EYC* p. 420, how is the child expressing creativity in movement?

▶ B. In the photos on the following *EYC* pages, how are children expressing creativity in movement?

① p. 36
② p. 152
   (left-hand photo)
③ p. 207

④ p. 311
⑤ p. 318
⑥ p. 325
⑦ p. 420

▶ C. How have you seen some of your study children moving creatively?

▶ D. During what kinds of play (exploratory play, constructive play, pretend play, games) might you see preschool children moving creatively? Why?

Exercise 7

Describing Movement

▶ A. What motions are the following children describing in the anecdotes on *EYC* pp. 422–423?

① Petey
② Callie
③ Mikey
④ Aimee

⑤ Brian
⑥ Callie
⑦ Brian
⑧ Christy

▶ B. How does Kayla represent movement in her drawing on *EYC* p. 423?

▶ C. How have you heard some of your study children describing movement?

▶ D. Exercises (1)–(3) concern how movement is related to language and literacy.

① How is *describing movement* related to the language and literacy key experience *describing objects, events, and relations?*

② Return to the 11 language and literacy anecdotes on *EYC* p. 353. In which of these anecdotes do children describe movement?

③ When during their play and interactions might children particularly want to describe movement?

Exercise 8

Making Up and Trying Out Movement Directions

▶ A. What movement directions are children making up or carrying out in the four anecdotes on *EYC* p. 424?

▶ B. What movement directions are children expressing in the seven bulleted examples on *EYC* p. 425?

▶ C. In terms of the ingredients of active learning—materials, manipulation, choice, language from children, support from adults—why is it important for young children to make up and try out their own movement directions?

Exercise 9

Feeling and Expressing Steady Beat

▶ A. What is *steady beat?*

▶ B. How is *steady beat* different from *rhythm?*

▶ C. How are the following children feeling and expressing steady beat in the anecdotes on *EYC* pp. 425–426?

① Kenneth
② Joanie
③ LJ

④ Sarah
⑤ Athi
⑥ Kenneth/ Douglas

D. How have you seen some of your study children expressing steady beat?

E. Exercises (1)–(4) concern *steady beat as part of everyday life.*

❶ What experiences have you had as a child and as an adult in which steady beat has played an important role?

❷ Under what circumstances does steady beat create a communal bond among people? How?

❸ What kinds of human endeavors rely on steady beat?

❹ How is steady beat related to clocks, timers, wheels turning on axles?

Exercise 10

Supporting Children as They Move Throughout the Day

A. *Providing space and materials:* What space and materials **are available** in your early childhood setting or in the setting of one of your study children to provide opportunities for each of the following types of locomotor movement? What **would you add** to the setting to enhance the opportunity for each type of movement?

❶ Running	**❹** Skipping
❷ Jumping	**❺** Marching
❸ Hopping	**❻** Climbing

B. In your current early childhood setting or in the setting of one of your study children, what objects of the following types (1)–(5) **are available** for children to move with? What objects of each type would you **like to add?**

❶ Materials that are light, floating, easy to set in motion as children move

❷ Novel materials to hold and move with

❸ Foot-focused materials

❹ Tossing, throwing, catching, striking, kicking materials

❺ Big things for pushing and pulling

C. In your current early childhood setting or in the setting of one of your study children, what objects **are available** for children to **rock,** to **swing,** and to **pedal?** What objects for rocking, swinging, and pedaling would you **like to add?**

D. *Supporting movement as it occurs in children's play and interactions throughout the day:* Look through the text of *EYC* pp. 412–429. What kind of spontaneous **movement** do adults observe in children? During what **type of play** does it occur? What movement **key experience** does it involve? How does the adult provide **support?** The sample chart below contains one example to get you started.

E. *Playing movement games with children:* Again, look through the text of *EYC* pp. 412–429. What kind of **movement games** do adults play with children? What movement **key experience** does each game encourage? The sample chart below contains an example to get you started.

EYC Page #	Movement Game	Movement KE
p. 413	"Statues"—twirl and freeze	Moving in nonlocomotor ways (freezing) Moving in locomotor ways (twirling)

F. In *EYC* Chapter 13, find all the examples of adults *incorporating children's ideas into movement games and experiences.* The

EYC Page #	Movement	Play Type	Movement KE	Adult Support
pp. 412–413	As Kenneth stays on carpet square to avoid "hot lava," he twists, bends, curls, stretches.	Pretend play	Moving in nonlocomotor ways	Watched. Talked with Kenneth at recall time about how he moved.

sample chart below contains an example to get you started.

EYC Page #	Movement Game or Experience	Child's Idea
p. 413	Stretch, bend, twist to music	(Watch for and imitate children's modifications.)

▶ G. Select a movement game you enjoy playing with children or a game from the list you made for exercise E. How might you use words but not motions to describe the game to children? How might you use motions but not words?

▶ H. Read through the *movement support strategies* in the checklist on the following page (which is from *EYC* p. 430). Under each movement key experience on the checklist, check off the support strategies you are already using, write "E" in front of the strategies you have not used but would like to explore, and read about each of these strategies in *EYC*.

Child Study: Creating a Movement Portfolio

As you teach, student teach, or observe your study child(ren), create a movement portfolio by collecting materials such as the following:

- Anecdotes related to each movement key experience
- Recordings or transcripts of children describing movement, making up movement directions

- Videotape clips or photographs of children moving in nonlocomotor and locomotor ways, moving with objects, moving creatively, feeling and expressing steady beat

When your movement portfolio is complete, find an opportunity to present it to teaching teams in your center, parents of preschoolers, or fellow early childhood students. Assembling and explaining your portfolio to others will add to your understanding of the ways young children move and understand movement.

Movement Scenarios: What Would You Do?

Based on your understanding of the movement key experiences and the support strategies listed on *EYC* p. 430, decide how you might interact with and support the preschool children in the following scenarios.

▶ A. *At work time, Malika is curled up in the wooden baby bed, playing "baby" all by herself. She turns over on her back and begins to "bicycle" her legs and wave her arms, saying "Ga-ga, ma-ma."*

How might you support Malika's nonlocomotor movement within the context of her play?

▶ B. *At work time, Jason and Elron are running up a ramp they have built of boards and large hollow blocks and jumping off the high end. "Let's see who jumps farthest!" Elron says to Jason.*

How might you support Jason and Elron's locomotor play?

▶ C. *Justin is pretending to be a horse at cleanup time. He is "galloping" on all fours from area to area, pawing the ground, rearing up on his "hind legs," and neighing.*

How might you support Justin's creative movement as a way to involve him in the cleanup process?

▶ D. *At outside time, Maggie is standing at the bottom of the slide, rolling a big rubber ball up and down the slide.*

How might you support Maggie's movement experience?

▶ E. *After small-group time, Maxwell is the first person to arrive at the rug for large-group time. He pats his knees to a steady beat and, after a bit, begins to chant, "Come to circle time. Come to circle time."*

How might you support Maxwell's expression of steady beat?

▶ F. *At large-group time, Hansi describes how he wants everyone to move: "Shake your hands fast and then really fast!"*

How might you support Hansi's movement idea and directions?

▶ G. *At large-group time, following a field trip to the local high school's marching band rehearsal, you, your teaching partner, and all the children are marching around the room to the steady beat of a Sousa march. After marching awhile, Cara says, "I tired." She sits down on a large hollow block and moves her feet up and down to the beat of the march music.*

How might you support Cara's way of keeping a steady beat?

Movement Strategies: A Summary

Moving in nonlocomotor ways (anchored movement: bending, twisting, rocking, swinging one's arms)

___Encourage children to explore a wide variety of positions:

___Watch for and acknowledge positions children assume as they play.

___Play position games with children.

___Look for opportunities to swing, bend, rock, and twist with children.

___Play games that focus on one movement at a time.

___Attend to the direction, size, level, intensity, shape, and timing of children's nonlocomotor movement.

Moving in locomotor ways (nonanchored movement: running, jumping, hopping, skipping, marching, climbing)

___Provide space and time for children to move.

___Encourage children to move about in a variety of ways:

___Look for and acknowledge all the ways children move about.

___Play games that call for nonanchored movement.

___Attend to the direction, size, level, pathway, intensity, and timing of children's nonanchored movement.

Moving with objects

___Provide children with time and space to move with objects.

___Provide a wide variety of easy-to-manipulate materials:

___Add light, floating materials that are easily set in motion by children's movement.

___Add novel objects to hold and move with.

___Add foot-focused materials.

___Add balls and other materials for tossing, throwing, kicking, striking, and catching.

___Add big things for pushing and pulling.

Expressing creativity in movement

___Watch for and acknowledge children's creative use of movement.

___Encourage children to solve movement problems at small-group, large-group, and transition times.

___Talk with children about how they are moving.

___Encourage children to represent their experiences through movement.

Describing movement

___Listen as children describe movement in their own way.

___Find opportunities to comment on how children are moving.

___Encourage children to plan, do, and recall movement.

___Plan large-group experiences in which children use a single word to describe a single movement.

Acting upon movement directions

___Listen for the movement directions children generate as they play.

___During group games, give or demonstrate simple movement directions:

___Provide verbal directions.

___Give children visual movement demonstrations.

Feeling and expressing steady beat

___Provide equipment on which children can rock, swing, and pedal.

___Build rocking to the beat and patting the beat into music and language experiences:

___Distinguish *beat* from *rhythm*.

___Rock, sway, and pat a steady beat while singing and chanting.

___Pat a steady beat when children are playing musical instruments.

___Provide opportunities for children to walk to a steady beat.

___Look for and acknowledge children's movement to a steady beat as they play.

___Play group games with a steady beat.

Moving in sequences to a common beat

___Name the body part associated with each movement in the sequence.

___Keep movement sequences clear and simple.

Implementation Study: Trying Out Movement Support Strategies

If you are currently teaching or student teaching or can work in an early childhood setting over a period of time, try out the movement support strategies listed on *EYC* p. 430 as opportunities arise during the child-initiated and adult-initiated times of the day. Support children's movement at work time and outside time. Plan and carry out a small-group time and a large-group time around children's interests in movement. Collect anecdotes, photographs, and recordings for your movement portfolio. At the end of each day of teaching, reflect on and record your discoveries about the ways young children move.

This implementation exercise is crucial for your understanding of the movement key experiences and ways to support them. Do not be discouraged if things do not go the way you expect them to. It is only with practice that adults learn from children how they construct knowledge about movement and how to encourage children's movement initiatives.

Child Assessment: COR Items Related to Movement

One way to assess preschool children's understanding and use of movement is to match the children's anecdotes (collected each day and discussed at daily team planning time) with the most relevant level descriptors for items M–P from the High/Scope Child Observation Record (COR) for Ages 2½–6. These COR items are presented on the next page. Based on the following anecdotes, at what level (1–5) would you place Erica on COR item M? (After making your own assessment, you may wish to look at the item M level suggested for Erica on p. 179 of this chapter.)

1/9 Erica held the small wastebasket with one hand and walked around the art table, brushing paper scraps into the basket with the other hand.

2/7 Erica walked several steps as she bounced the large playground ball.

3/16 Erica pushed a small rubber tire ahead of her as she climbed up the steps of the slide. At the top, she let the tire roll down the slide, then slid down after it.

3/30 At cleanup time, Erica carried two hollow blocks on her arms, and with her feet, shoved a third block over to the block shelf.

4/15 At outside time, Erica figured out how to get onto the neck of the dinosaur climber, put her feet through the hole, and slide down the pole.

Movement Issues to Ponder and Write About

▶ A. How is the movement key experience *expressing creativity in movement* related to the creative representation key experiences?

▶ B. How might culture, climate, and social norms influence the ways people move?

▶ C. How is human movement influenced by the movement of plants, animals, water, wind, and other natural elements?

▶ D. What causes people to want to move their bodies?

▶ E. What is the relationship between movement and nonverbal communication?

▶ F. What is the relationship between movement key experiences and the ingredients of active learning?

Related Publications

High/Scope Child Observation Record (COR) for Ages 2½–6. 1992. Ypsilanti, MI: High/Scope Press.

Strubank Ruth. 1991. "Music and Movement Throughout the Daily Routine." In *Supporting Young Learners: Ideas for Preschool and Day Care Providers,* Nancy A. Brickman and Lynn S. Taylor, eds., 104–111. Ypsilanti, MI: High/Scope Press.

Weikart, Phyllis S. 1990. *Movement in Steady Beat.* Ypsilanti, MI: High/Scope Press.

Weikart, Phyllis S. 1991. "Movement Experiences: Needed, But Neglected." In *Supporting Young Learners: Ideas for Preschool and Day Care Providers,* Nancy A. Brickman and Lynn S. Taylor, eds., 96–103. Ypsilanti, MI: High/Scope Press.

Weikart, Phyllis S. 1997. *Movement Plus Rhymes, Songs, & Singing Games: Activities for Children Ages 3–7,* 2nd Edition. Ypsilanti, MI: High/Scope Press.

Weikart, Phyllis S. 1999. "Moving with Purpose: Rhymes, Action Songs, and Singing Games." *High/Scope Extensions* (January-February): 1–3.

COR Item M. Exhibiting body coordination

Level 1   Child's movements are not yet coordinated.

Level 2   Child shows coordination in climbing steps and walking and seldom runs into objects or other children.

Level 3   Child alternates feet while walking up the stairs without holding on to the bannister; tosses and catches a ball or a beanbag.

Level 4   Child moves around while manipulating an object.

Level 5   Child engages in complex movements (skipping, dribbling a ball).

Supporting Anecdotes:

COR Item N. Exhibiting manual coordination

Level 1   Child uses whole hand to grasp and pick up small objects.

Level 2   Child uses appropriate finger and hand motions to handle or pick up small objects.

Level 3   Child fits materials together and takes them apart (pegs and pegboards, nuts and bolts).

Level 4   Child manipulates small objects with precision (threading a large needle, stringing small beads, fitting tiny pegs into holes).

Level 5   Child performs precise actions involving opposing hand movements (buttoning clothing, starting and zipping up a zipper).

Supporting Anecdotes:

COR Item O. Imitating movements to a steady beat

Level 1   Child does not yet imitate actions performed to a beat.

Level 2   Child imitates single movements presented one at a time (puts hands on knees).

Level 3   Child responds to the beat of songs or instrumental music with simple movements (patting knees to the steady beat).

Level 4   Child responds to the beat of songs or instrumental music with more complex movements (walking or jumping to the beat).

Level 5   Child chants or sings while performing a sequence of movements to the beat.

Supporting Anecdotes:

COR Item P. Following music and movement directions

Level 1   Child does not follow spoken instructions for music and movement.

Level 2   Child follows spoken instructions for a single movement ("Raise your hands").

Level 3   Child follows spoken instructions for a two-part or two-step movement ("Put your hands on your head; now put your hands on your shoulders").

Level 4   Child follows spoken instructions for more complex sequences of movements ("Put your hands on top of your head; now put one hand on your ear and the other hand on your nose").

Level 5   Child describes and carries out movement sequences (patting and saying the name of two body parts twice each: "Head, head, shoulders, shoulders, knees, knees, toes, toes").

Supporting Anecdotes:

Weikart, Phyllis S. 1997. *Teaching Folk Dance: Successful Steps.* Ypsilanti, MI: High/Scope Press.

Weikart, Phyllis S., and Elizabeth B. Carlton. 1995. *Foundations in Elementary Education: Movement.* Ypsilanti, MI: High/Scope Press.

Weikart, Phyllis S. 2000. *Round the Circle: Key Experiences in Movement for Children,* 2nd ed. Ypsilanti, MI: High/Scope Press.

Related Recordings

Movement Plus Rhymes, Songs, & Singing Games: Music Recordings. 1997. Available on cassette and CD. (Produced by Phyllis S. Weikart). Ypsilanti, MI: High/Scope Press.

Rhythmically Moving 1–9. 1982–1988. Series of musical recordings, available on cassettes, LP records, or CDs (Phyllis S. Weikart, creative director; *Guides to Rhythmically Moving* by Elizabeth B. Carlton and Phyllis S. Weikart are also available). Ypsilanti, MI: High/Scope Press.

Answer to Exercise 14

Erica's level on COR item M:

Level 3 on the basis of anecdote from *4/15*

Level 4 on the basis of anecdotes from *1/9, 2/7, 3/16, 3/30*

Level 4 overall

Music is an important ingredient of early childhood because young children are so open to hearing, making, and moving to music. Music actually becomes another language through which young music-makers learn about themselves and others.

—**Educating Young Children**, *p. 433*

Music

14

Exercise 1

Exploring Music

Experiencing the Preschool Music Key Experiences.

To carry out this activity, you will need a partner or several friends.

- Together, choose and play a recorded musical selection. As the music plays, sway from side to side or rock back and forth to the steady beat of the music. Then, each move in place or around the room in whatever way the music inspires you to move.

- Go outside, and silently listen to and list all the sounds you hear.

- Use your voices to make a variety of sounds. For example, you might try yodeling, sighing, or making siren noises, animal noises, or ghost noises.

- Take turns singing your names, using just two notes or pitches. Then, make up a song using a simple phrase (such as "Good morning"), your names, and just two notes or pitches.

- List some of the children's songs you know. Then, together, sing one of them that you all know. To begin, have one person give the starting pitch by singing "One, two, ready, sing. Row, row, row, your boat" (use the opening words of whatever song you decide to sing).

- Explore some simple musical instruments (for example, drum, tambourine, bells, rhythm sticks, cymbals, rattles). Play them in as many ways as you can think of.

Listening to and Watching Music-Makers

To carry out this activity, find a group of live musicians, and watch and listen as they play, rehearse, or improvise.

Based on your activities *experiencing the preschool music key experiences* and *listening to and watching music-makers,* how would you define music? Why do people make and listen to music?

Exercise 2

Recalling Your Own Experiences With Music

With a partner or several friends, discuss and record your answers to the following questions.

► A. What kinds of *live* music (at home, at church, in school, in the community) do you remember hearing as a child?

► B. What kinds of *recorded* music do you remember hearing as a child?

► C. What kinds of sounds do you recall making as a child? Under what circumstances?

► D. What experiences as a music-maker—singing, playing instruments, making up songs or tunes—did you have as a young child? As an older child?

► E. What *choices* did you have about making music as a young child? As an older child?

► F. Who in your family, school, or community encouraged and supported your interest in music?

▶ G. What kinds of music do you particularly like to listen to? To play? To sing?

▶ H. For a week, keep a sound and music log. Note which sounds and music you hear (on the radio, at the movies, and so forth) and the music you make as you hum, whistle, sing, play, compose. At the end of the week, review your entries, and describe your reflections about music in your daily life.

Exercise 3

Moving to Music

▶ A. How are children moving to music in the four anecdotes on *EYC* p. 434?

▶ B. How are children moving to music in the photographs on the following *EYC* pages?

❶ pp. 49 and 272

❷ p. 65

❸ p. 156 (left-hand photo)

❹ p. 267

❺ p. 276

❻ p. 278

❼ p. 291

❽ p. 428

❾ p. 432

❿ p. 435

⓫ p. 440

⓬ p. 443

⓭ p. 445

▶ C. For each anecdote in exercise A and photograph in exercise B, indicate the *movement* key experience(s) involved. For example, in the first anecdote on *EYC* p. 434, the 18 preschoolers who are rocking forward and back to the beat of "Row, Row, Row Your Boat" are *moving in nonlocomotor ways* and *feeling and expressing steady beat.*

▶ D. How have you seen some of your study children moving to music?

▶ E. What evidence do you have from your work with young children to support Gardner's observation (on *EYC* p. 433) about how young children relate music and movement?

▶ F. How have you seen young children respond to *live* music?

Exercise 4

Enjoying the World of Sound

▶ A. What sounds are children hearing and identifying in the four anecdotes on *EYC* p. 435? In the photograph on *EYC* p. 436?

▶ B. What sounds have some of your study children noticed and identified during the course of their play?

▶ C. How is the music key experience *exploring and identifying sounds* related to the creative representation key experience *recognizing objects by sight, sound, touch, taste, and smell*? How is it related to the classification key experience *exploring and describing similarities, differences, and the attributes of things*?

▶ D. What sounds do you associate with different parts of your day? With certain familiar places? With locales to which you have traveled?

▶ E. What sounds are heard daily by the children in your early childhood setting or by some of your study children in their setting? What sounds attract their attention?

Exercise 5

Vocal Exploration

▶ A. How are children exploring their singing voices in each of the three anecdotes and in the photograph on *EYC* p. 437?

▶ B. Look again at the children mentioned in exercise A. As they explore their singing voices, what kinds of play are they engaged in—exploratory play, constructive play, pretend play, or games?

▶ C. How have you heard some of your study children exploring their singing voices?

Exercise 6

Developing Melody

▶ A. In the anecdotes on *EYC* p. 438, how are the following children developing melody?

❶ Deola/Corrin

❷ Vanessa

❸ Brian/Alana

❹ Children at snack time

❺ Jonah

❻ Brian

B. How have you observed some of your study children developing melody?

Exercise 7

Singing Songs

▶ A. In the six anecdotes on *EYC* p. 440, what songs are the children singing?

▶ B. What songs do some of your study children know and like to sing?

▶ C. What songs do you remember singing as a young child?

▶ D. What songs have you sung with young children? What have you heard young children singing?

▶ E. During what kinds of play have you heard young children *initiate* singing?

▶ F. Read "Andrew's Song" (*EYC* p. 442) and "Trey's Basketball Song" (*EYC* p. 444). What connections have Andrew and Trey made between singing and writing?

Exercise 8

Playing Musical Instruments

▶ A. In the anecdotes on *EYC* pp. 442–443, what simple musical instruments are the following children playing?

❶ Sarah

❷ Audie/Douglas/Jalessa/Sarah

❸ Alana

❹ Brianna

❺ Nathan/Trey

❻ Jalessa

❼ Lanie/Louie

▶ B. In the photos on the following *EYC* pages, what instruments are children playing?

❶ p. 432 (bottom left photo)

❷ p. 433

❸ p. 442

❹ p. 444

▶ C. What characterizes the instruments children are playing in the photographs on *EYC* pp. 57 (bottom right), 291, and 443?

▶ D. What is the relationship between playing pretend musical instruments and the creative representation key experiences?

▶ E. What real and pretend instruments have you seen and heard some of your study children playing?

Exercise 9

Supporting Young Children as They Hear, Move to, and Make Music Throughout the Day

(Exercise A(3) involves a computer.)

▶ A. Exercises (1)–(3) relate to *providing materials.*

❶ What **musical instruments**, other **sound-producing objects, recorded selections,** and **children's illustrated song books** are available for children in your early childhood setting or in your study child(ren)'s setting? What materials of this kind would you like to add?

❷ What song books do you have as a resource for yourself, to help build your repertoire of songs to sing with young children?

❸ If you have access to a computer and preschool software, try out the programs that provide children with interactive music experiences. (For titles of appropriate software, see the software reviews in the bimonthly magazine *Children's Software Revue:* www.childrenssoftware.com.) Which programs do you or would you like to provide for the children in your early childhood setting?

▶ B. How are adults *following children's musical ideas* in the *EYC* scenarios listed below?

❶ Ruth, p. 435 (second column)

❷ Mikey's teacher, p. 438

❸ Rosa, p. 438

❹ Jackie, p. 439

❺ Beth, p. 439

▶ C. Read through the *music support strategies* in the checklist on the following page of this study guide (which is from *EYC* p. 445). Under each of the music key experiences on the checklist, check off the support strategies you are already using, write "E" in front of the strategies you have not used but would like to explore, and then read about each of these strategies in *EYC*.

Music Strategies: A Summary

Moving to music

___Play a wide variety of music for children.

___Encourage children to create their own ways of moving to music.

___Create simple movement sequences to music with children.

Exploring and identifying sounds

___Assess your environment for sound:

   ___Provide simple musical instruments.

   ___Provide other sound-generating materials.

   ___Provide quiet moments for listening.

___Be aware of sounds that attract children.

___Play "sound" guessing-games with children.

___Encourage children to describe the sounds they hear.

Exploring the singing voice

___Listen for and acknowledge children's creative vocalizations.

___Encourage children to play with their voices.

Developing melody

___Listen for and acknowledge children's use of pitch and melody.

___Play pitch-matching games with children.

___Sing your comments to children.

___Play "Guess This Tune" with children.

Singing songs

___Sing songs with children:

   ___Sing at large-group time.

   ___Sing at work time.

   ___Sing at small-group time.

   ___Sing at outside time.

   ___Sing during parent meetings.

___Begin with motions.

___Encourage children to create their own songs.

Playing simple musical instruments

___Set up a music area.

___Provide opportunities for children to play musical instruments on their own.

___Play musical instruments at small- and large-group times:

   ___Encourage children to create *parades* with musical instruments.

   ___Encourage children to play musical instruments as other children *dance*.

   ___Encourage children to use musical instruments to create sound effects to accompany *storytelling*.

   ___Play musical *stop-and-start games* with some children playing the game and others providing the musical accompaniment.

___Use musical instruments to signal transition times.

Child Study:
Creating a Music Portfolio

As you teach, student teach, or observe your study children, create a music portfolio by collecting materials such as the following:

- Anecdotes related to each of the music key experiences

- Recordings of children exploring sound and melody, singing, and playing musical instruments

- Samples of instruments children make and "music" children "write"

- Videotape clips or photographs of children making and moving to music

When your music portfolio is complete, find an opportunity to present it to teaching teams in your center, parents of preschoolers, or fellow early childhood students. Assembling and explaining your portfolio to others will add to your understanding of young children as music-makers.

Music Scenarios:
What Would You Do?

Based on your understanding of the music key experiences and the support strategies discussed on *EYC* pp. 434–444, decide how you might interact with and support the preschool children in the following scenarios.

▶ A. *At work time in the music area, Kendell, Neil, Babs, and Billy are "band guys" playing drums, bells, tambourine, and xylophone. Neil, the xylophone player, begins to sing "Band guys, band guys, froggy, froggy dew."*

How might you support the "band guys"?

▶ B. *"Ow-ooo, ow-ooo," howls Delise, "ow-ooo, ow-ooo." "What you doing, Delise?" Everlena asks. "I'm not Delise," says Delise, "I'm coyote howling at night time." "Oh," says Everlena, who then joins Delise and also begins to howl.*

How might you support Delise and Everlena as they explore their singing voices?

▶ C. *At large-group time, after singing several of the children's favorite songs, including "The Bear Went Over the Mountain" and "Yellow Bird," Jack says, "I've got a song." Using three notes, he sings, "A rocket goes to the moon and crashes. The people get off and see the aliens. Then they fix up their ship and fly away." The rest of the children listen transfixed as Jack sings.*

How might you support Jack's singing?

▶ D. *"I got to go down to babies," says Kristen, meaning that she wants to go to the infant room down the hallway, a common occurrence in this family-oriented child care center. "That's my baby brother crying!"*

How might you support Kristen's alertness to sound and her sensitivity to her little brother?

▶ E. *At cleanup time, David picks up a rattle in the house area, shakes it with a steady beat, and sings, "Jingle bells, jingle bells . . ." to his own steady beat.*

How might you support David's music experience?

▶ F. *At outside time, the maintenance staff is on a scaffolding, painting the upper story of the building just beyond the playground fence. They are listening to Jamaican reggae music as they paint. Tina and Crystal, as they stand nearby watching the painters, twist from side to side and wave their arms to the beat of the dance music.*

How might you support Tina and Crystal as they move to music?

▶ G. *"Sshh, be quiet!" Tanya tells the other children at the snack table, "I hear something!" Everyone stops what they are doing to listen. "I think it's that hooting thing," says Mack.*

How might you support the children's interest in the sound they hear?

Implementation Study:
Trying Out Music
Support Strategies

If you are currently teaching or student teaching or can work in an early childhood setting over a period of time, try out the music support strategies listed on *EYC* p. 445 as opportunities arise during the child-initiated and adult-initiated times of the day. Support children's music at work time and outside time. Plan and carry out a small-group time and a large-group time around children's interests in music. Collect anecdotes, photographs, recordings, and music samples for your music portfolio. At the end of each day of teaching, write down your reflections about the ways young children construct knowledge about music.

This implementation exercise is crucial for your understanding of the music key experiences and ways to support them. Do not be discouraged if things do not go the way you expect them to. It is only with practice that adults learn from children how they construct knowledge about music and how to encourage their musical initiatives.

Child Assessment: COR Item Related to Music

One way to assess preschool children's understanding and use of music is to match the children's anecdotes (collected each day and discussed at daily team planning time) with the most relevant level descriptors for item O from the High/Scope Child Observation Record (COR) for Ages 2½–6. This item appears at the lower right. On the basis of the following anecdotes, at what level (1–5) would you place Jack on COR item O? (After making your own assessment, you may wish to look at the item O level suggested for Jack on p. 187 of this chapter.)

9/20 At large-group time, Jack swayed from side to side to the steady beat of "Gaelic Waltz."

10/3 At recall time, Jack patted the table to the steady beat of the recall song that Beth, his teacher, sang: "Recall, recall, recall time . . ."

10/14 At large-group time, Jack jumped up and down to the steady beat of "La Raspa."

2/7 At the beginning of recall, while waiting for the rest of his group to gather, Jack used both fists to pound the table to his own steady beat and chanted, "We want recall! We want recall!"

2/20 At outside time, Jack and Daniel sang a three-note song: "We don't want the bad snow. We don't want the bad snow . . ." as they hit piles of snow with the backs of their shovels to the beat of the song.

Music Issues to Ponder and Write About

▶ A. What is the role of music within a culture? Within a community?

▶ B. What attracts young children to music?

▶ C. Why is music an integral part of cinema?

▶ D. What sounds do you hear on a regular basis that your parents and grandparents probably did not hear? What sounds were they used to hearing that you are not?

▶ E. Why do people all over the world rock and sing to their babies?

▶ F. How is the music key experience *singing songs* related to the language and literacy key experience *having fun with language*?

▶ G. Why does music from around the world include some sort of drums?

▶ H. How is the music key experience *playing simple musical instruments* related to the movement key experience *moving in nonlocomotor ways*?

COR Item O. Imitating movements to a steady beat

Level 1   Child does not yet imitate actions performed to a beat.

Level 2   Child imitates single movements presented one at a time (puts hands on knees).

Level 3   Child responds to the beat of songs or instrumental music with simple movements (patting knees to the steady beat).

Level 4   Child responds to the beat of songs or instrumental music with more complex movements (walking or jumping to the beat).

Level 5   Child chants or sings while performing a sequence of movements to the beat.

Supporting Anecdotes:

Related Publications

Carlton, Elizabeth B., and Phyllis S. Weikart. 1994. *Foundations in Elementary Education: Music.* Ypsilanti, MI: High/Scope Press.

High/Scope Child Observation Record (COR) for Ages 2½–6. 1992. Ypsilanti, MI: High/Scope Press.

Strubank, Ruth. 1991. "Music and Movement Throughout the Daily Routine." In *Supporting Young Learners: Ideas for Preschool and Day Care Providers,* Nancy A. Brickman and Lynn S. Taylor, eds., 104–111. Ypsilanti, MI: High/Scope Press.

Weikart, Phyllis S. 1990. *Movement in Steady Beat: Activities for Children Ages 3–7.* Ypsilanti, MI: High/Scope Press.

Weikart, Phyllis S. 1997. *Movement Plus Rhymes, Songs, & Singing Games: Activities for Children Ages 3–7,* 2nd Edition. Ypsilanti, MI: High/Scope Press.

Weikart, Phyllis S. 1999. "Moving with Purpose: Rhymes, Action Songs, and Singing Games." *High/Scope Extensions* (January-February): 1–3.

Related Recordings

Movement Plus Rhymes, Songs, & Singing Games: Music Recordings. 1997. Available on cassette and CD (Produced by Phyllis S. Weikart). Ypsilanti, MI: High/Scope Press.

Rhythmically Moving 1–9. Series of musical recordings, available on cassettes, LP records, or CDs (Phyllis S. Weikart, creative director; *Guides to Rhythmically Moving* by Elizabeth B. Carlton and Phyllis S. Weikart are also available). Ypsilanti, MI: High/Scope Press.

Answer to Exercise 13

Jack's level on COR item O:

Level 3 based on anecdotes from *9/20, 10/3*

Level 4 based on anecdote from *10/14*

Level 5 based on anecdotes from *2/7, 2/20*

Level 5 overall

Classification, the process of grouping things together based on common attributes and properties, is one basic strategy children use to organize the materials, people, and events involved in their play. Through the process of classification, young children begin to construct relationships between similar things and to treat similar materials and situations equivalently.

—*Educating Young Children, p. 447*

15

Classification: Recognizing Similarities and Differences

Exploring and Describing Attributes and Organizing Things Into Groups

Carry out each of the following three activities with one or more partners.

Exploring, Describing, and Grouping Chairs

This activity needs to be done in a room in which there is a moderate to wide variety of chairs.[29]

- Sit in, look at, and otherwise explore all the features of the chairs. Examine and discuss the attributes of each type of chair.

- Together find all the *regular* shapes the chairs incorporate. Then, find and take turns describing all the *irregular* shapes they include.

- Take turns, with one person grouping the chairs that according to some attribute go together, and the other(s) guessing the sorting criteria that was used. Devise at least four ways of grouping the chairs.

- Pick one chair, and together use the chair in as many ways as you can think of.

- Pick another chair, and together make as many *both . . . and* statements about it as you can think of. For example, "This chair is made of both wood and cloth."

- Take turns making *some* and *all* statements about the chairs. For example, "Some chairs have thick cushions," and "All the chairs in this room have rungs."

- Take turns describing a characteristic that does *not* belong to one or more of the chairs. For example, "This chair does not have claw feet," or "These three chairs do not have arms."

Identification of "Flubbyloofers"[30]

All of these objects are flubbyloofers.

Each of these objects is not a flubbyloofer.

Which of these objects are flubbyloofers?

---

[29]*If you cannot locate an assortment of chairs, substitute another set of objects—for example, a variety of shoes, books, dishes, blocks, cups.*

[30]*The flubbyloofer activity appears in David Webster's book* **Brain Boosters** *(Garden City, NY: Natural History Press, 1966), p. 13. Copyright © 1966 by David Webster. The activity was used in an earlier version of this study guide with permission from David Webster and Natural History Press, Garden City, NY.*

- How many attributes distinguish a flubby-loofer from a non-flubbyloofer? What are they?

- Look at your collection of chairs (or other objects) used in the previous activity. Pick out two or more attributes that only some of the chairs have in common. Label the chairs having these attributes with a non-sense name (like "flubbyloofer") that does not reveal what their common attributes are. Then arrange all the chairs in three rows: first, a row containing only "flubby-loofer" chairs; second, a row containing "non-flubbyloofer" chairs; and third, a row containing both "flubbyloofer" and "non-flubbyloofer" chairs.

- Have your partner(s) look at all three rows of chairs and figure out which chairs in the third row are "flubbyloofer" chairs and why.

Sorting Papers[31]

For this activity, you will need a set of 4 in. × 4 in. samples of noticeably different kinds of paper (for example, newspaper, construction paper, glossy paper, kraft paper, facial tissue, wallpaper, waxed paper, cellophane) and a magnifying glass.

- With your partner, examine the properties of the all the paper samples.

- Tear the edge of each paper sample, and look at it with the magnifying glass to examine similarities and differences in the density and coarseness of the papers' fibers.

- Take turns sorting the papers into groups and having the partner(s) figure out your sorting criteria.

---

[31]*This exercise is adapted from the* **High/Scope K–3 Curriculum Series: Science,** *pp. 122–123, 126–127.*

Based on your activities with the *chairs*, with the *flubbyloofers*, and with the *paper samples*, how would you define *classification*?

Exercise 2

Recalling Real-Life Experiences With Classification

With a partner or several friends, discuss and record your answers to the following exercises.

▶ A. What do you remember about sorting and organizing your toys and possessions as a child? What collections did you make?

▶ B. What experiences can you recall that had to do with cleaning up your room?

▶ C. How were dishes, silverware, and cooking utensils organized in your childhood home? To what extent does your current living space reflect these same organizing strategies?

▶ D. Recall your early experiences in a library, a museum, or a store. How were you able to find what you wanted to read, see, or buy?

▶ E. Think of an institution you know fairly well, for example, a school, church, or work place. How are people and tasks sorted and organized within the institution?

▶ F. Think of some paper or report that you have written. In it, how did you sort and organize the ideas you presented?

▶ G. Look at "The High/Scope Preschool 'Wheel of Learning' " on *EYC* p. 6. How does

this chart sort and organize the ideas underlying the High/Scope educational approach?

▶ H. For a week, keep a log of the classification activities you engage in or encounter in your daily life. At the end of the week, write down your reflections on these findings.

Exercise 3

Understanding Classification

The following exercises are based on the discussion of classification on *EYC* pp. 447–448.

▶ A. What does Sugarman mean (on *EYC* p. 447) when she says that "classification is said to exist when two or more distinguishable objects are treated equivalently"?

▶ B. According to Inhelder (on *EYC* p. 447), what is the relationship between classification and active learning?

▶ C. In the child's statement "Anyone who has a thermos is a baby 'cause the thermos has a nipple on top" (on *EYC* p. 447), what equivalency is the preschool-aged speaker constructing? What strikes you about this child's thinking?

▶ D. What do Inhelder and Piaget mean (on *EYC* p. 447) when they say that "the origins of classification . . . can be traced to the prior evolution of language and symbolic representation"?

▶ E. What sorting criteria are preschool-aged children likely to initiate and use in the course of their play?

F. During play, a preschool child (on *EYC* p. 448) says, "We just need the long squares." What strikes you about this child's thinking?

G. What is the difference in logic between the pair of statements in exercise (1)? Between the pair of statements in exercise (2)?

❶ "Only kings and queens wear the crown jewels."

"Only little kids sleep in boxes."

❷ "Bats only leave the cave after sunset."

"I only get married when it's dark."

Exercise 4

Exploring and Describing Similarities, Differences, and Attributes

A. In the anecdotes on *EYC* pp. 448–449, **what object** is each of the following children exploring and **how is the child describing** his or her findings? Use a chart like the following to organize your answers.

Child	Object	Description

❶ Jonah

❷ Kacey

❸ Jacob

❹ Jalessa

❺ Brian

❻ Alana

❼ Kenneth

❽ LJ

❾ Erica

❿ Kenneth

⓫ Audie (last paragraph of p. 449)

⓬ Alana (last paragraph of p. 449)

B. What objects have some of your study children explored and described?

C. How is the classification key experience *exploring and describing similarities, differences, and the attributes of things* similar to the language and literacy key experience *describing objects, events, and relations*? How are these two key experiences different?

D. In which anecdotes on *EYC* p. 353 are children describing similarities, differences, or the attributes of things?

Exercise 5

Shapes

A. Exercises (1)–(7) list the children from the anecdotes on *EYC* p. 451. What strikes you about each child's thinking about shapes?

❶ Trey

❷ Abby

❸ Kenneth

❹ Anna

❺ Jacob

❻ Rachel

❼ Pookie/Angie

B. In the three bulleted examples on *EYC* p. 452, what strikes you about each child's thinking about shapes?

C. What do the photographs on *EYC* pp. 452, 508, 511, and 513 suggest about children's use of shapes during play?

D. How have you seen and heard some of your study children using and describing shapes?

Exercise 6

Sorting and Matching

A. In the anecdotes on *EYC* p. 452, **what** and **how** are the following children sorting and matching?

❶ Tracey

❷ Kacey

❸ Douglas

❹ Julia

❺ Isaac

❻ Alana

❼ Noah

❽ Aimee

❾ Trey

❿ Kristan

⓫ Jason

B. **What** and **how** are the children sorting and matching in the photographs on the following *EYC* pages?

1 p. 14

2 p. 48

3 p. 110 (bottom right photo)

4 p. 122 (top photos)

5 p. 126 (bottom left photo)

6 p. 146 (left-hand photo)

7 p. 211

8 p. 322

9 p. 335

10 p. 446

11 p. 447

12 p. 453

13 p. 454

14 p. 479

▶ C. In the sorting and matching anecdotes on *EYC* p. 452, what objects are children **treating equivalently?** For example, Tracey treats the red pegs and the yellow pegs equivalently—they are all "birthday candles."

▶ D. **When** and **what** have you seen some of your study children sorting and matching?

▶ E. **What** and **how** is Chris sorting and matching in the work time scenario on *EYC* p. 454?

Exercise 7

Using and Describing Something in Several Ways

▶ A. In the anecdotes on *EYC* p. 454, **what** are the following children using or describing and **how** are they using or describing it in several ways?

1 Corey   **4** Lainie/Athi

2 Darla   **5** Douglas/Sarah

3 Lisa

▶ B. What have you seen some of your study children using or describing in several ways?

▶ C. Recall and list common items *you* regularly use in a variety of ways.

▶ D. Are there items that adults in your life tried to persuade you to use only in the "proper" way? Which ones and why?

▶ E. What does a person have to understand about an object to be able to use it in a variety of ways?

Exercise 8

Focusing on Two or More Attributes at Once

▶ A. In the anecdotes on *EYC* p. 456, what two attributes are the following children focusing on?

1 Callie   **5** Hannah

2 Deola   **6** Trey

3 Kenneth   **7** Hannah

4 Douglas   **8** Amanda (second column)

▶ B. In the guessing game scenario on *EYC* pp. 457–458, what strikes you about the types and number of attributes the children keep in mind?

Exercise 9

Some and *All*

▶ A. Under what circumstances are children in the anecdotes on *EYC* pp. 458–459 making observations about *some* and *all?*

▶ B. Based on the anecdotes and discussion on *EYC* pp. 458–459 and based on your own observations, summarize your understanding of preschool children's emerging ability to distinguish between *some* and *all.*

▶ C. How is the classification key experience *distinguishing between "some" and "all"* related to the language and literacy key experiences *talking with others about personally meaningful experiences* and *describing objects, events, and relations?* How is it related to the initiative and social relations key experience *making and expressing choices, plans, and decisions?*

Exercise 10

Using *Not* Statements

▶ A. Read through the anecdotes on *EYC* pp. 459–460 and the bulleted scenarios on *EYC* p. 461. What strikes you about the contexts in which Corey, Jeff, Anna, Jacob, Chelsea, Martin, Deola, Corrin, Kenneth, and Mikey are making *not* statements?

▶ B. How are the bulleted scenarios about Kenneth and Mikey on *EYC* p. 461 related to emergent literacy?

Supporting Children's Classification Throughout the Day

(Exercise B involves a computer.)

▶ A. If you are currently teaching or student teaching, think of your early childhood setting for this exercise about *providing materials* for classification; if you are not teaching, think about the early childhood setting of one of your study children. For each type of classification-related material listed in (1)–(6), list materials **currently in the setting** and list materials **you would like to add.** Use a chart like the following to organize your answers.

Type of Classification-Related Material	Have	Add

❶ Household/natural materials with attractive characteristics

❷ Materials with moving parts

❸ Materials that change

❹ Materials related to children's current interests/immediate purposes

❺ Materials having regular shapes

❻ Loose materials suited to sorting and matching

▶ B. If you have access to a computer and preschool software, try out the programs that provide children with interactive classification experiences. (For titles of appropriate software, see the software reviews in the bi-monthly magazine *Children's Software Revue:* www.childrenssoftware.com.) Which programs do you or would you like to provide for children in an early childhood setting?

▶ C. How are adults *being alert and attentive to children's classification* in the *EYC* scenarios and photographs listed in (1)–(9)?

❶ Jackie, p. 450, first-column scenario

❷ Beth/Becki, p. 450, first-column scenario

❸ Linda, p. 454 scenario

❹ Beth, p. 455, three scenarios

❺ Peter, p. 455 scenario

❻ Becki, p. 456 scenario

❼ Teacher, pp. 457–458 scenario

❽ Rose, p. 459 scenario

❾ Barbara, pp. 460–461 photos

▶ D. In the bulleted scenario on *EYC* p. 451, first column, what step in the problem-solving process is Ann using? (You may wish to review the six problem-solving steps listed in this study guide on p. 164.)

▶ E. How does organizing children's play space into interest areas and labeling materials provide children with ongoing daily experiences with classification?

▶ F. Read through the *classification support strategies* in the checklist on the next page

(which is from *EYC* p. 462). Under each of the checklist's classification key experiences, check the support strategies you are already using, write "E" in front of the strategies you have not used but would like to explore, and then read about each of these strategies in *EYC*.

Child Study: Creating a Classification Portfolio

As you teach, student-teach, or observe some of your study children, create a classification portfolio by collecting materials such as these:

- Anecdotes related to each classification key experience

- Samples of children's drawings and paintings in which children have created similar objects or grouped similar things together; labels children have made for new materials

- Recordings or transcripts of children describing objects, referring to more than one attribute, using *some, all, not*

- Videotape clips or photographs of collections children gather, materials children sort and match as part of their play, children sorting and matching at cleanup time

When your classification portfolio is complete, find an opportunity to present it to teaching teams in your center, parents of preschoolers, or fellow early childhood students. Assembling and explaining your portfolio to others will add to your understanding of the way young children create equivalencies.

Classification Strategies: A Summary

Exploring and describing similarities, differences, and the attributes of things

___Provide interesting materials.

___Support children as they collect things.

   ___Make time for collecting.

   ___Listen for children's comments and descriptions.

___Accept the descriptive names children use for objects.

___Encourage children to make labels for new materials.

___As children solve problems, listen for their references to attributes, similarities, and differences.

Distinguishing and describing shapes

___Provide a variety of regularly shaped materials.

___Use regularly shaped materials at small-group time.

___Watch for shape-making play.

___Listen for shape talk.

Sorting and matching

___Provide materials for sorting and matching.

___Consider times for choosing and storing toys as ongoing opportunities for children to sort and match materials.

___Watch for and acknowledge children's spontaneous sorting and matching.

___Ask children to make things that are the same.

Using and describing something in several ways

___Be aware of the various ways children use materials.

   ___Observe children's use of materials.

   ___Acknowledge children's uses of materials.

   ___Refer one child to another.

___Support children's use of materials in problem solving.

Holding more than one attribute in mind at a time

___Listen for children's references to more than one attribute at a time.

___Try using labels that encourage children to sort a set of materials according to two attributes.

___Appreciate the complexity of children's guessing games.

Distinguishing between "some" and "all"

___Store similar materials together.

___Listen for children's use of the words "some" and "all."

Describing characteristics something does not possess or the class it does not belong to

___Encourage children to use the symbol for the "no" concept (∅).

___Watch and listen for children's everyday use of "not."

Classification Scenarios: What Would You Do?

Based on your understanding of the classification key experiences and the support strategies discussed on *EYC* pp. 448–462, decide how you might interact with and support the preschool children in the following scenarios.

▶ A. *At work time, Raina carries an armload of long, rectangular unit blocks to the block shelf and places them carefully, one on top of another. Then she goes back and gathers all the square unit blocks she can carry and stacks them together on the block shelf.*

How might you support Raina's sorting and matching?

▶ B. *At large-group time, Jack, pretending to be an old man, says, "Abracadabra! I'm turning all the children into round, smooth rocks. Now roll, rocks! Roll away from the witch's house."*

How might you support Jack's reference to several attributes within the context of this story re-enactment?

▶ C. *At work time, Frances works intently with clay. After a while she pauses and shows you her "long-neck dinosaur" and her "spiny-back dinosaur."*

How might you support Frances's interest in and attention to the particular attributes of her dinosaur models?

▶ D. *At cleanup time, Brendan tells you, "I found the red button that turns off all the computers!"*

How might you support Brendan's observation of attributes and understanding of *all*?

▶ E. *At snack time outside, Leah looks closely at the popsicle she is eating and at the popsicles the others in her group are eating. "Guess what," she says, "if you have orange on the top, then you have pink on the bottom!"*

How might you support Leah's observations about popsicle attributes?

▶ F. *At work time, Jack and Daniel "fly" to the house area "restaurant" in their "spaceship" by moving their arms up and down. At the restaurant, Daniel says, "We're weightless. We need some spacefood to go."*

How might you support Daniel's and Jack's idea of weightlessness in their spaceship play?

▶ G. *Looking out the window at snack time, Frances notices something about the dinosaur climber. "Look at that orange spot on the dinosaur," she says. The other children look at the climber. "It's shaped like a hand," says Carleen. "Somebody put their hand in paint and stuck it on the dinosaur's head," says Kevin.*

How might you support these children's observations and attention to shape?

▶ H. *At work time, Andy snaps two necklaces together. "Now there's a big circle," he says, putting it over the head of Rover, a friendly dog who is visiting the center for the day.*

How might you support Andy's attention to shape?

▶ I. *At greeting circle, Megan looks up from her book and observes that "Frances is not here yet." Later, as Megan is putting her book away,* she tells you, "If Frances is not coming today, I'm working with Kelly and Leah."

How might you support Megan's observations and use of *not*?

▶ J. *At outside time, Kayla turns over the big tub of balls. "Let's find just the soccer balls," she says to Kacey.*

How might you support Kayla's and Kelly's sorting task?

▶ K. *At outside time, you watch Alex place a small rock in front of his tricycle tire. "That's for a brake," he tells you, "so it won't move while I open this." Then he uses another small rock to pound on a walnut he has placed on the asphalt bike path. "Let's pound this open and see what's in here!" he says, still pounding on the walnut with a rock.*

How might you support Alex's ways of using and describing rocks?

▶ L. *At work time, Kayla works with assorted colors of modeling dough. "This is going to be a cool design," she says, "because I'm going to make it part rainbow and part twisted." As she works on her three-dimensional design, she follows her plan.*

How might you support Kayla's various ways of using modeling dough?

▶ M. *At work time in the art area, Alana watches Megan make a paper fan. "I'm going to do just like that!" Alana says.*

How might you support Alana's desire to make a fan like Megan's?

▶ N. *On a walk around the block, Kevin stops to collect some chestnuts. "Do you know why this one is brown and these ones are green?" he asks you. Then, answering himself, he says, "Because this one [the brown chestnut] is older!"*

How might you support Kevin's observations of similarities and differences?

▶ O. *At the sand table at work time, Rachel makes a "chocolate chip cupcake." "It's not for you," she explains, "it's not for Carol [the other teacher], it's just for the kids."*

How might you support Rachel's description of the classes of people who may and may not eat her cupcake?

Exercise 14

Implementation Study: Trying Out Classification Support Strategies

If you are currently teaching or student teaching or can work in an early childhood setting over a period of time, try out the classification support strategies on *EYC* p. 462 during the child-initiated and adult-initiated times of the day. Support children's classification at work time, cleanup, and outside time. Watch for the classification key experiences as children work with materials at small-group time and as they offer their ideas during large-group experiences. Collect anecdotes, photographs, recordings, and children's drawings and paintings for your classification portfolio. At the end of each day of teaching, write down your reflections about the ways young children create equivalencies.

This implementation exercise is crucial for your understanding of the classification key experiences and ways to support them. Do not be discouraged if things do not go the way you expect them to. It is only with practice that adults learn from children how they construct knowledge about similarities and differences and how to encourage their classification initiatives.

Exercise 15

Child Assessment: COR Items Related to Classification

One way to assess preschool children's understanding and use of classification is to match the children's anecdotes (collected each day and discussed at daily team planning time) with the most relevant level descriptors for items W and X from the High/Scope Child Observation Record (COR) for Ages 2½–6. These items are presented on the facing page. Based on the following anecdotes, at what level (1–5) would you place Carleen on COR item W? (After making your own assessment, you may wish to look at the item W level suggested for Carleen on the facing page.)

> *10/12* At work time, Carleen filled her pegboard with tall and short green pegs. When she noticed that Megan was filling her pegboard with tall pegs of assorted colors, she told Megan, "I did mine by color."

> *10/23* At work time, Carleen sorted out all the purple barrettes (shaped like hearts, bows, stars, cats) and clipped them to her dolly's hair.

> *11/8* At small-group time, Carleen drew three different-sized people holding hands. "This is the big-foot family," she said, " 'cause they all have big feet."

> *11/11* At work time at the sand table, Carleen, using tongs, picked up all the kitty counters of various colors and put them in a bucket.

12/10 At work time at the computer, Carleen played the Fribble game.[32] She selected the Fribbles asked for, including a Fribble with big eyes and straight hair, a green Fribble with stripes, and a red Fribble with curly hair.

Exercise 16

Classification Issues to Ponder and Write About

▶ A. What is the role of active learning and intrinsic motivation in young children's classification experiences?

▶ B. How does the way a learning environment is arranged and equipped affect a child's opportunities to explore attributes, sort, and match things?

▶ C. What relation do you see between the preschool classification key experiences and young children's creative representations?

▶ D. What classification abilities do adults have that preschoolers have not yet developed?

▶ E. How do nonverbal children distinguish between *some* and *all* and communicate the idea of *not?*

▶ F. Why are many early childhood educators focused on teaching children to identify and distinguish shapes but unconcerned about children being able to explore and distinguish other attributes of objects?

---

[32]*This anecdote refers to "Fribble Shop," an activity on the software program* **Thinkin' Things Collection 1** *(Edmark Corporation, 1993).*

COR Item W. Sorting

Level 1 Child does not yet sort objects into groups.

Level 2 Child groups identical objects together.

Level 3 In sorting, child groups objects together that are the same in some way but different in other ways (combines red stars and red circles).

Level 4 In sorting, child groups objects together that are the same in some way and occasionally describes what has been done.

Level 5 In sorting, child groups objects together on the basis of two or more characteristics (includes all the big red circles but not the big red stars or the big blue circles).

Supporting Anecdotes:

COR Item X. Using the words *not, some,* and *all*

Level 1 Child does not yet use the words *not, some,* or *all* or uses them incorrectly.

Level 2 Child uses the words *not, some,* or *all* in conversation, but sometimes uses them incorrectly.

Level 3 Child correctly uses the words *not, some,* and *all* in conversation.

Level 4 Child uses the word *not* to identify the characteristic that excludes an object from a category ("This block is not red like the other ones, so it doesn't go in that group").

Level 5 Child distinguishes between *some* and *all* and uses these terms in categorizing ("We are all children, but some of us are girls").

Supporting Anecdotes:

Related Publications

Blackwell, Frank F., and Charles Hohmann. 1991. *High/Scope K–3 Curriculum Series: Science.* Ypsilanti, MI: High/Scope Press.

Frede, Ellen. 1984. *Getting Involved: Workshops for Parents,* 211–43. Ypsilanti, MI: High/Scope Press.

Graves, Michelle. 1989. *The Teacher's Idea Book: Daily Planning Around the Key Experiences,* 37–43. Ypsilanti, MI: High/Scope Press.

Graves, Michelle. 1996. "Classification: Collecting, Sorting, and Organizing." In *Supporting Young Learners 2: Ideas for Child Care Providers and Teachers,* Nancy A. Brickman, ed., 207–14. Ypsilanti, MI: High/Scope Press.

High/Scope Child Observation Record (COR) for Ages 2½–6. 1992. Ypsilanti, MI: High/Scope Press.

Hohmann, Charles. 1996. "Science in the Elementary Grades: Beyond Dinosaurs and Volcanoes." In *Supporting Young Learners 2: Ideas for Child Care Providers and Teachers,* Nancy A. Brickman, ed., 203–6. Ypsilanti, MI: High/Scope Press.

Post, Jackie. 1996. "Science: Here, There, and Everywhere." In *Supporting Young Learners 2: Ideas for Child Care Providers and Teachers,* Nancy A. Brickman, ed., 193–200. Ypsilanti, MI: High/Scope Press.

Wheel of Learning/Key Experience Card. Laminated card, 8½ × 11 inches. Ypsilanti, MI: High/Scope Press.

Related Video

Thinking and Reasoning in Preschool Children. 1976. Black and white video, 23 min. Ypsilanti, MI: High/Scope Press.

Answer to Exercise 1, "Identification of 'Flubbyloofers'"

A flubbyloofer has two essential attributes: It contains a solid black square and has a corkscrew tail. Therefore, in the last row, the third, fourth, fifth, and sixth objects are flubbyloofers.

Answer to Exercise 15

Carleen's level on COR item W:

Level 3 on the basis of anecdotes from *10/23, 11/11*

Level 4 on the basis of anecdotes from *10/12, 11/18*

Level 5 on the basis of anecdote from *12/10*

Level 4 overall

$\longrightarrow$ Seriation, like the related process of classification, builds on children's awareness of attributes . . . and is another way children learn about their world. . . . In seriation, children assign a logical order to a series of objects based on gradual variations in a single attribute (toy fire engines arranged from largest to smallest) or on a sequence of attributes that repeats (red sequin, blue sequin, red sequin, blue sequin, red sequin, blue sequin).

—*Educating Young Children*, p. 465

16

Seriation: Creating Series and Patterns

Creating Series and Patterns

Carry out the following three activities with two other partners.

Comparing and Seriating Chairs

For this activity, you will need a room in which there is a moderate to wide variety of chairs.[33]

- With your partners, take turns selecting a pair of chairs and comparing the two chairs in the pair in as many ways as you can. For example, within a pair, decide which chair is heavier or which chair has the softer cushion.

- With your partners, take turns arranging three or more chairs in order according to some attribute and having the others look at the arrangement and guess what ordering criteria was used. For example, you might arrange four chairs in order from the *chair with the lowest back* to the *chair with the highest back*.

- With your partners, take turns arranging four or more chairs in a pattern and having the others describe the chosen patterning strategy and decide which chair should be added next to continue the pattern. For example, you might create a simple pattern such as wooden chair, metal chair, wooden chair, metal chair.

- Select as many chairs as there are people in your group, and order the chairs according to some attribute. For example, you might order the chairs from *lowest chair seat* to *highest chair seat*. Then arrange yourselves in order in some way, for example, from shortest person to tallest person. Finally, bring these two ordered sets together by having the shortest person sit in the chair with the lowest seat, the next taller person sit in the chair with the next higher seat, and so on.

Seriating Creatures
(Flubbyloofers and Non-flubbyloofers)

For this activity, photocopy the flubbyloofer and non-flubbyloofer creatures pictured on page 189 of this study guide. You will also need some scissors.

- Cut out two of the creatures, and compare them in as many ways as you can.

- Cut out several of the creatures, and arrange them in some repeating pattern.

- Cut out at least three creatures, and arrange them in order according to some attribute.

- For each of the creatures you arranged in order, create an accessory that can be ordered according to some attribute (for example, boxes in varying sizes, bags of varying heights), and then put the two ordered sets together.

Seriating Paper by Absorbency[34]

For this activity, you will need 2 in. × 2 in. samples of several different types of absorbent paper—paper toweling, napkins, facial tissues—a small cup of water, an eyedropper, a magnifying glass, and a tray to contain spills.

---

[33]*If you cannot locate a room with an assortment of chairs, substitute another set of objects for chairs—for example, a variety of shoes, books, plates, plants, tools.*

[34]*This exercise is adapted from the **High/Scope K–3 Curriculum Series: Science**, pp. 126–127.*

- Test the absorbency of each paper sample by adding drops of water, one at a time, to a spill tray and blotting them up with the sample, one at a time, until the sample will hold no more water. Count and record the number of drops a sample will hold.

- Make a graph that compares the absorbency of the different samples (the number of drops absorbed by each).

- Look at the torn edge of each paper sample with a magnifying glass to see how structure and absorbency are related. What differences in the paper samples might explain why one absorbs more water than another?

Based on the three activities—seriating *chairs*, *creatures*, and *paper*—write your own definition of *seriation*.

Exercise 2

Recalling Seriation Experiences

With a partner or several friends, discuss and record your answers to the following questions.

▶ A. What experiences with seriation do you remember from your early childhood? For example, do you recall arranging your stuffed animals in patterns or in order from smallest to largest, or sorting your baseball cards from most valuable to least valuable?

▶ B. What do you recall from your later childhood about listing your likes or dislikes in order (for example, listing your favorite movies, musical groups, foods, teachers, books, things to do with friends)? How much importance did you and your friends place on rating or ranking things and places?

▶ C. Where did you and your friends fit in the social order of your high school? Looking back, how supportive did you find your system of social ordering to be?

▶ D. Think about seriation in your current life. What things do you arrange in patterns? What things or ideas do you now compare, rank, or order?

▶ E. Think of and discuss seriation you have encountered in your everyday life—for example in restaurants, airports, newspapers, stores, greenhouses.

▶ F. How are people ranked in the work place, the armed services, orchestras, sports teams, religious institutions, governments, political parties?

▶ G. Find a graph in a newspaper, magazine, or book. What relationship does the graph have to seriation?

▶ H. For a week, keep a log of seriation you engage in and encounter in your daily life. At the end of the week, record your reflections about your findings.

Exercise 3

Understanding Seriation

This exercise is based on the discussion of seriation on *EYC* pp. 465–466.

▶ A. What are Piaget and Inhelder (*EYC* p. 465) saying about the way toddlers arrange things in order?

▶ B. What does Charles Hohmann mean by finding order in difference (*EYC* p. 465, first column), and "the relations of difference" (*EYC* p. 465 display quote)?

▶ C. What is the relationship between arranging things in an ordered series and arranging things in a pattern?

▶ D. Why do you think preschool children are so interested in comparing the size of things—for example, "I've got big mittens . . . " "I want the biggest one . . . " "My mommy and daddy are bigger than my house . . . "?

Exercise 4

Comparing Attributes

▶ A. For exercises (1)–(15), what **materials** is the child comparing and what **attributes** is the child focusing on?

❶ Jacob, *EYC* p. 467 anecdote
❷ Jalessa, *EYC* p. 467 anecdote
❸ Brian, *EYC* p. 467 anecdote
❹ Corrin, *EYC* p. 467 anecdote
❺ Kenneth, *EYC* p. 467 anecdote
❻ Anna, *EYC* p. 467 anecdote
❼ Jason, *EYC* p. 467 anecdote
❽ Julia, *EYC* p. 467 anecdote
❾ LJ, *EYC* p. 467 anecdote
❿ Kacey, *EYC* p. 467 anecdote
⓫ Child in *EYC* p. 464 right-hand photo
⓬ Child in *EYC* p. 466 photo

⑬ Child in *EYC* p. 468 photo

⑭ Abby in *EYC* p. 468 bulleted scenario

⑮ Chelsea in *EYC* p. 468 bulleted scenario

▶ B. What comparisons have you seen or heard some of your study children making?

Exercise 5

Creating and Describing Series and Patterns

▶ A. **What materials** are the following children arranging, **how** are they arranging them (in an ordered series or in a pattern), and **what attributes are they focusing on** in the anecdotes on *EYC* p. 468? Use a chart like the following to organize your answers.

Child	Materials	How: Ordered Series or Pattern	Attribute

❶ Corrin

❷ Trey

❸ Chrysten

❹ Mikey

❺ Alana

❻ Athi

❼ Deola

❽ Jonah

❾ Corrin

❿ Jason

▶ B. For the children listed in (1)–(8) below, complete a chart like the one you completed for exercise A.

❶ Anna, *EYC* p. 469 bulleted scenario

❷ Andrew, *EYC* p. 469 bulleted scenario

❸ Hannah, *EYC* p. 469 bulleted scenario

❹ Leah, *EYC* p. 469 bulleted scenario

❺ Beth's group of children, *EYC* p. 469 bulleted scenario

❻ Child whose play dough is shown in photo on *EYC* p. 469

❼ Child whose drawing is shown on *EYC* p. 470

❽ Child whose drawing is shown on *EYC* p. 473

▶ C. What strikes you about the context in which children create series and patterns?

▶ D. What patterns or series have you seen some of your study children creating?

Exercise 6

Fitting Together Ordered Sets

▶ A. What **two ordered sets of materials** are the following children fitting together, and what **attributes** are they attending to?

❶ Alana, *EYC* p. 470 anecdote

❷ Jon, *EYC* p. 470 anecdote

❸ Hannah, *EYC* p. 470 anecdote

❹ Kenneth, *EYC* p. 470 anecdote

❺ Jonah, *EYC* p. 470 anecdote

❻ Hannah, *EYC* p. 471 anecdote

❼ Child in photo, *EYC* p. 471

❽ Oscar, *EYC* p. 471 anecdote

▶ B. Jon, Jonah, and Oscar, in exercises A(2), A(5), and A(8), create their own ordered sets. What does this suggest to you about their understanding of seriation?

▶ C. What strikes you about the way a child hung the pans in the photograph on *EYC* p. 464?

▶ D. How have you seen some of your study children fitting ordered sets together or creating ordered sets?

Exercise 7

Supporting Children's Seriation Throughout the Day

(Exercise B involves a computer.)

▶ A. If you are currently teaching or student teaching, think of your early childhood setting for this exercise about *providing materials*. If you are not teaching, think about the setting of one of your study children. For each type of seriation-related material in (1)–(6), list the materials **currently in the setting,** and list materials **you would like to add.** Use a chart like the following to organize your answers.

Material Type	Have	Add

❶ Sets of materials in two sizes

❷ Materials children can shape and change

❸ Materials with contrasting attributes other than size

❹ Sets of materials in three or four sizes

❺ Materials children can use to make their own series and patterns

❻ Ordered sets of materials that go together

▶ B. If you have access to a computer and preschool software, try out the software programs that provide children with interactive seriation experiences. (For titles of appropriate software, see the software reviews in the bimonthly magazine *Children's Software Revue:* www.childrenssoftware.com.) Which programs do you or would you like to provide for children in an early childhood setting?

▶ C. In the *EYC* scenarios and photographs listed in (1)–(7), how are adults *being alert and attentive to the ways children seriate* as they work and play?

❶ Adult, p. 466 photo

❷ Jackie, p. 468, first column

❸ Beth, p. 468, first column

❹ Isobel, p. 468, first column

❺ Leah's teacher, p. 469, third column

❻ Beth, p. 469, third column

❼ Manuel, p. 471, third column

▶ D. How might a teaching team arrange and label materials to provide opportunities for children to seriate at cleanup time?

▶ E. Read through the seriation support strategies in the checklist on the facing page (which is from *EYC* p. 472). Under each of the seriation key experiences on the checklist, check off the support strategies you are already using, write "E" in front of the strategies you have not used but would like to explore, and read about each of these strategies in *EYC.*

Exercise 8

Child Study: Creating a Seriation Portfolio

By yourself or with a partner, create a seriation portfolio by collecting materials such as the following as you teach, student teach, or observe one of your study children:

- Anecdotes related to each seriation key experience

- Samples of children's art in which children have created ordered series or patterns or matched ordered sets

- Videotape clips or photographs of children seriating materials in the course of their indoor and outdoor play or at cleanup time

When your seriation portfolio is complete, find an opportunity to present it to teaching teams in your center, parents of preschoolers, or fellow early childhood students. Assembling and explaining your portfolio to others will add to your understanding of how children create series and patterns.

Exercise 9

Seriation Scenarios: What Would You Do?

Based on your understanding of the seriation key experiences and the support strategies discussed on *EYC* pp. 465–472, decide how you might interact with and support the preschool children in the following scenarios.

▶ A. *At work time in the block area, Kevin is looking for additional blocks to build a room next to the doghouse he has made. "Here, use these," says Alex, holding out two square unit blocks. "No, they're too small," Kevin replies. "It's all that's left," Alex observes, looking at the block shelf. "Uh-uh, too small," says Kevin with determination.*

How might you support Kevin's desire to build with materials bigger than the unit blocks?

▶ B. *At small-group time, the children in your group are using paper strips and glue to construct three-dimensional designs, patterns, structures, and so forth. Carleen ignores the glue, gets a pair of scissors, and cuts her paper strips into tinier and tinier bits and pieces. "Look," she says, holding a very small piece she has cut, "this is even smaller!"*

How might you support Carleen's interest in cutting the paper strips into very tiny pieces?

▶ C. *While putting away blocks at cleanup time, Brendan keeps his eye on the sand timer. At one point, going over to the sand timer, he says, "It's getting lower and lower!" while moving his hand down to show how the sand level is going*

Seriation Strategies: A Summary

Comparing attributes (longer/shorter, bigger/smaller)

___Provide materials whose attributes children can easily compare.

   ___Sets of materials in two sizes

   ___Materials children can shape and change

   ___Materials with other contrasting attributes

___Store and label materials in a way that encourages children to compare attributes.

___Listen for and support the comparisons children make as they play and solve problems.

Arranging several things one after another in a series or pattern and describing their relationships (big/bigger/biggest, red/blue/red/blue)

___Provide collections and sets of materials.

   ___Sets of materials in three or four sizes

   ___Materials that children can use to make their own series and patterns

   ___Computer software programs that feature series and patterns

___Watch and listen for the series and patterns children make.

___Ask children to draw or make families, necklaces, and trains.

___Read stories and encourage children to represent stories in which size relationships play an important role.

Fitting one ordered set of objects to another through trial and error (small cup-small saucer/ medium cup-medium saucer/big cup-big saucer)

___Provide ordered sets of materials that go together.

___Label some materials so children match ordered sets to ordered labels.

___Watch to see how children put ordered sets together.

---

down in the top of the timer. Then he moves his hand to show how the pile of sand is building up in the bottom of the timer and says, "This is getting higher and higher!"

How might you support Brendan's observations and comparisons?

▶ *D. At work time in the toy area, Kelly dumps the basket of plastic animals, sorts them by type (putting all the deer together, all the cows together, all the horses together, and so on), and then lines up each type in order by size—the "baby" deer, "mommy" deer, and "daddy" deer, followed by the "baby" cows, "mommy" cows, and "daddy" cows, and so forth. "It's a parade," she tells you.*

How might you support Kelly's construction of series and patterns?

▶ *E. Frances and Megan are making a train by carefully lining up several chairs of various heights and sizes. They put the shortest, smallest chairs in the back; then some bigger chairs in front of those; and finally the metal folding chairs in front of those. They place puppets on the small chairs and dolls on the medium-sized chairs, and they themselves sit on the metal folding chairs.*

How might you support Frances's and Megan's ordering of chairs and (pretend and real) people?

▶ *F. At cleanup time, Chrysten hangs up the measuring spoons. She hangs the biggest spoon on the hook with the biggest label. She hangs the smallest spoon on the hook with the smallest label. Then she hangs the two remaining spoons arbitrarily, without regard to the size of their labels.*

How might you support Chrysten's fitting together of ordered sets?

G. *At work time, Leah rolls clay into three different lengths. When she has finished, she turns to you and says,"Look at my worms— mama, sister, baby!"*

How might you support Leah's creation of a seriated worm family?

H. *At large-group time, the children are deciding how to act out **The Three Billy Goats Gruff**, a story you have read to them many times. Some children decide to be trolls, some decide to be big-brother and big-sister goats, some decide to be middle-sister and middle-brother goats, but no one wants to be a baby goat. "You could be my baby brother," Avery says to Kyle. "I'm not playin' no baby," says Kyle.*

How might you support the children's ideas and choices and still end up with three sizes of goats?

I. *At work time, Jack and Dan use the hollow blocks to build steps. "You go up this side and down this side," they say as they show you how to use the steps.*

How might you support Jack's and Dan's ability to seriate?

Exercise 10

Implementation Study: Trying Out Seriation Support Strategies

If you are currently teaching or student teaching or can work in an early childhood setting over a period of time, try out the seriation support strategies on *EYC* p. 472 as opportunities arise during the child-initiated and adult-initiated times of the day. Support children's seriation at work time, cleanup time, and outside time.

Watch for seriation key experiences as children work with materials at small-group time and as they offer ideas at large-group time. Collect anecdotes, photographs, recordings, and samples of seriation for your seriation portfolio. At the end of each day of teaching, write down your discoveries about the ways young children create ordered series and patterns.

This implementation exercise is crucial for your understanding of the seriation key experiences and ways to support them. Do not be discouraged if things do not go the way you expect them to. It is only with practice that adults learn from children how they construct knowledge about series and patterns and how to encourage their initiatives related to seriation.

Exercise 11

Child Assessment: COR Items Related to Seriation

One way to assess preschool children's understanding and use of seriation is to match the children's anecdotes (collected each day and discussed at daily team planning time) with the most relevant level descriptors for items Y and Z from the High/Scope Child Observation Record (COR) for Ages 2½–6. These items are presented on the facing page. Based on the following anecdotes, at what level (1–5) would you place Daniel on COR item Z? (After making your own assessment, you may wish to look at the Item Z level suggested for Daniel on p. 205.)

9/20 At greeting circle, Daniel looked at a picture book about buildings and pointed out the elevators in a cutaway drawing of a building. "There are big ones, medium

ones, and small ones," he said. (The elevators were drawn in three sizes.)

10/13 At work time, listening to Carol and Rachel talk about getting their hair cut, Daniel said, "I go to a different barber shop where no girls go." When Carol asked why, he said, "Maybe because their hair is longer and it would take too long."

12/1 At small-group time, Daniel rolled some dough into two "worms or snakes." "This one's the baby," he said, pointing to the shorter one, "and this one's the bigger brother."

2/11 At small-group time, Daniel held up two foam pieces and said about the longer, fatter one, "Look, this one's bigger than the other one!"

3/6 At outside time, Daniel offered to push Kevin on the taxi because, he explained, "I'm bigger than you." (Daniel is taller and older than Kevin.)

Exercise 12

Seriation Issues to Ponder and Write About

A. How is seriation related to classification? To the concept of number?

B. During what segment of the day might you be most likely to observe children seriating? Why?

C. Why are size relationships so important to children and adults?

COR Item Y. Arranging materials in graduated order

Level 1   Child does not yet arrange items in graduated order.

Level 2   Child arranges two or three items in graduated order based on one characteristic such as size, shade of a color, or texture.

Level 3   Child arranges four or more items in graduated order based on one characteristic.

Level 4   Child places new items in their proper place within an ordered set of objects (not at the beginning or end of the series).

Level 5   Child matches one ordered set of items to another ordered set (arranges a set of balls by size next to a set of blocks arranged by size).

Supporting Anecdotes:

COR Item Z. Using comparison words

Level 1   Child does not yet use or respond to comparison words *(bigger, biggest).*

Level 2   Child follows directions that involve comparison words ("Take the biggest cookie").

Level 3   Child uses comparison words, but not always correctly.

Level 4   Child uses comparison words correctly ("This one is bigger than that one").

Level 5   Child compares three or more things using some comparison words appropriately *(smaller, smallest).*

Supporting Anecdotes:

Related Publications

Blackwell, Frank F., and Charles Hohmann. 1991. *High/Scope K–3 Curriculum Series: Science.* Ypsilanti, MI: High/Scope Press.

Graves, Michelle. 1989. *The Teacher's Idea Book: Daily Planning Around the Key Experiences,* 45–50. Ypsilanti, MI: High/Scope Press.

High/Scope Child Observation Record (COR) for Ages 2½–6. 1992. Ypsilanti, MI: High/Scope Press.

Answer to Exercise 11

Daniel's level on COR item Z:

Level 4 on the basis of anecdotes from *10/13, 12/1, 2/11, 3/6*

Level 5 on the basis of anecdote from *9/20*

Level 4 overall

→ *Forming a basic understanding of the assumptions that underlie the use of numbers is an important task for young children. To develop such an understanding, they need to be able to exercise their current numerical capacities, however simple and apparently erroneous their conclusions about numbers may be. As young children make observations and draw conclusions based on their emerging concept of number, they are building a base for logical thinking.*

—*Educating Young Children, p. 476*

17

Number

Comparing, Arranging Objects in One-to-One Correspondence, and Counting

For the following two activities, you will need a partner.

Exploring Number With Two Collections

Find two collections of countable objects, and put them in two separate bags, or containers (for example, use a bag of stones and a bag of buttons).

- Look at your two bags of objects. Which bag appears to contain more objects? Without counting, estimate how many objects are in each collection.

- Line up the two collections so you have a succession of pairs made up of one object from each collection (for example, one stone paired with one button). Form as many such pairs as possible. Are there objects from either collection that are left over? If so, which collection contains more items? If not, what does that tell you about the two collections?

- Count the objects in each collection. How many objects are there in each one?

- Put the collections back in their bags. Arbitrarily remove (or add) some objects from (or to) each collection, and then repeat the above three steps with these two altered collections.

Exploring Number With Toothpicks and Marshmallows

For this activity you will need a box of toothpicks, a bag of miniature marshmallows, and two markers (for example, red and green).

- You and your partner each build a structure using toothpicks and marshmallows.

- When you have each completed a structure, look at your structures side by side. Together with your partner, without actually counting, visually compare the number of toothpicks and marshmallows used in your two structures. Whose structure, if either, appears to incorporate more toothpicks? More marshmallows?

- Each choose a colored marker, and with it, mark the individual marshmallows and toothpicks in your structure. (For example, while you mark each toothpick and marshmallow with a red dot, your partner might mark each toothpick and marshmallow with a green dot.)

- Disassemble your structures, and line up first the marshmallows from the two structures in pairs and then the toothpicks from the two structures in pairs so there is a red and green color in each pair. Did one structure use more toothpicks? More marshmallows? If so, which used more?

- Count the toothpicks and marshmallows used in each structure, and record the results.

What fundamental *number* concepts were you and your partner working with in the activity with *two collections* and the activity with *toothpicks and marshmallows?*

Reconstructing the Pythagorean Theorem: A Concrete Math Experience for Adults

For this activity connected with exercises A–D, you will need a partner and a box of **square** crackers.

- With your partner, lay out three rows of square crackers so they form the three sides of a "3-4-5" *right* triangle (that is, a triangle with one "square corner"). Use 3 crackers for side A, 4 crackers for side B, and 5 crackers for side C (this longest side is the right triangle's *hypotenuse*). The right triangle you have made should look like this:

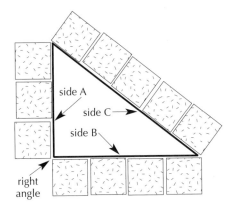

- Now, using the triangle you have made, use some more crackers to build a square on each side of the triangle. For example,

on the "3-cracker" side, the square you build will look like this:

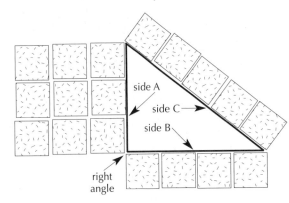

▶ A. How many crackers did you use for the square on side A? On side B? On side C? How is the number of crackers you used on side C related to the numbers used on sides A and B?

▶ B. With crackers, you have gained hands-on experience with the following theorem formulated by the sixth-century B.C. Greek mathematician Pythagoras: *In a right triangle, the sum of the squares on the sides that form the right angle is equal to the square on the hypotenuse.* Although working with this theorem is beyond the ability of preschoolers, why do you think this activity was included in this chapter?

▶ C. By doing this activity, what did you as an adult discover about the sides of a right triangle? What is the connection between this activity for older students and adults and the ingredients of active learning?

▶ D. Why might it be important for students of all ages to use manipulatives as they work with number concepts?

Recalling Number Experiences

With a partner or group of friends, discuss and record your answers to the following questions.

▶ A. What are your earliest memories of number awareness or working with numbers?

▶ B. What do you recall about your experiences with math in elementary school? In high school?

▶ C. What views about teaching or learning math have you encountered? What do you think of the following views?

- The math test scores of students make or break our country's economic future.
- Calculators and computers are vital [overrated] in math education.
- Boys are innately better at math than girls.
- Girls do better at math when they are taught in a same-sex setting.
- Computation is more important than [as important as] [less important than] creative problem solving.

▶ D. For a week, keep a log of number or math experiences you encounter in your daily life. At the end of the week, write down your reflections on your findings.

Understanding Number

This exercise is based on the discussion of number on *EYC* pp. 475–476.

▶ A. What is *object permanence?* Why must children have a sense of object permanence before they can form the concept of number?

▶ B. For a young child, how is forming the concept of number related to understanding *classification?*

▶ C. What role does *seriation* play in a child's understanding of number?

▶ D. What is *one-to-one correspondence?* How does it relate to children's understanding of number?

▶ E. What is *conservation of number?* How and under what circumstances do appearances conflict with young children's ability to conserve number?

▶ F. In "Counting on Appearances and Counting" (*EYC* p. 477), how would you describe Kevin's bean counting and scissors counting in terms of conservation of number?

Comparing Numbers of Things

▶ A. In each of exercises (1)–(13), what **sets of things** is the child comparing, and what **conclusions** is he or she drawing about the

number of things? Use a chart like the following to organize your answers.

Child	Sets of Materials Child Compares	Child's Conclusions

❶ Corey, anecdote on *EYC* p. 477

❷ Jonah, anecdote on *EYC* p. 477

❸ Chrysten, anecdote on *EYC* p. 477

❹ Andrew, anecdote on *EYC* p. 477

❺ Brianna, anecdote on *EYC* p. 477

❻ Douglas, anecdote on *EYC* p. 477

❼ Andrew, anecdote on *EYC* p. 477

❽ Wendy, anecdote on *EYC* p. 477

❾ Douglas, anecdote on *EYC* p. 477

❿ Trey, bulleted scenario on *EYC* p. 478

⓫ Callie, bulleted scenario on *EYC* p. 478

⓬ Jonah, "Comparing numbers of things in representations," *EYC* p. 478

⓭ Jonah/Hannah, "Comparing ages," *EYC* p. 478

▶ B. What number comparisons have you seen or heard some of your study children making?

Arranging Things in One-to-One Correspondence

▶ A. For each of these children from the anecdotes on *EYC* p. 479, indicate what sets of things the child is arranging in one-to-one correspondence.

❶ Hannah ❻ LJ

❷ Audie ❼ Corrin

❸ Amanda ❽ Mikey

❹ Brian ❾ Hannah

❺ Aimee ❿ Douglas

▶ B. In each of the four bulleted scenarios on *EYC* p. 480, what sets of objects are the children arranging in one-to-one correspondence?

▶ C. In the photos listed in (1)–(8), what are children arranging in one-to-one correspondence?

❶ p. 20, top photo

❷ p. 33

❸ p. 122, left-hand photo

❹ p. 240

❺ p. 471

❻ p. 475, top photo

❼ p. 479

❽ p. 480

▶ D. What strikes you about the *context* in which the children in exercises A–C arrange things in one-to-one correspondence?

▶ E. What experiences with one-to-one correspondence have some of your study children had?

Counting Things

▶ A. Gardner observes that young children arrive at a point when they are intrinsically motivated to count (*EYC* p. 482)—they see their world as full of countable objects. Gelman identifies five principles that distinguish and guide their counting (*EYC* pp. 481–482). In your own words, define each of these principles; they are listed in exercises (1)–(5).

❶ The *one-to-one* principle

❷ The *stable order* principle

❸ The *cardinal* principle

❹ The *abstraction* principle

❺ The *order-irrelevance* principle

▶ B. The children listed in (1)–(16) are from the anecdotes on *EYC* pp. 481–482. **What objects and actions** are they counting, and **which of Gelman's counting principles** do you find them to be using? Use a chart like the following to organize your answers.

Child	Objects/Actions Child Counts	Counting Principles Used

❶ Alana
❷ Audie
❸ Julia
❹ Brian
❺ Chrysten
❻ Douglas
❼ Kacey
❽ Trey
❾ Amanda
❿ Isaac
⓫ Chelsea
⓬ Kenneth
⓭ Abby
⓮ Douglas
⓯ Jalessa
⓰ Jeff

▶ C. What have you seen or heard some of your study children counting?

▶ D. What strikes you about the way young children incorporate numbers into their conversations in the three bulleted scenarios on *EYC* p. 485 and in the conversation about going to the movies on *EYC* pp. 485–486?

Supporting Children's Concept of Number Throughout the Day

(Exercise B involves a computer.)

▶ A. If you are currently teaching or student teaching, think of your early childhood setting for this exercise about *providing materials*. If you are not teaching, think about the setting of one of your study children. For each type of number-related material in (1)–(4), list materials **currently in the setting** and materials **you would like to add.** Use a table like the following to organize your answers.

Type of Number-Related Material	Have	Add

❶ Sets of discrete materials (suitable for number comparison)

❷ Sets of art materials (to use as countable objects or to make representations of countable objects)

❸ Sets of materials that fit together in one-to-one correspondence

❹ Sets that are countable, including blocks, small-object collections, messy things, materials with numerals, board games involving moving pieces from space to space

▶ B. If you have access to a computer and preschool software, try out the programs that provide children with interactive number experiences. (For titles of appropriate software, see the software reviews in the bimonthly magazine *Children's Software Revue:* www.childrenssoftware.com.) Which programs do you or would you like to provide for children in an early childhood setting?

▶ C. Exercises (1)–(4) deal with *accepting children's number logic.*

❶ In the last paragraph on *EYC* p. 478, why is Abby convinced that having her fifth birthday at last makes her the oldest child among her peers? Why does her teacher accept her logic?

❷ At the beginning of *EYC* p. 479, how is Wally using counting to determine the size of the two rugs? Why is Eddie unconvinced by Wally's rug-measuring system?

❸ In the first bulleted scenario on *EYC* p. 484, how and why does Jonah's teacher accept Jonah's count of 66 beads?

❹ Read the last bulleted scenario on *EYC* p. 486, and then look at Trey's cartoon shown on *EYC* p. 485. What strikes you about the numbers Trey has written and the order in which he has arranged them? What effect did Beth's acceptance of his work have?

▶ D. Read through the *number support strategies* in the checklist at the right (which is from *EYC* p. 486). Under each of the number key experiences on the checklist, check off the support strategies you are already using, write "E" in front of the strategies you have not used but would like to explore, and read about each of these strategies in *EYC*.

Child Study: Creating a Number Portfolio

By yourself or with a partner, create a number portfolio by collecting materials such as the following as you teach, student teach, or observe one of your study children:

- Anecdotes related to each number key experience

- Samples of children's art in which children have created sets that are in one-to-one correspondence or in which they have incorporated numbers

---

Number Strategies: A Summary

Comparing the numbers of things in two sets to determine "more," "fewer," "same number"

___Provide materials for comparing numbers of things.

___Discrete materials

___Art materials

___Listen for children's spontaneous number comparisons.

___Comparing numbers of materials

___Comparing numbers of things in representations

___Comparing ages

___Accept children's findings about number.

Arranging two sets of objects in one-to-one correspondence

___Provide materials that fit together in one-to-one correspondence.

___Watch for the sets of corresponding materials children generate.

___Encourage children to share and talk about their one-to-one arrangements at recall time.

___Encourage children to gather and distribute materials.

___At snack and meal times

___At small- and large-group times

___During card games

Counting objects

___Provide sets of countable objects.

___Blocks

___Collections of small things

___Messy things

___Computer software

___Materials with numerals

___Board games

___Listen for children's counting throughout the day.

___Accept children's numerical ordering.

___Listen for children's number talk.

___Watch for children's recognition of written numbers.

___Support children who are interested in writing numbers.

- Videotape clips or photographs of children comparing, forming one-to-one correspondence, and counting materials in the course of play

When your number portfolio is complete, find an opportunity to present it to teaching teams in your center, parents of preschoolers, or fellow early childhood students. Assembling and explaining your portfolio to others will add to your understanding of how children compare numbers of things, create one-to-one correspondences, and count objects.

Number Scenarios: What Would You Do?

Based on your understanding of the number key experiences and the support strategies discussed on *EYC* pp. 476–486, decide how you might interact with and support the preschool children in the following scenarios.

► A. *At greeting circle, Frances selects the book* **Have You Seen My Duckling?** *She sits on your lap, and Rachel leans up against you. On one page of the book, Frances points to and counts seven ducklings. Rachel looks at the same page and counts eight ducklings, explaining " 'cause one of them's still in the egg."*

How might you support each child's way of counting?

► B. *At work time in the art area, Megan and Frances paint together at the easel on the same large sheet of paper. First, Frances paints a line of color on her side of the paper, then Megan paints a line of the same color on her side of the paper. Then, using another color, they repeat this process. This continues until they have filled the paper with matching pairs of colored lines.*

How might you support Frances and Megan's creation of one-to-one correspondence in their painting?

► C. *At snack time, Brendan correctly counts the number of people at the other snack table, saying "One, two, three, four. Four people at that table." Then he looks at the people at his table (where you are also sitting). "There's lots more at this table," he observes without counting. (There are, in fact, nine people at his table.)*

How might you support Brendan's counting and comparing?

► D. *At work time, Mia tells someone how old she is by counting "One, two, three, four, five" on her fingers and then saying "I'm four, but I'll be five next."*

How might you support Mia's counting strategy?

► E. *At greeting circle, Levin looks at one blown-up balloon hanging on the wall. "When we break that one, then there's no balloons."*

How might you support Levin's ability to anticipate and compare numbers of things?

► F. *At work time in the art area, Kayla says, "I'm going to make a three-shaker with three tops." After taping the three tops together on her three-shaker, she decides, "I'm going to make a four shaker with four tops!" She does.*

How might you support Kayla's use of counting in her art creations?

► G. *At planning time, Jack selects two pieces of wooden fruit from the planning basket "because," he says, "I'm making two plans." He holds out a wooden banana in one hand and says, "One, make a zord in the toy area with the Lasy builders, and [as he holds out a wooden apple with the other hand] two, fly it on a fighter jet in the block area."*

How might you support Jack's use of one-to-one correspondence?

► H. *At outside time, Chris counts the walnuts in the sandbox. "One, two, three, four, six, eleven, eleventy-one! That's a lot!"*

How might you support Chris's counting?

► I. *For snack, Timmy has brought cupcakes made by him and his mom. The frosting of each one is decorated with eight randomly arranged chocolate chips. Lynnette is crying, and when you ask what is troubling her, she points to Timmy's cupcake, saying "He's got more chips!" "No, they're all the same. That's how we made them," Timmy tells her.*

How might you support Lynnette's and Timmy's observations about number?

► J. *At planning time, Jack asks you about his best friend, Daniel, who is visiting his grandma in another part of the state for the week: "When does Daniel come back?" "Next Monday," you reply. "Isn't that a lot of days, like six or twelve?" Jack asks.*

How might you help Jack figure out in a concrete way the number of days until Daniel returns?

Exercise 11

Implementation Study: Trying Out Number Support Strategies

If you are currently teaching or student teaching or can work in an early childhood setting over a period of time, try out the number support strategies on *EYC* p. 486 during the child-initiated and adult-initiated times of the day. Support children's use of number at work time, cleanup time, and outside time. Watch for number key experiences as children work with materials in small-group time and as they offer ideas at large-group time. Collect anecdotes, photographs, recordings, and samples of number experiences for your number portfolio. At the end of each day of teaching, write down your reflections about the ways young children compare numbers of things, create examples of one-to-one correspondence, and count.

This implementation exercise is crucial for your understanding of the number key experiences and ways to support them. Do not be discouraged if things do not go the way you expect them to. It is only with practice that adults learn from children how they construct knowledge about number and how to encourage their number-related initiatives.

Exercise 12

Child Assessment: COR Items Related to Number

One way to assess preschool children's understanding and use of number is to match the children's anecdotes (collected each day and discussed at daily team planning time) with the most relevant level descriptors for items AA and BB from the High/Scope Child Observation Record (COR) for Ages 2½–6. These items are presented on the next page. On the basis of the following anecdotes, at what level (1–5) would you place Alex on COR item BB? (After making your own assessment, you may wish to look at the item BB level suggested for Alex on page 214.)

> *9/30* At outside time, Alex climbed up behind the dinosaur's head on the dinosaur climber and said to Carol, as he pointed to the dinosaur's head, "This isn't just one piece of metal. It's two pieces of metal welded together. Did you notice that?"

> *10/14* At small-group time, Alex put together the 13-piece rocket-ship puzzle. "That's a lot of pieces," he said, and then he counted the 13 pieces. "That's thirteen pieces. That *is* a lot!"

> *11/17* At work time at the computer, Alex counted 10 rabbits in the magic hat game, and then he counted 9 salamanders. (There were 10 rabbits and 9 salamanders on the screen.)[35]

> *11/18* At recall time, Alex said, "I washed one, two, three, four, five, six windows," pointing to each of the six windows he had washed.

> *1/9* At work time in the art area, Alex cut a strip of stickers in what looked like the middle of the strip. Then he said, "I'm going to count to make sure they [the resulting two strips] are the same. "One, two, three, four, five, six, seven, eight, nine," he counted on one strip. Then he counted the stickers on the other strip: "One, two, three, four, five, six, seven, eight, nine. They *are* the same!" He kept one set of stickers and gave the other set to Kevin.

Exercise 13

Number Issues to Ponder and Write About

▶ A. Why are some adults intent on teaching young children to count?

▶ B. Why is facility with numbers highly valued in a technological society?

▶ C. Do early childhood teachers tend to be people who have majored in math and science? Why or why not? What impact does a teacher's comfort with math have on the young children in his or her care?

▶ D. What is the role of nursery rhymes such as "One, Two, Buckle My Shoe" in children's understanding of counting? Which, if any, of Gelman's counting principles might such counting rhymes support? How?

▶ E. What is the role of manipulative materials in math education?

---

[35]*This anecdote refers to an activity on the software program* **Counting Critters 1.0** *(MECC, 1985).*

COR Item AA. Comparing numbers of objects

Level 1 Child does not yet correctly compare the numbers of objects in two groups.

Level 2 Child compares the quantities of small groups of objects, correctly using words like *more* and *less*.

Level 3 Child correctly judges whether two groups of up to five objects each (pegs, blocks, cars, children) contain the same number of objects.

Level 4 Child uses one-to-one matching to tell whether one group of up to five objects has more, fewer, or the same number of objects as another group.

Level 5 Child correctly compares the sizes of groups of more than five objects.

Supporting Anecdotes:

COR Item BB. Counting objects

Level 1 Child does not relate number-words and objects.

Level 2 Child touches objects and names a number for each one, although the numbers may not be in the correct order.

Level 3 Child correctly counts up to three objects.

Level 4 Child correctly counts four to ten objects.

Level 5 Child correctly counts over ten objects.

Supporting Anecdotes:

Related Publications

Frede, Ellen. 1984. *Getting Involved: Workshops for Parents*, 183–209. Ypsilanti, MI: High/Scope Press.

Graves, Michelle. 1989. In *The Teacher's Idea Book: Daily Planning Around the Key Experiences*, 51–56. Ypsilanti, MI: High/Scope Press.

Graves, Michelle. 2000. "Young Children and Math." *High/Scope Extensions* (October), 1–3.

Hannibal, Sam. 1991. "Math Learning: Making It Happen Naturally." In *Supporting Young Learners: Ideas for Preschool and Day Care Providers*, Nancy A. Brickman and Lynn S. Taylor, eds, 87–95. Ypsilanti, MI: High/Scope Press.

High/Scope Child Observation Record (COR) for Ages 2½–6. 1992. Ypsilanti, MI: High/Scope Press.

Hohmann, Charles. 1991. *High/Scope K–3 Curriculum Series: Mathematics.* Ypsilanti, MI: High/Scope Press.

Answer to Exercise 12

Alex's level on COR item BB:

Level 3 on the basis of anecdote from *9/30*

Level 4 on the basis of anecdotes from *11/17, 11/18, 1/9*

Level 5 on the basis of anecdote from *10/14*

Level 4 overall

As preschoolers work with people and materials and solve spatial problems— "It couldn't fit so we biggered the door"—they gain an awareness of the spatial relationships in their immediate surroundings. This knowledge enables them to move and act with confidence in the physical world.

—*Educating Young Children, p. 490*

18

Space

Filling, Fitting, and Shaping Things; Observing, Describing, and Interpreting Spatial Relations

For the following two building activities, you will need a partner.

Building a Tower

For this activity, find two empty cans (such as tuna cans or coffee cans); two containers (such as bags, buckets, baskets) for collecting things; a place outdoors where you can find "foundation" materials (dirt, sand, gravel, or pebbles) and other natural materials for tower building (sticks, leaves, pine needles); and some pieces of thin wire or some wire twist-ties to fasten your tower together.

- You and your partner each fill a can with something like sand, dirt, stones, or pebbles, so the can serves as a sturdy base on which to construct a tower.

- Use your collecting containers to gather some outdoor materials suitable for tower building.

- Using the collected materials and wire fastening as needed, each of you build a tower, using the can of sand or pebbles for the tower's foundation. For example, you might begin by sticking several sticks into the sand and attaching a shell or a leaf to them.

- When you have each built a tower, make a drawing of it, and then write a description of it.

- Dismantle your towers, and exchange your drawings and written descriptions with each other. Based on your partner's drawing and description, rebuild your partner's tower. Your partner should do likewise, based on your drawing and description.

- Look at your partner's version of your tower, and vice versa. Decide how the two new towers resemble the originals.

Building a Structure to Support a Book

For this exercise, you and your partner need toothpicks, marshmallows or small balls of clay, and a textbook.

- Each of you build a structure no more than one toothpick high that is strong enough to hold the textbook.

- Examine each other's completed work. Which structure uses fewer toothpicks? Why? Does either structure use triangular supports or braces? What are the advantages of such braces?

- Together with your partner, build another structure that is one toothpick high and strong enough to hold a book. Incorporate triangles, and use as few toothpicks as possible.

What *spatial* concepts were you and your partner working with in building the *towers* and the *book-supporting structures?*

Recalling Space Experiences

With a partner or several friends, discuss and record your answers to the following:

A. What do you remember from your child-hood about things you liked to fill and empty? About things you liked to take apart and put together? About things you liked to shape and reshape, or arrange and rearrange?

B. What "tight-fit" experiences do you recall from your life—for example, experiences involving moving furniture, squeezing into a small space, closing a box or suitcase?

C. What experiences do you recall that involved seeing things from a different or an unusual point of view—for example, when you crawled around under a table, climbed a tree, or rode on a ferris wheel?

D. What do you recall about how people and places looked to you as a young child? About how these people and places "shrank" as you grew bigger?

E. What experiences do you recall about learning to find your way around your house, apartment building, or neighborhood? About taking short cuts through an alley, the neighbor's yard, or the woods?

F. What do you remember about looking at and making maps as a young child? What people did you see using maps? What did maps mean to you? When did they begin to make sense to you?

G. For a week, keep a daily log of your experiences with space. At the end of the week, write down your reflections on your findings.

Exercise 3

Understanding Space

This exercise is based on the discussion of space on *EYC* pp. 489–490.

A. What do these statements mean: "The child's space . . . is essentially of an active and operational character" (Piaget and Inhelder, *EYC* p. 489). "Spatial intelligence arises from the child's action upon the world" (Gardner, *EYC* p. 489)?

B. How do Piaget and Inhelder define the following spatial concepts?

❶ Proximity   ❸ Order
❷ Separation   ❹ Enclosure

C. According to Laurendeau, Pinard, and Furth (*EYC* p. 489), how might space appear to young children? Why is a young child's perception of space difficult for adults to imagine?

D. According to Gardner (*EYC* p. 490), how is young children's spatial ability related to their understanding of classification and representation?

Exercise 4

Filling and Emptying

A. What **materials** and what **containers** are children using for filling and emptying in the *EYC* anecdotes and photographs listed in (1)–(18)?

❶ Brian, anecdote p. 491
❷ Vanessa, anecdote p. 491

❸ Audie, anecdote p. 491
❹ Alana, anecdote p. 492
❺ Colin/Athi, anecdote p. 492
❻ Caroline, anecdote p. 492
❼ p. 13 right-hand photo
❽ p. 45 middle photo, p. 516 photos
❾ pp. 101 and 491 photos
❿ p. 125 photos
⓫ p. 129 bottom photo
⓬ p. 150 top middle photo
⓭ p. 201 left-hand photo
⓮ p. 246 photo
⓯ p. 300 photos
⓰ p. 301 photos
⓱ p. 492 photos
⓲ p. 494 photos

B. What have you seen some of your study children filling and emptying?

C. What strikes you about the materials young children use for filling and emptying?

D. Why might young children find it satisfying to fill and empty things?

Exercise 5

Fitting Together and Taking Apart

A. For exercises (1)–(30), what are children in the anecdote or photo(s) fitting together and/or taking apart?

① Jason, anecdote p. 493

② Amanda/Isaac, anecdote p. 493

③ Andrew, anecdote p. 493

④ Jaleesa, anecdote p. 493

⑤ Kenneth/Douglas, anecdote p. 494

⑥ Chrysten, anecdote p. 494

⑦ Johnny, anecdote p. 494

⑧ Julia, anecdote p. 494

⑨ Mikey, anecdote p. 494

⑩ Christy, anecdote p. 494

⑪ Joey, anecdote p. 494

⑫ Deola, anecdote p. 494

⑬ Max, anecdote p. 494

⑭ p. 30 top photo

⑮ p. 31 bottom left photo

⑯ p. 136 left-hand photo

⑰ p. 140 photo

⑱ p. 177 photo

⑲ p. 219 photo

⑳ p. 261 photo

㉑ p. 384 photo

㉒ p. 385 photo

㉓ p. 447 photo

㉔ p. 454 left-hand photo

㉕ p. 455 photo

㉖ p. 472 photo

㉗ p. 493 photo

㉘ p. 494 photos

㉙ p. 508 photos

㉚ pp. 501 and 509 photos

▶ B. What have you seen some of your study children fitting together and taking apart?

▶ C. Why do young children enjoy the challenge of fitting things together and taking them apart?

Exercise 6

Shaping and Arranging— Wrapping, Twisting, Stretching, Stacking, Enclosing

▶ A. For exercises (1)–(13), describe **what** the children are shaping and arranging and **how** they are doing it. The children appear in the anecdotes on *EYC* p. 496 and in the bulleted scenarios on *EYC* p. 498, first column. Organize your answers in a chart like the following.

Child(ren)	Material	How Child Shapes/Arranges

① Jason

② Brianna

③ Jacob

④ Jalessa

⑤ Jonah/Jason

⑥ Oscarina

⑦ Markie

⑧ Rachel

⑨ Douglas

⑩ Abby

⑪ Jason

⑫ Kacey

⑬ Callie

▶ B. For exercises (1)–(22) make a chart like the one you made for exercise A, answering the same questions about the children in the photos.

① Photos, p. 2 (top middle) and p. 109

② Photos, p. 2 (bottom right) and p. 488

③ Photos, pp. 14 and 15

④ Photo, p. 31 (top middle)

⑤ Photo, p. 33

⑥ Photos, pp. 49 and 272

⑦ Photo, p. 53 (right-hand)

⑧ Photo, p. 110 (bottom right)

⑨ Photo, p. 118

⑩ Photos, p. 119

⑪ Photo, p. 149

⑫ Photo, p. 220

⑬ Photo, p. 237

⑭ Photo, p. 291

⑮ Photo, p. 326

⑯ Photos, p. 382

⑰ Photo, p. 466

⑱ Photo, p. 472

⑲ Photos, p. 494

⑳ Photo, p. 496

㉑ Photo, p. 497

㉒ Photo, p. 507

▶ C. What have you seen some of your study children shaping and arranging?

▶ D. Why is shaping and arranging materials an important experience for young children?

Exercise 7

Observing Things From Different Spatial Viewpoints

▶ A. In the *EYC* anecdotes and the *EYC* photographs listed below, **what** are children observing, and **where** are they making the observation from? Use a chart like the following to organize your answers.

Child(ren)	What They See (or Can't See)	Where They Are

❶ Abby, anecdote p. 498

❷ Jacob/Isaac, anecdote p. 498

❸ Anna/Jessa, anecdote p. 498

❹ Douglas, anecdote p. 498

❺ Abby, anecdote p. 498

❻ Abby, anecdote p. 498

❼ Nathan/Brianna, anecdote p. 498

❽ Photos, pp. 14 and 15

❾ Photos, p. 19 (top left) and p. 521 (right)

❿ Photo, p. 19 (bottom left)

⓫ Photo, p. 26 (bottom)

⓬ Photo, p. 499 (top)

⓭ Photo, p. 499 (bottom)

⓮ Photo, pp. 500 and 521 (left)

⓯ Photo, p. 502

▶ B. How or when have some of your study children observed people, places, and things from different spatial viewpoints?

Exercise 8

Experiencing and Describing Positions, Directions, and Distances

▶ A. What are the following children describing in the anecdotes on *EYC* p. 500?

❶ Audie   ❽ Brianna

❷ Abby   ❾ Brian

❸ Colin   ❿ Amanda

❹ Kacey   ⓫ Douglas

❺ Jason   ⓬ Amanda

❻ Amanda   ⓭ Kenneth

❼ Jacob   ⓮ Callie

▶ B. What strikes you about the context of the children's descriptions?

▶ C. What descriptions of position, direction, or distance have you heard some of your study children making?

▶ D. In the anecdotes on *EYC* p. 500, children usually describe position and direction rather than distance. Why?

▶ E. Look through the photos in *EYC*, and list different kinds of positions you see children experiencing.

▶ F. How is the space key experience *experiencing and describing positions, directions, and distances* related to the movement key experiences *moving in nonlocomotor ways* and *moving in locomotor ways*?

Exercise 9

Interpreting Spatial Relations in Representations

▶ A. Read about the following children in the anecdotes on *EYC* pp. 503–504. What strikes you about each child's interpretation of what he or she sees in the drawing or photograph being described?

❶ Jonah   ❹ Alana

❷ Amanda   ❺ Jason

❸ Trey   ❻ Kenneth

▶ B. How have some of your study children interpreted spatial relations in drawings, pictures, and photographs?

Exercise 10

Supporting Children's Understanding of Space Throughout the Day

(Exercise B involves a computer.)

▶ A. If you are currently teaching or student teaching, think of your early childhood setting for this exercise about *providing materials*. If you are not teaching, think about your study children's early childhood setting. For each type of space-related material in (1)–(6), list the materials **currently in the setting,** and then list materials **you would like to add.** Use a chart like the following to organize your answers.

Type of Space-Related Material	Have	Add

❶ Materials for filling and emptying: continuous, discrete, containers, scoops

❷ Materials that fit together and come apart

❸ Materials to shape and arrange: blocks, paper, cloth, rubber bands, elastic, thread, wire

❹ Sturdy climbing equipment

❺ Materials children can set in motion

❻ Pictorial materials

❼ Art materials

▶ B. If you have access to a computer and preschool software, try out the software programs that provide children with interactive spatial experiences. (For titles of appropriate software, see the software reviews in the bimonthly magazine *Children's Software Revue:* www.childrenssoftware.com.) Which programs do you or would you provide for children in an early childhood setting?

▶ C. Exercises (1)–(3) concern *providing time for children to explore and work with spatial concepts.*

❶ How does the adult support Trey (*EYC* p. 495, middle column) as he fits together materials to make a robot?

❷ What characterizes the "sample openers" for recall time on *EYC* p. 495, third column? How might such statements from adults encourage children to describe spatial concepts?

❸ What expectations did Helena and Sara have for their children at small-group time (*EYC* p. 495, third column)? How did Helena and Sara support children's experiences with space?

▶ D. Exercises (1)–(4) concern *supporting children's spatial problem solving.*

❶ How does the adult support Traci's wheel problem (*EYC* p. 495, middle column)?

❷ What strikes you about Colin's solution to the out-of-reach dinosaurs (*EYC* p. 497)? Why did the adult refrain from handing Colin the dinosaurs he needed?

❸ What spatial problem was Erica encountering (*EYC* p. 497)? Why did Linda restrain herself from telling Erica to use a longer board?

❹ How does the adult support Brian and Deola's problem solving (*EYC* pp. 502–503)?

▶ E. Exercises (1)–(3) concern *commenting on what you see children doing.*

❶ How does the adult support Trey's arrangement of sticky pieces (*EYC* p. 498, first column)?

❷ How does Becki support Brianna's observations from the top of the climber (*EYC* p. 499, bottom of first column)?

❸ How does the adult support Abby's description of spatial relations (*EYC* p. 502)?

▶ F. Exercises (1)–(2) concern *listening to children as they talk about space.*

❶ How does Trent's teacher support his descriptions of space at recall time (photo caption

on *EYC* p. 505)? Since drawing is an important stage in emergent writing, how might the teacher have recorded Trent's comments in some way other than writing them on his drawing?

❷ How does Betsy support Jonah's interest in maps (*EYC* p. 505, first column)?

▶ G. Read through the space support strategies in the checklist on the following page (which is from *EYC* p. 507). Under each of the space key experiences on the checklist, check off the support strategies you are already using, write "E" in front of the strategies you have not used but would like to explore, and then read about each of these strategies in *EYC*.

Child Study: Creating a Space Portfolio

By yourself or with a partner, create a space portfolio by collecting materials such as the following as you teach, student teach, or observe your study children:

• Anecdotes related to each space key experience

• Samples of children's art in which children have created things that fit together and come apart; arranged and shaped things; or represented and described positions, directions, and distances

• Videotape clips or photographs of children filling and emptying; fitting things together and taking them apart; changing the shape and arrangement of things; and observing, describing, and interpreting spatial viewpoints and relations

Space Strategies: A Summary

Filling and emptying

___Provide materials for filling and emptying.

    ___Continuous materials for pouring

    ___Discrete materials

    ___A variety of containers and scoops

    ___Computer software

___Watch for children's filling and emptying play.

___Imitate children's actions.

___Anticipate repetition.

Fitting things together and taking them apart

___Provide materials that fit together and come apart.

    ___Commercial materials

    ___Common household materials

___Provide materials children can use to make things that fit together and come apart.

___Provide time for children to work with materials on their own.

___Support children as they solve fit problems.

___At recall time, encourage children to talk about things they put together and took apart.

___Include fit-together, take-apart materials at small-group time.

Changing the shape and arrangement of objects (wrapping, twisting, stretching, stacking, enclosing)

___Provide materials to shape and arrange.

    ___Blocks

    ___Paper and cloth

___Clay and dough

___Rubber bands and elastic

___Thread, string, yarn, ribbon, rope, wire, and pipe cleaners

___Support children as they rearrange things to solve problems.

___Listen for children's awareness of how they are shaping and arranging things.

___Take cues from children to comment on changes they have made.

Observing people, places, and things from different spatial viewpoints

___Provide sturdy play equipment.

    ___Outside

    ___Inside

___Encourage children to crawl, roll, bounce, lie on their backs.

___Join children in a variety of positions.

___Take walks with children.

Experiencing and describing positions, directions, and distances in the play space, building, and neighborhood

___Provide materials children can set in motion.

___Provide lots of opportunities for children to move.

___Converse with children about positions, directions, and distances.

    ___Listen.

    ___Comment.

___Take directions from children.

___Support children as they encounter and solve position problems.

___Encourage children to explore their immediate environment.

    ___Implement the plan-work-recall sequence.

    ___Value cleanup time.

    ___Go on walks with children.

Interpreting spatial relations in drawings, pictures, and photographs

___Provide a wide variety of pictorial materials.

___Provide materials children can use to make their own pictures.

___Provide opportunities for children to draw at recall time.

___Display photos and drawings of block structures.

___Look at picture books with children.

___Take photographs of children in action.

    ___Keep a "loaded" camera handy.

    ___Take photographs of the shaping and arranging process.

    ___Take photographs from different spatial viewpoints.

    ___Make photographs available to children.

When your space portfolio is complete, find an opportunity to present it to teaching teams in your center, parents of preschoolers, or fellow early childhood students. Assembling and explaining your portfolio to others will add to your understanding of how children construct an understanding of space.

Exercise 12

Space Scenarios: What Would You Do?

Based on your understanding of the space key experiences and the support strategies discussed on *EYC* pp. 491–507, decide how you might interact with and support the preschool children in the following scenarios.

▶ A. *At work time, several children wearing mittens and gloves play in the "snow table" (a sand table filled with snow). You notice that Vernecia has taken a glove and a mitten to the sand table (another table, filled with sand) and is filling them with sand.*

How might you support her filling and emptying experience?

▶ B. *At cleanup time, Alex is having a difficult time fitting two bins of yarn on the art shelf, so he empties all the yarn into one bin, puts that bin on the shelf, and fits the empty bin on top of the full one. "Look," he says to you, "I made a lid to fit on top."*

How might you support Alex's idea of fitting things together?

▶ C. *At work time in the house area, Fareed is trying to get a small plastic counting bear out of the adult-sized tea kettle. He turns the kettle upside down and shakes it, but the bear does not come out. Next he tries poking it out with a table knife while he holds the kettle upside down. "I know—tongs," Reena suggests. Fareed inserts the tongs, and after several tries with Reena holding the kettle upside down, he removes the bear. "We got it!" they cry.*

How might you support Fareed and Reena's spatial problem solving?

▶ D. *At planning time, Axel says he is going to use the hollow blocks to build "a big boat like yesterday, with a ramp to go up, a place on top to shoot missiles, and a place underneath to play games."*

How might you support Axel's description of position and direction?

▶ E. *At outside time, Kayla wraps yarn around parts of the climber. "I'm making a trap," she tells you.*

How might you support Kayla's wrapping, twisting, and enclosing?

▶ F. *At outside time, Tenisha and Layla are lying on their backs under the maple tree, watching the leaves come down. "Leaves are coming right on us," Tenisha says to Layla.*

How might you support Tenisha and Layla's observation of leaves from their unusual spatial viewpoint?

▶ G. *At work time in the computer area, Daniel and Carleen are together trying to find the hidden treasures in the "Sandbox Treasure Game."*[36] *Jack,*

[36]*This anecdote refers to a game on the software program* **The Backyard** *(Broderbund, 1993).*

another child, hears their struggles and joins them. Jack says to Daniel and Carleen, "You see the digger by the cup? You have to find the cup on the map, and go over here (he points to the × mark on the map), and then dig." The three children then work together, following Jack's instructions about how to find the buried treasure.*

How might you support their interpretation of spatial relations in drawings and pictures?

▶ H. *At work time in the toy area, Lourdes puts together the framed wooden dinosaur puzzle several times. Then she puts it together outside its frame.*

How might you support her fitting together and taking apart?

▶ I. *At work time in the toy area, Brendan is making a robot with the Lasy builders (interlocking plastic shapes). "Look," he says to you, "Philo, a big robot made out of vehicles." You can see that he has built and fit together three vehicles to make Philo.*

How might you support his fitting-together experience?

▶ J. *At small-group time, Jack folds a strip of tag board into a circular loop, fastens it together with tape, and wraps yarn around his "magic bracelet."*

How might you support Jack's interest in changing the shape and arrangement of things?

▶ K. *At work time, several children role-playing together in the house area decide to "move to Chicago." They pack up all the clothes and cooking utensils along with the stove, the refrigerator, and the mirror and take them to the area near the cubbies.*

How might you support their changing the shape and arrangement of things?

▶ L. *At recall time, Julia draws a picture of herself inside a box. "This is me when I was a kitty inside my kitty house," she tells you.*

How might you support Julia's understanding and description of spatial positions?

Exercise 13

Implementation Study: Trying Out Space Support Strategies

If you are currently teaching or student teaching or can work in an early childhood setting over a period of time, try out the space support strategies on *EYC* p. 507 during the child-initiated and adult-initiated times of the day. Support children's use of space at work time, cleanup time, and outside time. Watch for space key experiences as children work with materials at small-group time and as they offer ideas at large-group time. Collect anecdotes, photographs, recordings, and samples of space experiences for your space portfolio. At the end of each day of teaching, record your discoveries about the ways young children fill and empty; fit things together and take them apart; change the shape and arrangement of things; and observe, describe, and interpret spatial relations.

This implementation exercise is crucial for your understanding of the space key experiences and ways to support them. Do not be discouraged if things do not go the way you expect them to. It is only with practice that adults learn from children how they construct knowledge about space and how to encourage their space-related initiatives.

Exercise 14

Child Assessment: COR Item Related to Space

One way to assess preschool children's understanding and use of space is to match the children's anecdotes (collected each day and discussed at daily team planning time) with the most relevant level descriptors for item CC from the High/Scope Child Observation Record (COR) for Ages 2½–6. This item is presented on the facing page. Based on the following anecdote, at what level (1–5) would you place Kevin on COR item CC? (After making your own assessment, you may wish to look at the item CC level suggested for Kevin on page 225.)

10/11 At outside time, when Beth asked Alex to come down from the climber because his mother had arrived to take him home, Kevin said, "I'm not coming down, 'cause I'm not up!"

10/21 On a home visit, Kevin showed Carol, one of his teachers, the bunk beds he and his brother share, saying "Alex goes on the top, and I go under."

12/7a At work time in the block area, Kevin and Alex built a structure with the hollow blocks. Kevin crawled into one section of the structure, under some wooden planks, and said, "When there's a storm, I can crawl underneath here."

12/7b At recall time, as Kevin talked about his block structure, he described hiding from the storm: "I crawled out. I crawled back in."

1/18 At snack time, as he passed around the basket of apples, Kevin said to Rachel, "Take the one on top."

Exercise 15

Space Issues to Ponder and Write About

▶ A. How is the child's understanding of space related to his or her role as an active learner?

▶ B. How are *filling and emptying; fitting together and taking apart;* and *shaping and arranging things* similar experiences? How are they different?

▶ C. How is the space key experience *interpreting spatial relations in drawings, pictures, and photographs* related to the language and literacy key experience *reading in various ways: reading storybooks, signs and symbols, one's own writing?*

▶ D. How do the creative representation key experiences *making models out of clay, blocks, and other materials* and *drawing and painting* relate to children's understanding of space?

▶ E. What is a map? What do you have to know to create a map? To use a map?

▶ F. How does the arrangement of the learning environment affect children's experiences with space?

COR Item CC. Describing spatial relations

Level 1   Child does not follow directions that describe the relative positions of people or things (on, over, under, behind) or the direction of movement of things (up, down, forward, back, into, out of).

Level 2   Child follows directions including such words, but does not use them correctly in speaking.

Level 3   Child uses words that describe the relative positions of things (over, under, behind, in front of).

Level 4   Child uses words that describe the direction of movement of things (up, down, forward, back, into, out of).

Level 5   Child uses words that describe the relative distances between things (closer, farther away).

Supporting Anecdotes:

Related Publications

Blackwell, Frank, and Charles Hohmann. 1991. *High/Scope K–3 Curriculum Series: Science.* Ypsilanti, MI: High/Scope Press.

Graves, Michelle. 1989. *The Teacher's Idea Book: Daily Planning Around the Key Experiences*, 57–62. Ypsilanti, MI: High/Scope Press.

High/Scope Child Observation Record (COR) for Ages 2½–6. 1992. Ypsilanti, MI: High/Scope Press.

Tompkins, Mark. 1996. "Spatial Learning: Beyond Circles, Squares, and Triangles." In *Supporting Young Learners 2: Ideas for Child Care Providers and Teachers*, Nancy A. Brickman, ed., 215–22. Ypsilanti, MI: High/Scope Press.

Related Video

Spatial Learning in the Preschool Years. 1977. Black-and-white video, 22 min. Ypsilanti, MI: High/Scope Press.

Answer to Exercise 14

Kevin's level on COR item CC:

Level 3 on the basis of anecdotes from *10/21, 12/7a, 1/18*

Level 4 on the basis of anecdotes from *10/11, 12/7b*

Level 4 overall

Preschool children experience and conceive of time in very personal ways. Their measurement of time has little to do with the standard time units of clocks and calendars. Rather, children relate time intervals and the passage of time to familiar events, places, and feelings.

—*Educating Young Children, p. 512*

Time

Experiencing Time Rates, Intervals, and Sequences[37]

Do each of the three activities in this exercise with a partner.

Rolling Balls

For this activity, use two identical balls (such as two golf balls, tennis balls, or baseballs); two boards, each 3 to 4 feet long and wide enough to use as a ramp for rolling the balls (two lengths of eaves trough will also work); an even number of unit blocks to support each ramp at various heights; and two blocks to set up at the end of the ramps, as targets.

- You and your partner each make a low ramp by setting one end of a board (or trough) on a unit block and the other end on the floor, and then place a block at the end of the ramp as a target.

- Each experiment with releasing (rather than pushing) a ball to make it roll down your low ramp and hit the target. Then each experiment with changing the height of your ramp. Discuss your observations with your partner.

- Set up the two ramps (yours and your partner's) side by side, so when you each release a ball, the two balls roll down the ramps at the same rate of speed. Then change the height of one or both ramps, so when you release the two balls, one rolls faster than the other. Based on your observations, discuss what makes the two balls roll at different rates of speed.

[37]The three activities in this exercise are adapted from the **High/Scope K–3 Curriculum Series: Science**, pp. 170–171, 172–173, and 154–155.

Making Pendulum Clocks

This exercise requires a meter stick, a spool of string or thread, two large washers for weights, two dowel rods, two heavy books (or some other similar objects) to act as anchors to secure the sticks to a table or other high surface, and a watch or clock (either digital or with a second hand).

- You and your partner each construct a pendulum clock by tying a piece of string (or thread) to a rod, attaching one washer to the end of the string, and using a book to secure the rod to a table in such a way that the string and its weight (the washer) can swing freely.

- Each set your pendulum in motion, and count the swings the pendulum makes. Consider "one swing" to be the weight moving completely from right to left (or completely from left to right).

- Each use your pendulum to time a simple activity. For example, count how many swings it takes for you to tie a bow or to take off both shoes and put them back on.

- Compare the two pendulums—which one swings faster? When you change the length of either pendulum's string, what happens to the swing?

- Together with your partner, make a pendulum with a string that is 1 meter long. What do you notice about the swing of this pendulum? For example, approximately how many swings does it make in 1 minute?

Making a Sun Clock

For this exercise, use a 3- to 4-inch pencil or dowel rod and a flat board about 1-foot square with a hole drilled in the center to hold the pencil or dowel rod upright.

- Put the pencil or dowel rod in the center of the board to construct a sundial, and place this sundial outside in a spot that has full sun all day.

- Over several days, record the position of the pencil's (or dowel's) shadow at various times of the day. For example, you might record the position of the shadow every hour on the hour or you might mark the positions of the shadow to indicate lunch time, specific class times, or other significant events in your day.

- After you have recorded your marks, check your sun clock over the next several days to see what time it is.

- With your partner, discuss what causes the shadow and how the shadow changes over the day.

In your own words, describe the time concepts involved in the *ball-rolling* activity, the *pendulum* activity, and the *sundial* activity.

Exercise 2

Recalling Experiences With Time

With a partner or several friends, discuss the following:

▶ A. What do you remember about your concept of time as a young child, before you could read clocks and calendars? How did you experience time in your pre-clock and pre-calendar world?

▶ B. How did our earliest ancestors reckon time?

▶ C. What do you recall about learning to tell time?

▶ D. When did you begin using a calendar in a way that was meaningful to you?

▶ E. What kind of internal clock do you have?

▶ F. What, if any, experiences can you recall when you were lost in time or when time seemed to stand still?

▶ G. What experiences have you had with people whose concept of time is different from yours?

▶ H. Record all the stock phrases you know involving time, such as "We'll be there in no time." "Time out!" "How many times have I told you . . ." "Time is money." "Please proceed in a timely manner." "What good timing!"

▶ I. Why does our language include so many time-worn references to time? How do young children make sense of these phrases?

Exercise 3

Understanding Time

Exercises A–D are based on the discussion of time on *EYC* pp. 511–512.

▶ A. What does Piaget mean when he describes young children's sense of time as "local" (*EYC* p. 511)?

▶ B. According to Phillips, how do infants perceive time (*EYC* p. 511)?

▶ C. How has a 3- or 4-year-old child's understanding of time developed since infancy?

▶ D. In what ways do preschoolers make the abstract notion of time concrete for themselves?

Exercise 4

Stopping and Starting

▶ A. How are these children (from the anecdotes on *EYC* pp. 512–513) expressing their understanding of stopping and starting?

1 Lynette and Markie   5 Abby
2 Kenneth   6 Mikey
3 Sarah   7 Alana and LJ
4 Jacob   8 Brian

▶ B. How have you seen some of your study children engaging in stopping and starting?

Exercise 5

Rates of Movement

▶ A. What are the following children experiencing or describing related to rates of movement?

1 Corey, anecdote on *EYC* p. 515
2 Jessa, anecdote on *EYC* p. 515
3 Jason, anecdote on *EYC* p. 515
4 Kelli, anecdote on *EYC* p. 515
5 Douglas, anecdote on *EYC* p. 515
6 Children in photos on *EYC* p. 516

▶ B. How have you seen and heard some of your study children experiencing and describing rates of movement?

Exercise 6

Time Intervals

▶ A. Read through the anecdotes on *EYC* p. 517, in which children experience and compare time intervals. How are these anecdotes expressions of what Piaget calls "local" time?

▶ B. What strikes you about the *context* in which these children experience and make observations about time intervals?

▶ C. What have you observed about some of your study children's experiences and talk about time intervals?

Exercise 7

Sequences of Events

▶ A. The children listed in (1)–(15) appear in the anecdotes on *EYC* pp. 518–519. For each exercise, identify the **event experienced or described** and the **event anticipated or recalled.** To organize your answers, use a chart like the following, in which Mikey is shown as an example.

Child(ren)	Event Experienced or Described	Event Anticipated or Recalled
Mikey	Sees a parent arrive	Anticipates end of outside time and riding bike the next day

❶ Kacey
❷ Erica
❸ Alana
❹ Jonah
❺ Corrin
❻ Douglas
❼ Brian
❽ Brianna
❾ Kacey
❿ Brian
⓫ Sarah
⓬ Alana
⓭ Isaac/Amanda
⓮ Hannah
⓯ Kacey

▶ B. What strikes you about the kinds of events these children anticipate and recall and about the context in which they talk about them?

▶ C. What events and interactions have you heard some of your study children anticipating and recalling?

▶ D. How would you analyze Andrew's "color soup" recipe (*EYC* p. 520) in terms of his understanding and use of time concepts, creative representation, language and literacy, and classification?

Exercise 8

Supporting Children's Understanding of Time Throughout the Day

(Exercise B involves a computer.)

▶ A. If you are currently teaching or student teaching, think of your early childhood setting for this exercise about *providing materials.* If you are not teaching, think about your study children's early childhood setting. For each type of time-related material in (1)–(3), list materials **currently in the setting,** and then list materials **you would like to add.** Use a chart like the following to organize your answers.

Type of Time-Related Material	Have	Add

❶ Materials children can use to signal stopping and starting

❷ Materials children can set in motion

❸ Living things

▶ B. If you have access to a computer and preschool software, try out the programs that provide children with interactive time experiences. (For titles of appropriate software, see the software reviews in the bimonthly magazine *Children's Software Revue:* www.childrenssoftware.com.) Which programs do you or would you like to provide for the children in your early childhood setting?

▶ C. Exercises (1)–(2) concern *listening for* and *supporting children's observations about time.*

❶ How does Beth support Brian's observations about his fast-moving bus (*EYC* p. 517, first column)?

❷ How does the adult support Jonah's anticipation of what he is going to do at work time (*EYC* p. 520, first column)?

▶ D. Exercises (1)–(3) concern *referring to time in concrete terms that children will understand.*

❶ How does the adult refer concretely to time intervals in the bulleted sentences on *EYC* pp. 517–518?

❷ How did the adults help children anticipate their turns for passing out the snacks on *EYC* p. 520?

❸ How do adults support children's anticipation and recall of holiday celebrations on *EYC* pp. 521–522?

➤ E. Read through the *time support strategies* in the checklist at the right, which is from *EYC* p. 523. Under each of the time key experiences on the checklist, check off the support strategies you are already using, write "E" in front of the strategies you have not used but would like to explore, and then read about each of these strategies in *EYC*.

Exercise 9

Child Study: Creating a Time Portfolio

By yourself or with a partner, create a time portfolio by collecting materials such as the following as you teach, student teach, or observe your study children:

- Anecdotes related to each time key experience

- Samples of children's planning and recall drawings in which they anticipate work time plans and recall what they have done

- Videotape clips or photographs of children stopping and starting, experiencing rates of movement, comparing time intervals, and anticipating and recalling events

Time Strategies: A Summary

Stopping and starting an action on signal

___Provide materials children can use to signal stopping and starting.

___Let children know when time periods begin and end within the daily routine.

___Sing, dance, and play musical instruments together.

___Watch for and support children's interest in stopping and starting.

Experiencing and describing rates of movement

___Provide materials children can set in motion.

___Provide opportunities for children to move at different rates.

___Play fast and slow music.

___Re-enact stories that incorporate different rates of movement.

___Encourage children to pour their own juice and milk.

___Listen for and support children's observations about speed.

Experiencing and comparing time intervals

___Establish and follow a consistent daily routine.

___Relate lengths of time to familiar actions and events.

___Accept children's observations about time.

___Provide sand timers for children to play with.

Anticipating, remembering, and describing sequences of events

___Establish and maintain a consistent routine.

___Help children learn the daily routine and anticipate what comes next.

___At planning time, converse with children who are ready to make detailed plans.

___Encourage children to recall events.

___Illustrate the order of daily events with children.

___Watch for children's sequenced representations.

___Inform children about changes in the daily routine.

___Include children in the change process.

___Include living things indoors and outdoors.

___Look at seasonal change through preschoolers' eyes.

___Plan holiday celebrations around children's understanding of time.

When your time portfolio is complete, find an opportunity to present it to teaching teams in your center, parents of preschoolers, or fellow early childhood students. Assembling and explaining your portfolio to others will add to your understanding of how children construct an understanding of time.

Exercise 10

Time Scenarios: What Would You Do?

Based on your understanding of the time key experiences and the support strategies discussed on *EYC* pp. 512–523, decide how you might interact with and support the preschool children in the following scenarios.

▶ A. *At outside time Megan and Raina are swinging side by side on the swings. Megan asks Raina, "How did you get so high?" Raina replies, " I started slow, and then I pumped and I went faster and higher."*

How might you support Raina's experience and description of her rate of movement?

▶ B. *At work time in the toy area, Alex is building with the Lasy builders. "I'm making a neat thing!" he tells you. "Oh, I see," you reply, "what does your neat thing do?" Continuing working, Alex says, "I'm not finished. I can't tell you about it when I'm not finished." Pausing, he adds, "I'll tell you later when I'm finished."*

How might you support Alex's plan for telling you about his construction?

▶ C. *After Kevin arrives and takes off his jacket, he comes to you and says, "See this Band-Aid? When it comes off today or the next day, I'll need another one, because it has a really bad hurt underneath."*

How might you support Kevin's understanding of time intervals and sequences?

▶ D. *At work time, Rachel flips over the sand timer and says to you, "In two more minutes all of the sand comes to the bottom."*

How might you support Rachel's interest in time intervals?

▶ E. *Several days after the children return from winter break in February, Andy brings in a fresh pine bough his dad trimmed from a tree that has "broken in the ice storm." At the beginning of work time, Andy, Jack and Raina set up this bough as a "Christmas tree" in the house area and then make decorations for it in the art area.*

How might you support Andy's, Jack's, and Raina's recollections of past holiday experiences?

▶ F. *On a walk to the farmer's market, seeing a familiar landmark, Kelly says, "We are almost there. It's just a little time now till we get to the market."*

How might you support Kelly's anticipation of events and awareness of time intervals?

▶ G. *At greeting circle, Rachel tells you about a family outing: "We got strawberries, and there were boats there! It was on a river!"*

How might you support Rachel's recollection of events?

▶ H. *When Kacey's cousin comes to your center to visit for the day, Kacey takes her to the photo chart of the daily routine, "This is how we do it, we read books," she explains, pointing to the photograph of children and adults reading at greeting circle, "and then we go to planning." After explaining each photo and part of the day, she adds, "And then after, at the end of outside time, our moms come."*

How might you support Kacey's understanding of the sequence of the daily routine?

▶ I. *While eating cereal at snack time, the children in your group talk about their favorite cereals. When someone mentions Very Berry Kix, Kevin says, "I had some of those. If you wait long enough, even the milk turns pink!"*

How might you support Kevin's observation about time intervals?

▶ J. *At work time in the block area, Carleen points to her shoes and says to you, "These are new. I only weared them two days. This is my second time."*

How might you support Carleen's observations about time?

▶ K. *At greeting circle, several days before he is about to move to another city, Jack says to you, "You better draw my name up there (on the message board), because I'm moving soon."*

How might you support Jack's anticipation of this important event? Also, how would you interpret his use of the word "draw" in terms of emergent literacy?

Exercise 11

Implementation Study: Trying Out Time Support Strategies

If you are currently teaching or student teaching, or if you can work in an early childhood setting over a period of time, try out the time support strategies on *EYC* p. 523 during the child-initiated and adult-initiated times of the day. Support children's use of time concepts at work time, cleanup time, and outside time. Watch for time key experiences as children work with materials at small-group time and as they offer ideas at large-group time. Collect anecdotes, photographs, recordings, and samples for your time portfolio. At the end of each day of teaching, write down your reflections about the ways young children experience and describe rates of movement, compare time intervals, and anticipate and recall sequences of events.

This implementation exercise is crucial for your understanding of the time key experiences and ways to support them. Do not be discouraged if things do not go the way you expect them to. It is only with practice that adults learn from children how they construct knowledge about time and how to encourage children's time-related initiatives.

Exercise 12

Child Assessment: COR Item Related to Time

One way to assess preschool children's understanding and use of time is to match the children's anecdotes (collected each day and discussed at daily team planning time) with the most relevant level descriptors for item DD from the High/Scope Child Observation Record (COR) for Ages 2½–6. This item is presented on the facing page. On the basis of the following anecdotes, at what level (1–5) would you place Megan on COR item DD? (After making your own assessment, you may wish to look at the item DD level suggested for Megan on p. 233.)

> 3/1 At greeting circle, Megan explained why the sun kept shining even when the power went off during a city-wide power outage the previous day: "Yesterday the sun didn't go out, because the electricity doesn't go up in the sky, and the sun's in the sky."

> 3/15 At the end of small-group time, when all the other children went to the door to go outside, Megan showed them the daily routine chart, pointing to the small-group picture, the large-group picture, and the outside time picture: "We just had small-group time," she explained, "and then we go to large-group time, and *then* we go outside."

> 4/6 At planning time, Megan said, "I am going to play with the trains with Frances and Raina."

> 4/9 At recall time, Megan recounted what she, Frances, and Raina did in the house and block areas: "We made a castle, and then we put in food, dishes, silverware, and necklaces. We were the princesses, and Beth was the queen. We called the king on the phone, and then we got ready for the ball, and we pretended the step-sister ripped up our dresses."

> 4/22 At work time, Megan said to Carol, "I remember last week we went to a place and got ice cream with N & M's. I got chocolate N & M's."

Exercise 13

Time Issues to Ponder and Write About

▶ A. What did early Chinese, Egyptian, or Mayan calendars look like?

▶ B. Why do people's views of time vary from place to place and from culture to culture?

▶ C. How much time do children need for childhood?

▶ D. In an educational setting, how is it possible to accommodate both children's need for a leisurely pace and adults' need to stay on schedule?

▶ E. How is the movement key experience *feeling and expressing steady beat* related to children's emerging concept of time?

COR Item DD. Describing sequence and time

Level 1   Child does not yet show an understanding of time or of routine sequences of events.

Level 2   Child plans or anticipates the next event in a sequence.

Level 3   Child describes or represents a series of events in the correct sequence.

Level 4   Child compares time periods correctly (a *short time* is shorter than a *long time*).

Level 5   When describing or representing a series of events in the correct sequence, child uses words for conventional time periods (*morning, yesterday, lunch time*).

Supporting Anecdotes:

Related Publications

Blackwell, Frank, and Charles Hohmann. 1991. *High/Scope K–3 Curriculum Series: Science.* Ypsilanti, MI: High/Scope Press.

Graves, Michelle. 1989. *The Teacher's Idea Book: Daily Planning Around the Key Experiences,* 63–69. Ypsilanti, MI: High/Scope Press.

High/Scope Child Observation Record (COR) for Ages 2½–6. 1992. Ypsilanti, MI: High/Scope Press.

Johnston, Diana Jo. 1996. "Primary-Grade Holiday Activities." In *Supporting Young Learners 2: Ideas for Child Care Providers and Teachers,* Nancy A. Brickman, ed, 255–56. Ypsilanti, MI: High/Scope Press.

Terdan, Susan M. 1996. "Celebrating With Preschoolers." In *Supporting Young Learners 2: Ideas for Child Care Providers and Teachers,* Nancy A. Brickman, ed, 247–54. Ypsilanti, MI: High/Scope Press.

Tompkins, Mark. 1996. "It's About Time!" "Alternatives to 'Calendar Time'" In *Supporting Young Learners 2: Ideas for Child Care Providers and Teachers,* Nancy A. Brickman, ed, 223–32. Ypsilanti, MI: High/Scope Press.

Related Video

Learning About Time in the Preschool Years. 1977. Black-and-white video, 38 min. Ypsilanti, MI: High/Scope Press.

Answer to Exercise 12

Megan's level on COR item DD:

Level 2 on the basis of anecdote from 4/6

Level 3 on the basis of anecdote from 4/9

Level 5 on the basis of anecdotes from 3/1, 3/15, 4/22

Level 5 overall

INDEX

A

Active learning, 7–13. *See also* **Opening activities.**
  adult collaboration to promote, 39–45
  arranging, equipping spaces for, 49–62
  creating an environment for, based on family life, 27
  daily routine as framework for, 65–68
  defining daily routine for, 65
  expressing intentions, 158
  ingredients of, 7–8, 9, 11, 12, 27
  involving families in settings for, 27–36
  making large-group times participatory, 110–111
  planning large-group times for, 106–110
  planning small-group times for, 97–101
  relation to sense of self, 16
  at small-group time, 95–96
  within supportive climate, 67
  watching, listening to active learner, 8

Adult-child interactions, 15–25

Adult support. *See also* **Adult-child interactions.**
  balancing with adult initiative at small-group time, 96
  of children as they hear, move to, make music, 183
  of children's classification, 193
  of children's concept of number, 210–211
  of children's creative representation, 138
  of children's initiative, social relations, 161–162
  of children's language, literacy, 149–150
  of children's outdoor play, 117
  of children's seriation, 201–202
  of children's understanding of space, 220–221
  of children's understanding of time, 229–230
  of children throughout the day, 174–175
  classification support strategies, 194
  creative representation support strategies, 139
  identifying, 10
  initiative, social relations support strategies, 164

  language, literacy support strategies, 150
  at large-group time, 111
  movement support strategies, 176
  music support strategies, 184
  number support strategies, 211
  participating in children's role play, 138
  of planning process, 74
  providing a supportive atmosphere, 149
  of recall process, 90
  remembering supportive adults, 10
  seriation support strategies, 203
  at small-group time, 103
  space support strategies, 222
  taking cues from children, 149–150
  throughout the daily routine, 67
  time support strategies, 230
  at transition time, 119–120
  at work time, 83

Anecdotal notes. *See* **Anecdotes.**

Anecdotes, 125–127
  classification, 196
  creative representation, 141
  initiative, social relations, 165
  language, literacy, 152
  movement, 177
  music, 186
  number, 213
  seriation, 204
  space, 224
  time, 232

Arnheim, Rudolf, 134

Arranging, equipping spaces for active learners, 49–62. *See also* **Materials.**
  effects of room arrangement on work time interactions, 79

Asher, Steven, 158

Assessment. *See High/Scope Child Observation Record (COR).*

Ayers, William, 160

with meaning for children, 50, 53
for movement, 174
for music, 183
number-related, 210
planning around new, unexplored, 100
scrap, natural, "real", 53
for seriation, 201–202
for small-group-time, 101–102
space-related, 218, 219, 220–221
storing, labeling, 56
study child's favorite, 54
that worry adults, satisfy children, 55
time-related, 229

McClellan, Diane, 161

McCoy, Charles, 160

Moore, Shirley, 158

Movement, 171–179

Music, 181–187

N

Number, 207–214

O

Observing children. *See* Child observation.

Opening activities
building-blocks of human relationships, 15
childhood memories of play, 40
choosing to collaborate, 40
comparing, arranging one-to-one correspondence, counting, 207
consideration of nature of transitions, 119
creating active learning environment based on family life, 27
creating representations, 133
creating series, patterns, 199–200
experiencing active learning, 7
experiencing elements of support, their opposites, 17–18
experiencing, recalling representations, 133

experiencing time rates, intervals, sequences, 227–228
exploring, describing attributes; organizing into groups, 189–190
exploring music, 181
filling, fitting, shaping; observing, describing, interpreting spatial relations, 217
ideal place to be, 49
initiating, carrying out individual and group work, 157
intentions you have expressed, plans you have made, 71
learning to level: open communication, 40, 41
moving in a variety of ways, 171
recalling experiences with language, literacy, 145–146
recalling experiences with music, 181
recalling experiences with time, 228
recalling initiatives, relationships, 157
recalling large-group experiences, 105
recalling movement experiences, 171
recalling number experiences, 208
recalling real-life experiences with classification, 190
recalling seriation experiences, 200
recalling space experiences, 217–218
recalling team experiences, 39
reconstructing the Pythagorean theorem, 208
remembering outdoor play, 114
speaking, listening, writing, reading, 145
working as a team, 39

Opper, Sylvia, 134

Outside time, 114–118

P

Painter, Marjorie, 73

Parent Report Form (COR), 31, 32

Pellegrini, Anthony, 88

Phillips, John, 228

Piaget, Jean, 133, 190, 200, 218, 228

Pinard, Adrien, 218

Plan-do-review process, 71–93